# Addiction to Perfection

Marie-Louise von Franz, Honorary Patron

**Studies in Jungian Psychology
by Jungian Analysts**

Daryl Sharp, General Editor

# Addiction to Perfection

## The Still Unravished Bride

A Psychological Study by

## MARION WOODMAN

For Ross

With much gratitude to Fraser Boa, Shirley Grace Jeffries,
Daryl Sharp and my analysands.

Some of the material in this book was originally presented in
public lectures. Names and circumstantial details have been changed.

**Canadian Cataloguing in Publication Data**

Woodman, Marion
   Addiction to perfection

(Studies in Jungian psychology by Jungian analysts; 12)

Bibliography: p.
Includes index.

ISBN 0-919123-11-2

1. Femininity (Psychology).   2. Obesity—Psychological
aspects.   3. Anorexia nervosa.   4. Jung, C.G. (Carl
Gustav), 1875-1961.   I. Title.   II. Series.

HQ1206.W66      155.6'33      C82-095165-X

· INNER CITY BOOKS
Box 1271, Station Q, Toronto, Canada M4T 2P4


Honorary Patron: Marie-Louise von Franz.
Publisher and General Editor: Daryl Sharp.
Editorial Board: Fraser Boa, Daryl Sharp, Marion Woodman.

INNER CITY BOOKS was founded in 1980 to promote the
understanding and practical application of the work of C.G. Jung.

*Cover:* "The Black Cape." Pen and ink drawing by Aubrey Beardsley,
for an illustration in *Salome.* (Princeton University Library)

*Back Cover:* Perseus decapitating the Gorgon Medusa. Athena is on
the left. Metope, Temple C, Selinus, Sicily. (National Museum, Palermo)

Glossary and Index by Daryl Sharp.

Printed and bound in Canada by Webcom Limited

# CONTENTS

*See last pages for descriptions of other INNER CITY BOOKS*

*. . . look like the innocent flower,/But be the serpent under't.*
                    —Shakespeare, *Macbeth.*

The Woman with the Skeletons (Lady Macbeth), 1906.—Gustav-Adolf Mossa.

# Preface

This book is about taking the head off an evil witch. Lady Macbeth, glued to the sticking-place of insatiable power, unable to countenance failure to the point of rejecting life, will serve as a symbol of the woman robbed of her femininity through her pursuit of masculine goals that are in themselves a parody of what masculinity really is. And though in Shakespeare's tragedy it is Macbeth who is beheaded, the head he loses is fatally infected by the witches' evil curse. Macbeth and Lady Macbeth are metaphors of the masculine and feminine principles functioning in one person or in a culture, and the deteriorating relationship between them clearly demonstrates the dynamics of evil when the masculine principle loses its standpoint in its own reality, and the feminine principle of love succumbs to calculating, intellectualized ambition. Shakespeare's beheading of his hero-villain is, in the total context of the play, the healing of the country.

This book is about a beheading. It has been hewn out of the hard rock of an addiction to perfection. Repeatedly, I have done battle with the black crow sitting on my left shoulder croaking, "It isn't good enough. You haven't anything new to say. You don't say it well enough." Repeatedly, I have had to stop trying to perfect a sentence here, a paragraph there, while the rest of the book remained unwritten. Fortunately there were deadlines to be met, or I would never have struck this book out of the rock in which it was buried. And the crow croaks, "Just as well." I counter that with the interest of the audiences to whom much of this material was first presented, and the encouragement of friends and analysands who so generously opened their own souls to make this book possible. Thus I have steered my course through the Scylla and Charybdis of rigid

7

scholarly methods and a whirlpool of material and landed my creation, rough-hewn, as delicately as possible without falling into my
own addiction.

By nature I like to work with cameos. I like to work in fine detail,
perfect that, and fall back in exhaustion until another cameo comes
along. Writing a book is not cameo work and putting a rough-hewn
rock into the world is not easy for a perfectionist. Reading it over
now, I find some parts boring, some parts running away with themselves in true compulsive style, and some parts mired in detail. I
could cut them out, but when I wrote them they were important as
part of a whole process—a process that takes infinite patience, with
heartbreaking setbacks and long periods of moving ahead while
looking backward into the mirror.

Linear thinking does not come naturally to me; moreover, it kills
my imagination. Nothing happens. No bell rings; no moment of
HERE and NOW. No moment that says YES. Without those mo-
ments I am not alive. And so, rather than driving toward a goal, I
prefer the pleasure of the journey through a spiral. And I ask my
reader to relax and enjoy the spiral too. If you miss something on
the first round, don't worry. You may pick it up on the second or
the third or the ninth. It doesn't matter. The important thing is that
you are relaxed so that if the bell does ring you will hear it and
allow it to resonate through all the rungs of your own spiral. The
world of the feminine resonates. Timing is everything. If it doesn't
ring, either it is the wrong spiral or the wrong time or there is no
bell.

Many of my analysands have eating disorders, and therefore
much of the illustrative material, especially in the first half of the
book, centers on obesity and anorexia nervosa. These syndromes,
however, are simply particular symptoms of a malaise that is general
in Western society, and while the anguish of a distorted feminine
body brings the problem into sharp focus, the psychology involved
does not apply only to the obese or the anorexic. Indeed, as the
weight problem is brought under control, images of emptiness, pris-
ons, glass coffins, etc., begin to appear in the dreams, pointing to
sexual and spiritual problems common to most modern women.
These emerge in the latter half of the book. I might add that the cry
of the witch that underlies most of the material may well be recognized by men too.

*

A Greek version of the witch motif concerns Medusa, a beautiful
woman until she offended the goddess Athena (born "fully armed,
with a mighty shout" from the head of Zeus after he had swallowed

her pregnant mother Metis).[1] In reprisal, Athena changed Medusa's hair into snakes and made her face so hideous that all who looked on her were turned to stone. It fell to the hero Perseus to kill the Medusa, and to do this Hermes gave him a curved sword and winged sandals, Athena a mirror-shield, and Hades a helmet which made Perseus invisible. Thus accoutered, Perseus slew Medusa, avoiding being turned into stone by keeping his eyes on the mirror-shield. From the pregnant Medusa's neck, Pegasus and Chrysaor were released. On his homeward journey Perseus rescued the princess Andromeda from a sea monster and released her from the rock to which she had been chained as a sacrifice. Later they were married.

If we look at the modern Athenas sprung from their father's foreheads, we do not necessarily see liberated women. Many of them have proven beyond question that they are equal to or better than men: excellent doctors, excellent mechanics, excellent business consultants. But they are also, in many cases, unhappy women. "I have everything," they say. "Perfect job, perfect house, perfect clothes, so what? What does it all add up to? There's got to be more than this. I was born, I died, I never lived." Often, behind the scenes, they are chained to some addiction: food, alcohol, constant cleaning, perfectionism, etc. As already mentioned, much of this book concentrates on eating disorders, but I am convinced that the same problem is at the root of all addictions. The problem manifests differently, of course, with the individual, but within everyone there are collective patterns and attitudes that unconsciously influence behavior.

One of these patterns is illustrated in Athena's cruel revenge on the once beautiful Medusa, whose snaky locks twist and writhe in constant agitation, reaching, reaching, reaching, wanting more and more and more. Is it possible that the modern Athena is not in contact with her Medusa because somewhere back in the dark patriarchal ages she was shut up in a cave? Our generation scarcely knows of her existence, but she is making her presence increasingly felt in her unquenchable cravings for something. What that something is depends on the individual's personal history. To try to fight her directly is almost certain defeat because she is so angry and so full of repressed energy that to face her brings on a paralysis of fear, as Margaret Laurence with devastating but moving accuracy has described in *The Stone Angel*. We have to find our own inner Perseus and arm him with the right weapons and let him move in, wearing his helmet or cloak of invisibility, in order to remove the tormented head. He dare not look the Medusa in the eye; neither dare he take his eyes off her in the mirror. Once the head is off, Pegasus, winged horse of creativity, is released along with Chrysaor, he of the golden sword. Then the hero, full of victory, finds the virgin who was to have been sacrificed to the sea monster, unchains her and takes her as his bride.

Essentially I am suggesting that many of us—men and women—are addicted in one way or another because our patriarchal culture emphasizes specialization and perfection. Driven to do our best at school, on the job, in our relationships—in every corner of our lives—we try to make ourselves into works of art. Working so hard to create our own perfection we forget that we are human beings. On one side we try to be the efficient, disciplined goddess Athena, on the other we are forced into the voracious repressed energy of Medusa. Athena is chained to Medusa as surely as Medusa is chained to Athena. We are trapped in the extremes of the gods, territory that doesn't belong to us. Meanwhile the one who is forgotten is the maiden Andromeda, chained to the rock, in danger of being sacrificed to a monster from the unconscious. She is the forgotten one—the "still unravished bride" in our culture. So long as she is chained to a rock she must remain still and unravished. She remains like a figure on Keats' Grecian urn, with all her passionate loveliness frozen into marble immobility,

> *For ever warm, and still to be enjoyed,*
> *For ever panting, and for ever young;*
> *All breathing human passion far above,*
> *That leaves a heart high-sorrowful and cloyed,*
> *A burning forehead, and a parching tongue.*[2]

This book looks into the heart of the driven Athena, the anguish of the writhing Medusa, and suggests ways of releasing the maiden into her vibrant womanhood before she is sacrificed to the perfection of death. Only by loving our own maiden, and allowing her to find the deep down passion within herself, can we dare to open ourselves to the raging goddess at the core of the addiction. Only through love can we transform her and allow her to transform us.

When my own maiden falters, I encourage her with a Zen koan:

> *Ride your horse along the edge*
> *of the sword*
> *Hide yourself in the middle*
> *of the flames*
> *Blossoms of the fruit tree will*
> *bloom in the fire*
> *The sun rises in the evening.*[3]

# 1

## Introduction

*DA*
*Damyata: The boat responded*
*Gaily, to the hand expert with sail and oar*
*The sea was calm, your heart would have responded*
*Gaily, when invited, beating obedient*
*To controlling hands*
—T.S. Eliot, "What the Thunder said," *The Waste Land.*

One night several years ago, we had a party—a memorable party. It was the closing night cast party of what had been an excellent production. Everyone was exhilarated, glad the last curtain was the best of all, glad the discipline was momentarily over, yet still holding on to a world which no longer existed. The sets had been struck before we left the theater.

And so we danced and ate and drank in that no man's land in which we hadn't quite left our roles behind and hadn't quite returned to the person we could recognize as "I." About two o'clock in the morning, in the midst of our Dionysian fun, one of the lead men crossed the room to thank me for the party. His step was deliberate; his face was serious.

"But the party's not over," I said. "There's no performance tomorrow."

"Great party!" he said. "But I have to go now. I have some serious drinking to do."

His tone was quiet and decisive. It was as if he had a rendezvous with the woman he had loved all his life but could never marry. I remember standing in the midst of the dancers looking into his proud eyes. It was on my tongue to tell him there was plenty of booze on the table. But I sensed that was irrelevant.

Serious drinkers are like serious eaters or serious noneaters. They are like serious drug-addicts. Their addiction holds a spell over them which acts as some powerful secret at the center of everything they do. The serious eater listens to others talking of diets, Weight Watchers, exercises; she hears them excitedly comparing pounds lost, pounds gained. She hears them encouraging each other, joking, consoling. She is not one of them. She knows the diets better than they do; she knows Weight Watchers is useless for her; she knows her life is on some Almighty Scale that she has to step on alone. She

11

is in some covenant with food—a covenant which she probably does not understand, but which nevertheless exerts some magical, compelling power over her. She hates it; she loves it; she keeps her covenant silent.

This book is about serious eaters and serious drinkers, serious house cleaners, serious anyones. As an analyst I share the secret anguish of men and women trapped in various types of compulsion. Most of them are highly respected professionals who know there is no problem with their work, but who also know their inner collapse repeats itself in a cyclic pattern—daily, weekly, monthly. They know their right hand does not know what their left hand is doing and they know their left hand is undermining what appears to be a very successful life. This book is also about serious workers or workaholics who say, "I know I'll get the promotion. I can handle the job perfectly. But if that's all there is, I'm not interested. It's all adding up to nothing. I do nothing but work. My personal life is the pits."

Behind the masks of these successful lives, there lurks disillusionment and terror. One common factor appears repeatedly. Consciously the individuals are being driven to do better and better within the rigid framework they have created for themselves; unconsciously they cannot control their behavior. There are countless individual and collective reasons for the outbreak of chaos as soon as the daily routine is completed. Will power can only last so long. If that will power has been maintained at the cost of everything else in the personality, then nothingness gapes raw. When in the evening it's time to come back to oneself, the mask and the inner Being do not communicate.

Compulsions narrow life down until there is no living—existence perhaps, but no living.

Ernest Becker in *The Denial of Death* makes this dichotomy quite clear:

> On the one hand, we see a human animal who is partly dead to the world, who is most "dignified" when he shows a certain obliviousness to his fate, when he allows himself to be driven through life; who is most "free" when he lives in secure dependency on powers around him, when he is least in possession of himself. On the other hand, we get an image of a human animal who is overly sensitive to the world, who cannot shut it out, who is thrown back on his own meagre powers, and who seems least free to move and act, least in possession of himself, and most undignified. Whichever image we choose to identify with depends in large part upon ourselves.[1]

Whether we are human animals "partly dead to the world" or human animals who are "overly sensitive to the world," many of us are being driven either by some force which we experience as coming from outside or some equally powerful force coming from inside, or we are battered by both until "I" cease to have control in my own life. This "I" has no value system of its own. It is not master in its own house. All day the mask, or persona, performs with perfect efficiency, but when the job is done, those frenzied, foreign rhythms continue to dominate body and Being. There is no "I" to call a halt, no strong, differentiated ego to gear down to the natural rhythms.

If those natural rhythms have dropped into total unconsciousness, *being* disappears, and the body, like a beaten, neurotic, terrified animal attempts to persevere with the rhythms totally foreign to its nature. The wolf attitude which demands more and more and more during the day, howls I want, I want, I want at night. Society's values based on the work ethic and perfectionist standards, ambitions and goals uphold the wolf attitude in the professional jungle, but society can do nothing to feed the lonely wolf at night. Some people go with the crowd to alcohol, to sex, to food, to drugs. In their efforts to escape they say, "It's better to be drunk than crazy, better to be vomiting than crazy, better to be fat than crazy." But nobody is drinking, loving, eating or vomiting because there's nobody and no body consciously there. The instincts, which have a natural satiation point, are not operating. The emptiness can never be filled.

Some people I meet in my practice refuse to go with the crowd, but are nevertheless caught in the wolf syndrome. They are gulping alcohol they don't taste, devouring food they don't chew, cleaning their clean houses all night, or running off whatever bit of flesh is still left on their poor bones. They come for therapy because they know "It's crazy." Their "I" is possessed by some demon over which they have no control. The demon who wears the mask of respectibility during the day shows his real face at night. He demands perfection—perfect efficiency, perfect world, perfect clean, perfect body, perfect bones, but they being human, and not prime-time TV advertisements, falter into perfect chaos and perfect death. The demon obliterates them and, being obliterated, they at last fall asleep.

What is missing is the balance which would restore the quality of the living. The goal-oriented, rational, perfectionist, masculine principle has to be balanced by the feminine. These two words, masculine and feminine, are so highly charged these days that I would like to clarify their psychological meaning by describing a simple incident.

Last summer my friend Tony and I, barefoot and hair flying, were sailing our small craft through the rough waters of Georgian Bay—skimming, tossing, veering with the treacherous currents and the vagaries of the bay winds. I am no sailor but I love to crew for my sailor friend. He takes easy command of the boat and as I watch him poised and excited, straining every muscle to keep the craft upright, I suddenly see him as a metaphor of the balance between masculine and feminine. I see the strong body and the keen mind fused in perfect harmony, at once concentrated and relaxed, sensitive to the fierce energies through which we sail. His right hand firmly controls the lines, his fingers sensitive to the shifts in the energy of the wind. His left hand holds the rudder with the same tension, which isn't tension at all but rather a poised surrender to the energies of the water. We know that we are dependent on the wind and the waves to move us, but we are equally dependent on his sailing expertise. One slip in judgment, one moment of indecision, would hurl us headlong into the bay. Sails full blown, our tiny craft cuts its way on a razor's edge. We hang on with our toes and strain back over the water as far as we can to hold the balance. Always his hands are responding to the messages conveyed through the rudder and ropes.

Safely moored, I step out of the boat, feet bloody from hanging on too hard and thighs burning with charlie horses. Tony quietly takes down the sails, ties the ropes and smiles, knowing. That knowing informs his walk as he moves up the cliff, confident, erect, easy. He knows his own strength; he trusts his own animal body; he is able to surrender his strength to a strength infinitely beyond his personal strength. The eternal has blown through him because he has tuned himself so exactly to receive it.

Now I am not for one moment suggesting that I, weak female, deliberately put myself in a situation dependent on a big strong man. In fact I am just as happy to crew for my friend Mary, whose expertise as a sailor is just as good as Tony's. And that's just the point. Masculinity and femininity have nothing to do with being locked into a male or female body. If we are biologically female the ego is feminine and we carry within us our own inner masculinity, what Jung calls the animus. If we are biologically male, the ego is masculine and the man carries within himself his own inner femininity, the anima. Masculinity and femininity are not matters of gender, though historically in our Western culture their long identification with gender still makes it difficult for us to view them in this "liberated" way. It is this liberated view of masculinity and femininity with which I shall be dealing throughout this book. It is a matter of psychic rather than biological differentiation.

The *I Ching*, the Chinese Book of Changes, recognizes the continual shifts that go on within the individual. The Yang power, the creative masculine, moves ahead with steadfast perseverance toward a goal until it becomes too strong, begins to break—and then the Yin, the receptive feminine, enters from below and gradually moves toward the top. Life is a continual attempt to balance these two forces. With growing maturity the individual is able to avoid the extreme of either polarity, so that the pendulum does not gain too much momentum by swinging too far to the right only to come crashing back to the left in a relentless cycle of action and reaction, inflation and depression. Rather one recognizes that these poles are the domain of the gods, the extremes of black and white. To identify with one or the other can only lead to plunging into its opposite. The ratio is cruelly exact. The further I move into the white radiance on one side, the blacker the energy that is unconsciously constellating behind my back: the more I force myself to perfect my ideal image of myself, the more overflowing toilet bowls I'm going to have in my dreams.

The man who identifies with his own ideal becomes like Swift's adoring lover who cries,

> *Nor wonder how I lost my Wits;*
> *Oh! Caelia, Caelia, Caelia shits!*[2]

He cannot accept that the white radiance of his beloved can be stained by the humanity of her excremental functions.

As human creatures, not gods, we must go for the grey, the steady solid line that makes its serpentine way only slightly to left and right down the middle course between the opposites.

And that's the differentiated ego, whether male or female, cutting a course between wind and water. Positive masculine energy is goal-oriented and has the strength of purpose to move toward that goal. It disciplines itself to make the most of its gifts—physical, intellectual, spiritual—attempting to bring them into harmony. It comes to recognize its own individuality, and paradoxically the stronger it becomes the less rigid it becomes and the more flexible. It does not have to depend on old patterns of behavior, old habits, old traditions. With growing confidence, it experiences the excitement of new modes of behavior, the continual unfolding of new energies. It learns to hold perfect tension between a firm standpoint and the surrender to the creative feminine forces within. Its penetrating power inseminates and releases the creativity of the feminine.

The feminine is a vast ocean of eternal Being. It was, is and shall be. It contains the primordial animals "red in tooth and claw"; it contains the potential seeds for life; it knows the laws of nature and exacts those laws with ruthless justice; it lives in the eternal Now. It has its own rhythms, slower than those of the masculine, meandering, moving in a spiral motion, seemingly turning back on itself, but inevitably attracted to the light. It finds what is meaningful to it and plays. It may work very hard, but its attitude is always one of play because it loves life. It loves, and if that love is penetrated by the positive masculine, its energies are released to flow into life with a constant flow of new hope, new faith, new dimensions of love. But the spiritual feminine is always grounded in the natural instincts so that no matter how spiritualized it becomes, it is always on the side of life. In this it is different from the overspiritualized masculine (in man or woman) which tends to seduce us into the sleep that ends "the heartache . . . that flesh is heir to."[3]

Good sailors in the storms of life use their own "I," their own ego, to discriminate in what situation to use their masculinity and in what situation to use their femininity. They build their ego strong enough to ride with the power of wind and wave. And that ego can only be strong enough if it is supported by the wisdom of the body whose messages are directly in touch with the instincts. Without that interplay between spirit and body, the spirit is always trapped. At the very moment when it could soar, it is undermined by fear and lack of confidence because it cannot depend on its instinctual ground even for survival. Without that ground, the body is experienced as the enemy. Like a boat without a rudder whirling in panic-stricken circles, the sailor may be dragged into a vortex of paralysis or terror. If, on the other hand, spirit and body are attuned to each other, each complements the other with its own special wisdom.

We are living in a technological age that puts its faith in the perfection of the computer. Human beings tend to become like the god they worship, but fortunately for us, our agony does not allow us to become perfect robots. However hard we try to eradicate nature it eventually exerts its own value system and its own painful price. Our generation is a bridge generation attempting to make a giant stride in consciousness. Faced with atomic power, faced with the possibility of our own self-destruction, we are trying to reconnect to roots that have lain dormant underground for centuries in the hope that the nourishment from those depths may somehow counterbalance the sterility of the perfect machine. Most of us have no model. Although we may have loved our homes and our families we have to be ruthlessly honest in evaluating our heritage.

Most of our mothers "loved" us and did the very best they could to give us a good foundation for a good life. Most of their mothers from generation to generation did the same, but the fact remains that most people in this generation, male and female, do not have a strong maternal matrix out of which to go forward into life. Many of our mothers and grandmothers were the daughters of suffragettes who were already on the way to a new role for women. Some of them longed to be men; some related to their masculine side and dominated the household with masculine values so the atmosphere was geared to order, to goal-oriented ideals, to success in life, success that they themselves felt they had missed. The gall of their disappointment their children drank with their mother's milk. Unrelated to their own feminine principle, these mothers could not pass on their joy in living, their faith in being, their trust in life as it is. Geared to doing things efficiently, they could not surrender to allowing life to happen. They dared not allow themselves to react spontaneously to the unexpected. And since their children were sometimes the unexpected, these infants had three strikes against them before they were put in their cradles, unexpected not only in their person but in their temperament since they had feelings and thoughts that were not in accordance with their parents' projections of what their children should be. Within that attitude there is no room for life to be lived as it is, no room for either parent or child to relax into "I am"; consequently, the child lives with an elusive sense of guilt, the personification of the mother's disappointment less in her child than in herself. The child grows up attempting to justify its very existence, an existence which in psychic reality it has never been granted.

Where the mother is not at home in her own body, she cannot joyously interact with her unborn child, nor can she triumph in its actual birth, nor feed it with the tender nourishment of caresses that should accompany the long hours of breastfeeding. In *Magical Child,* Joseph Chilton Pearce builds a strong argument for the matrices through which we pass. Of the first matrix, in the womb, he says:

> If the mother's body is producing massive amounts of adrenal steroids during pregnancy, as a result of chronic anxiety, maltreatment, or fear, the infant in the womb automatically shares in these stress hormones; they pass right through the placenta. That infant is locked into a free-floating anxiety, a kind of permanent body stress.... Locked into this tension, the infant in utero cannot develop intellectually or establish the bonding with the mother in preparation for birth.[4]

He goes on to point out:

> If the first matrix formation is incomplete or insufficient, the next matrix formation will be doubly difficult. The young life is more and more jeopardized because the shifts of matrices must take place automatically.[5]

Pearce makes a devastating attack on technological delivery-room procedures; as he describes what takes place at birth, one is surprised that the baby survives at all and wonders what part is permanently destroyed in the trauma that is so distorted by modern medical techniques. Surely the imprint of that first passage from one world to another must leave indelible traces on the infant psyche. Pearce says,

... it works like a time bomb, none of the parties to the crime ever has to pay, for the explosion takes place in slow fusion over the years and creates such widespread and diverse havoc that few bother to trace it back to see who lit the fuse.[6]

## The infant moves slowly out from the mother, but it

can do this fully and successfully only to the extent that the mother is his absolutely unquestioned safe place to which he can always instantly return and be nurtured. Only when the infant knows that the mother matrix will not abandon him can that infant move into childhood with confidence and power.... The physical mother remains the primary matrix even though we separate from her and move into larger matrices.... No matter how abstract our explorations of pure thought and created reality, the mind draws its energy from the brain, which draws its energy from the body matrix, which draws its energy from the earth matrix.... We have, in effect, only two matrices: the physical matrix, progressing from womb, mother, earth, and physical body, and the abstract matrix of thought, progressing from relationships, the ability for interaction.[7]

Clearly, in Pearce's system, most of us have not, or have only in part, those early matrices that would give us faith in ourselves and in our own life. The extreme form to which the unrealized feminine assuming masculine ideals foreign to its own nature can lead is perhaps epitomized in Shakespeare's *Macbeth*.

In the first act Macbeth recognizes the power of his own imagination. He sees clearly enough the dagger which would lure him on to his own destruction. He carefully evaluates the moral values involved in killing his king and the destruction to his own soul if he persists in his ambition. He decides to "proceed no further in this business." But Lady Macbeth has other ideas. She is locked into an ideal of Kingship. To achieve that goal, she betrays her own feminine nature "in deepest consequence," and in one of the darkest soliloquies Shakespeare ever wrote surrenders her soul to "the spirits that tend on mortal darkness." Thus, instead of fulfilling her feminine role in relation to her man—that is, instead of helping him to keep in touch with his own feeling values—she mocks his masculine ego and points him in a direction which alienates him from himself, from her, and eventually from the whole cosmic structure. Encapsulated in their ideals and their projections, they lose contact with the intimate bond that kept them human.

Macbeth and Lady Macbeth began with intimate endearments: "Dearest Chuck, My Dearest Love." As each became more intent on the ideal of Kingship, they lost each other. In the crucial moment of decision, she challenged his manhood: "But screw your courage to the sticking place and we'll not fail." Had her feeling function been active in that moment, had she been in touch with her own heart, she might rather have turned his face toward hers and whispered, "Why are you afraid?" The outcome would have been quite different. Our last image of her is of a woman in her nightdress, moving in a trance toward the bedroom they once shared, clutching empty space for the hand she once loved and crying, "To bed, to bed, to bed." Her eyes are open but their sense is shut. The candle might as well be out. She created the wrong image. She might have made a great king of Scotland, but she did not have the imagination to recognize that her husband would not. Her masculinity burned out her femininity—a fatal error for any woman. For when this happens, life inevitably becomes

> *. . . a tale*
> *Told by an idiot, full of sound and fury,*
> *Signifying nothing.*[8]

The masculine, when divorced from the feminine and given an autonomous life of its own, produces a false notion of Kingship—power for its own sake, reducing Kingship to a demonic parody of the real thing. Thus, when Lady Macbeth's masculinity usurps her femininity, Macbeth confronts her not as "My Dearest Love" but as a triple-headed witch who takes possession of him.

This theme of the destruction of true Kingship Shakespeare explores again and again, always showing the woman denying her true nature as she simulates masculine values in a power-play alien to her feminine identity.

While it is apparent that there are more and more Lady Macbeths among so-called emancipated women, a reaction has already set in. Many women are now refusing to be Lady Macbeths. They are refusing to be caught up in "the dunnest smoke of hell," refusing to dedicate themselves to a Kingship that careens toward madness. They refuse to push their men in that direction and refuse to be dragged that way themselves. Consciously or unconsciously, they know that all the perfumes of Arabia will not sweeten a little hand that has performed murder on itself.

The murder which has been committed is in effect the murder of the Great Mother, understood as the inner psychic life expressing itself in a world of symbols that feed the spirit. As Jung has pointed out, we are so busy doing and achieving that we have lost touch with our inner life, that life which gives meaning to symbols and conversely the symbols which give meaning to life. No other era has so totally divorced outer reality from inner reality, the matrix of which is the Great Mother. Never before have we been so cut off from the wisdom of nature and the wisdom of our own instincts. The literary world from Eliot to Beckett cries out for water or food; the art world creates distortions ranging from Giacometti's anorexic skeletons to Botero's obese bourgeoisie.

The goddess at the center of our wasteland culture is a Lady Macbeth. We don't call her that. We don't know she's there. Like her, we go about sleepwalking with our eyes open and our senses shut. Lady Macbeth personifies the extreme negative mother, one who would dash her baby's brains out and sacrifice love to power. She is not to be confused with the Black Madonna in Christian mythology (below, pages 79-82) who lives through our dark, uncanny, instinctual nature and who can, if she is given the chance, bring her healing to our despair. Through her, our divine child can be born. But nothing divine can come out of a Lady Macbeth. She is without love and without any redeeming power because she has cut herself off from her feminine instincts; her so-called "love," therefore, alienates rather than joins. Hers is the voice that whines, "How can you do this to me?"

It's true Lady Macbeth did not know what she was doing. And neither do her worshipers. Some of the sweetest, kindest, most unselfish witches suck the life-blood out of those they "love." They do not understand when their children cannot eat the food they so devotedly prepare. Only by seeing her, and naming her, can we recover the power she insidiously sips away. She is still sleepwalking among us; she is still going to bed in total unconsciousness, with her feminine agony crying out in her dreams. Hers is the power principle that castrates men and kills feminine relatedness. That goddess is at the center of many addictions. We cannot redeem her unless we wrench the veils from our own eyes and see her and the seductive witchery behind her.

In my practice, I see this battle between inner and outer reality, between the feminine and the masculine, between being and doing, between the unconscious and consciousness, raging in dramatic terms in my obese and anorexic analysands. Most of them are college-trained, sensitive, efficient young women whose education has been dedicated to achieving good grades, whose sensitivity has been honed to a degree which makes ordinary life nasty, mean and brutish. Their allegiance to the masculine principle has split their feminine principle into white and black: on the one hand the good mother, cherishing, nurturing, unconditionally loving; on the other, the ruthless whore, jealous, unrelated, sexual. Their feelings toward their own mother are usually ambivalent: both unconscious identification with her masculine-oriented ideals and/or total rejection of them, and unconscious identification with the nurturing mother and clinging daughter—at the same time totally rejecting both roles. Often unconscious of the duality of their feelings and the contradic-

*Fair is foul and foul is fair;/Hover through the fog and filthy air.*
—Shakespeare, *Macbeth.*

Circle Limit IV, 1960.—M.C. Escher. (© Escher-heirs 1982 c/o Beeldrecht Amsterdam; Collection Haags Gemeentemuseum, The Hague)

tion that lies at the center of their personality, on the one hand they seem to be clinging to life, on the other they are systematically destroying themselves. Once they become aware of this duality, they are careful to hide the real conflict behind a passive, silent mask.

They are accused of being dramatic, hysterical, orgiastic. These accusations are perhaps true, but seen in perspective the reason is clear. They have no sense of everlasting arms to uphold them through the crises of life; the early matrix with the mother isn't there. That deprivation propels them to make violent attempts to hold onto life; momentarily they may do so, and then sink back into a lethargy of nonexistence. Their existence is precarious at best because they have no sense of a daily continuum. Such girls seek husbands who will provide that loving day-to-day cherishing, and therefore in marriage they may lock themselves yet again into the mother they sought to escape.

The obese and the anorexic are fighting their battles for consciousness through food—the acceptance or rejection of it. Food in our culture is a catalyst for almost any emotion—a positive way of expressing love, joy, acceptance; or negatively, a way of expressing guilt, bribery, fear of rejection. Food and the quality of the food are at the center of every festival. To share the food is to be a part of the festival; to reject it is to be left out of life.

Increasingly, I see the food complex as a neurosis compelling intelligent women toward consciousness. This is to view the food complex positively, in terms of its purpose. That that consciousness may not be endurable is the other side. It begins in what looks like a weight problem; where the conflict is not yet in consciousness, it takes psychosomatic form. Fat in our culture is taboo, so the neurosis hits where it hurts most—at the heart of the female ego. The fat girl is not one with her peers: she cannot eat the junk foods, she is not invited to the adolescent parties, she cannot wear jeans, she is not attractive sexually. In short, in our society she is not a female, and no one knows it as well as she. Isolation forces her into her own inner world where fantasies compensate for the unlived life and the images of the imagination gradually take on numinous power. The forbidden becomes at once the revered and the dangerous object.

Where the unconscious drive behind the food that involves the girl's relationship to her mother is not understood, it will be acted out destructively. If it is understood, there is some chance of its being worked out creatively. What consciousness demands is a recognition of the difference between appearance and reality which defines the girl's ambivalent feelings toward the mother. On the one hand she recognizes all the mother has given; on the other she senses the negativity behind the gifts, especially the rejection of herself as a person.

The women I have worked with, and those I have in mind in this book, are conscious enough to make the distinction between appearance and reality. They are grappling with their ambivalent feelings having been in analysis from one to three years. In the world they function efficiently, many in highly responsible professional positions. They have some understanding of the matriarchal dynamics behind the food complex. They are struggling to come to grips with a false Lady Macbeth matriarchal value system in which their own femininity is contaminated by masculine values which the unconscious rightly refuses to accept, even as their body refuses to assimilate the food. The longer they are the victims of this false value system, the more they come to realize that whatever the outward show of achievement, their lives are increasingly "full of sound and fury, signifying nothing."

While young women often come into analysis merely to lose weight, the more mature recognize that they must seek out its underlying causes and adjust their conscious values and attitudes accordingly. They are, as women, locked into a false view of Kingship inherent in the woman possessed by a drive alien to her nature. Their task is to rescue themselves from a drive that is destroying them. Food embodies the false values that their own bodies refuse to assimilate, by which I mean that their bodies become edemic, bloated, allergic, or resort to vomiting the poison out. The unconscious body, and certainly the conscious body, will not tolerate the negative mother.

I stress here that this book is not a condemnation of mothers—or fathers. It is about recognizing the enemy and giving it a name in order to deal creatively with it. Of course, children have to recognize negative as well as positive feelings toward their parents, but most of us, at some point in analysis, realize that our parents were in a worse situation than we. Many of them knew they were trapped, but they had no means of finding a way out. The sins of one generation are visited on the next; that is the human situation, and to the extent that parents are unconscious, their children suffer. It is the task of mature individuals to differentiate infantile imagos from the actual parents, to differentiate what was wholesome in their heritage from what was destructive, and to forgive.

The creative purpose of the neurosis is to bring the woman to confront within herself the negative mother which her feminine body naturally rejects. The negative mother is a foreign substance; it is alien; it does not belong to her any more than do two pounds of chocolates before she goes to sleep. Her body is demanding that she differentiate herself out from it so that she can discover who she is as a mature woman. The task which her own mother may have failed to perform, she must perform. That is the new consciousness, the giant leap, the healing in her own life which she is being called upon to incorporate.

I sat before my glass one day,
    And conjured up a vision bare,
Unlike the aspects glad and gay,
    That erst were found reflected there—
The vision of a woman, wild
    With more than womanly despair.

Her hair stood back on either side
    A face bereft of loveliness.
It had no envy now to hide
    What once no man on earth could guess.
It formed the thorny aureole
    Of hard unsanctified distress.

Her lips were open—not a sound
    Came through the parted lines of red.
Whate'er it was, the hideous wound
    In silence and in secret bled.
No sigh relieved her speechless woe,
    She had no voice to speak her dread.

And in her lurid eyes there shone
    The dying flame of life's desire,
Made mad because its hope was gone,
    And kindled at the leaping fire
Of jealousy, and fierce revenge,
    And strength that could not change nor tire.

Shade of a shadow in the glass,
    O set the crystal surface free!
Pass—as the fairer visions pass—
    Nor ever more return to be
The ghost of a distracted hour,
That heard me whisper, "I am she!"

　　　—Mary Elizabeth Coleridge, "The Other Side of the Mirror."


Phlebas the Phoenician, a fortnight dead,
Forgot the cry of gulls, the deep sea swell
And the profit and loss.
　　　　　　　　　A current under sea
Picked his bones in whispers. As he rose and fell
He passed the stages of his age and youth
Entering the whirlpool.
　　　　　　　　　Gentile or Jew
O you who turn the wheel and look to windward,
Consider Phlebas, who was once handsome and tall as you.

　　　　—T.S. Eliot, "Death by Water," *The Waste Land.*

# 2

## Ritual: Sacred and Demonic

*All ages before us have believed in gods in some form or other. Only an unparalleled impoverishment of symbolism could enable us to rediscover the gods as psychic factors, that is, as archetypes of the unconscious.*

     —C.G. Jung, "Archetypes of the Unconscious."

Asking ourselves why oral addictions have permeated our Western culture at this particular time helps us not only to open our eyes to our own sacred cow, but also to the dark angel that we are being forced to wrestle with. According to recent statistics, about 30% of American males are overweight, 40% of American females are twenty pounds or more overweight,[1] and 7% of Canadian, university-aged women induce vomiting to control their weight.[2] The anorexic population varies radically in age, sex and social group, but using rigorous diagnostic criteria it is estimated that 7% of modeling students suffer from anorexia nervosa.[3] Why this great hollow at our center?

In a recent TV interview, Leonard Bernstein, commenting on the fact that Mahler's music is now very popular with young people, said that he did not find this extraordinary because everything is in every note of Mahler. Young people can deal with that, he suggested, because they are so constantly confronted with the end of the world that they can bring all of themselves to those majestic notes.

This sense of finality is partly why compulsions, particularly those having to do with the body, are constellating so forcibly in our culture. In every newscast we are confronted with destruction—wars, airplane crashes, rape, murder. Books, movies, theater—from every side we are bombarded with the possibility of our imminent annihilation. At the same time, the structures which once would have supported us are crumbling: the nuclear family, the community, the Church. Rituals which were once the cornerstone of living are now hollow and rosaries are worn as adornments. Coupled with this dread of extinction is the natural propensity of compulsives to live in the future. Often intuitive by nature, they don't clasp the here-and-now reality with which they cannot cope; rather they dream about what they could be, should be, were meant to be in the future. The gap between reality and dream is often filled by the obsession.

25

Furthermore, the technological age is propelling us into a space quite unrelated to our instincts. We have forgotten how to listen to our bodies; we pop pills for everything that goes wrong with us; we can have an intestinal bypass or we can have our stomach stapled. We can turn ourselves over to medicine without ever questioning what the body is trying to tell us. To our peril, we assume it has no wisdom of its own and we attempt to right our physical ills without making the necessary psychic corrections. We may temporarily succeed but the body has its way and soon another symptom appears, attempting to draw our attention to some basic problem. If we ignore the small symptoms, the body eventually takes its revenge. As a culture we are not in touch with our instinctual roots, and parents tend to treat their children as if they too were machines instead of human beings with feelings and fears. If the child is treated that way, consciously or unconsciously, it in turn treats itself that way and the malaise deepens with each generation until someone in the family becomes conscious enough to stop it.

If, for example, a mother looks into her mirror and sees her body, not as her own self, but as the raw stuff of art which can be manipulated as she pleases, then a "mirror, mirror on the wall" attitude develops in her daughter. Her body may become an art object, to the extent that she fails to recognize herself in it as a human being. She does not inhabit that body. Thus a terrifying dichotomy develops: she appears like a young girl, sweet, compliant, passive, with a voice like a child, but what comes out of her mouth is murderous. In her "innocence," she is unaware of the killer at large inside her. The following statement is typical of a twenty-year-old anorexic woman:

> When can I get out of this box? I drag my body around as if it's some gross foreign object. I'm so scared of cancer and war and school and what people think. Now I'm so upset my head is going to explode and I'm so scared I'm going to be huge and the world will end and I'm just nowhere. I'm not here and I'm certainly not there. What am I doing? I keep setting these standards for myself and I just can't do it. I can't do anything. NOTHING. NOTHING. Ugly, filthy, fat slob!

Her reaction to the affluent world in which she is living is withdrawal. She hates everything superfluous. Her patriarchal value system based on the Kingdom of Beauty, Purity and Light forces her into deeper enmity toward her "filthy body," which she would reduce to "minimal" or even "conceptual" art in which the object is no longer there. Nor can society offer a Great Mother image to reach out to, a mother who could help her to bridge the gap between herself and her femininity. That archetype is not yet constellated. Without that maternal matrix she moves alone in the landscape of her own terror, shrinking from the chaos of a new life and paralyzed by dreams of the old. For her, life is not the issue. Her sole purpose is to fashion the object in the mirror into a work of art, totally acceptable, ironically, to the collective value system she despises.

Aloneness is a crucial component in compulsive syndromes, as it is a crucial component in modern society. Real compulsives carry out their rituals alone. To quote from the journal of another anorexic young woman:

> I go in various stages of perfection. When my life is organized, it is perfectly organized, so that if something goes wrong, I can't just make the best of it. I totally fall apart. Everything goes. There has to be a logical reason for everything I do, right down to the food I eat. "The skinnier the better" is my philosophy. It's not only attractive; it shows discipline and control. But everything I do is centered around food and worrying that people will make me eat. Once that statement would have seemed bizarre to me. That is why I feel it is hopeless to try to explain myself to people who aren't anorexics. They are on a different thought-plane. They don't understand that when I am gripped by the compulsion I could go forever without food.

The same sense of orbiting alone is expressed by an obese young woman:

> I've graduated from crap food to granola cookies. I lost ten pounds. I feel great until I look in the mirror—that's the killer. I can feel the blood being sucked out of me. I hear mocking laughter echoing to the bottom of my gut. I don't believe anymore. I don't believe I can stay with life. I grab a cookie to stop that terrible laughter. And then the guilt! Who would ever believe that? Narrowing life down to making a cookie a crime!

One of the greatest difficulties in dealing with food addicts, as with alcoholics, is helping them to overcome their sense of despair when they lose the high associated with these addictions. In fact the overcoming of one addiction may activate another, and many an anorexic or obese girl has been born in full armor from an alcoholic's brain. It is not uncommon for such a girl to find her own healing through a religious conversion. Certainly, Jung recognized the confusion between physical and spiritual thirst when he wrote to Bill Wilson, cofounder of Alcoholics Anonymous:

> [The] craving for alcohol [is] the equivalent on a low level of the spiritual thirst of our being for wholeness; expressed in medieval language: the union with God. . . .
> I am strongly convinced that the evil principle prevailing in this world leads the unrecognized spiritual need into perdition, if it is not counteracted either by a real religious insight or by the protective wall

of human community. An ordinary man, not protected by an action from above and isolated in society, cannot resist the power of evil, which is called very aptly the Devil. . . .

You see, "alcohol," in Latin is *spiritus* and you use the same word for the highest religious experience as well as for the most depraving poison. The helpful formula therefore is: *spiritus contra spiritum.*[4]

The first two steps in the Alcoholics Anonymous program are:

1. We admitted we were powerless over alcohol—that our lives had become unmanageable.
2. Came to believe that a Power greater than ourselves could restore us to sanity.[5]

Food and alcohol hold an overwhelming fascination for a vast majority in our society, and it may well be that the numinosity of food and drink reflects the central crisis in our 20th-century culture: the crisis in faith. We live in a predominantly Christian culture which has lost its living connection to the symbolism of wafer and wine. Lacking spiritual sustenance there is genuine hunger and thirst. The archetypal structure behind the wafer and wine is slowly giving way to a new configuration, but we are in chaos during the transition. That chaos breeds loneliness, fear and alienation. While that sense of aloneness is hard to endure, it can be of supreme value in the analytic process. The new life always comes out of the dispossessed, as Christ came from the cow stable.

The danger in joining a group is that one can become identified with its image, or the image that society has put upon it. Thus a woman who joins a feminist group may be locked into 1970's ideas of repression instead of flowing with her own creative process. If an obese woman gets locked into "Big is Beautiful" and starts preaching that philosophy, she has effectively stopped her own inner development—just as an alcoholic who joins AA and becomes the best speaker on the circuit may find himself once again on the bottle.

I have a deep respect for both Alcoholics Anonymous and Overeaters Anonymous and I encourage my analysands to join those groups, because understanding from others can be tremendously liberating. But the fact remains that if we are to find our own inner truth, we have to go into our darkness alone and stay with our inner process until we find our own healing archetypal pattern. Once that relationship is established, we are on our individual path whether we are with a group or not. It takes great courage to break with one's past history and stand alone.

In fairytales, the movement toward wholeness—often symbolized by a quest for prince, princess or treasure—is constellated by the lack of something in the kingdom. Similarly, in any human society a new archetypal pattern will be constellated in the collective unconscious to compensate for what is missing in the consciousness of the collective. Hence I tend to see what is happening today with food and drink as Mater's way of concretizing a new archetypal pattern— a feminine one—that is constellating to compensate for the specious masculine ideals and the loss of numinous spiritual values in our culture.

Matter is accumulating in heaps all around us, more and more material. We can't get enough. We are burying ourselves in it, whether in possessions or flesh. We rape nature, the Great Mother, with very little sense of guilt. The devouring mother is taking over but we don't open our eyes to see her. The anorexic girl unconsciously says a flat NO to the witch, but is unconsciously devoured. The fat girl, caught between her hatred of the witch outside and the witch within, builds her own fortress in an effort to escape. The alcoholic escapes through his trickster spirit. Meanwhile the Eros principle, the spirit of love, cannot relate to the daily ravaging of human instincts. The love that once existed between nature and man has almost been annihilated. It is at the point of death, indeed, that new life can appear. Yet the archetype of the feminine, as it is constellating now, is not clear. Maybe the darkness is not yet deep enough.

Many people in our society are being driven to addictions because there is no collective container for their natural spiritual needs. Their natural propensity for transcendent experience, for ritual, for connection to some energy greater than their own, is being distorted into addictive behavior. Rituals on whatever level are a very important part of daily life. We love our little routines that help us to float through a day. We imagine we are conscious when we wake up. We move through our ablution rituals, we exercise, we have our coffee, orange juice and toast. We move from bedroom to bathroom to kitchen. Then one morning there is a guest in the house. We can't get into the bathroom. We go to the kitchen and drop our favorite coffee mug. We're cranky. We hate small talk over breakfast. We miss our bus. The whole day is shot. On such small details we build our profane rituals, rituals to which we are basically indifferent until they go wrong. Then we realize how unconscious we can remain so long as we have those repetitive patterns to hold our world together.

Spraying fixative on our daily lives, establishing comfortable daily routines, is to some extent necessary. Some people manage very well within a highly organized life. Others, compulsives for example, move through the fixed world with a seeming equilibrium, but are actually enslaved to rigid routine, hence a great part of their energy is seething in some secret chamber which even they may fail to recognize. Psychologically speaking, their energy is locked into a complex—a taboo area which is at once forbidden and magnetic, terrifying and numinous. Periodically or regularly they are compelled to contact that awesome energy in themselves. If food is the taboo object, they eat until the ego lets go, surrenders, submits itself to the archetypal energy that is then released. If they are anorexic, they perform their rituals with the food and then exercise until the "lightness" begins to take over. They go into the Light and then experience themselves lit with an inner radiance. If they are bulimics (ritual vomiters), they may eat as much as 50,000 calories and purge themselves six times in a single day, with vomiting, diuretics or laxatives. All are setting up a thoroughly schizophrenic pattern: one side of the personality is in fierce rebellion against the society that is starving them; the other side is killing them in order to attain the image of slimness that society requires.

There is, in fact, a criminal mentality at work. If ice cream is forbidden, then they will have one cone and hate themselves for the rest of the day. If chocolate macaroons are spilled on the supermarket shelf, they'll have a handful. If this behavior is looked at carefully, it is clear that almost all the food they eat is stolen—even from their own refrigerators. They tell themselves they will fast but they don't; in effect they steal the food from themselves. This craving to do the forbidden often comes from a lifelong relationship with the negative mother who is constantly judging, so that if "I" am doing what I want to do, it is wrong, and therefore I must do it quickly and surreptitiously if I am to enjoy it without condemnation.

During the conflict their energy swings from one pole to the other. This sudden reversal of energy is called *enantiodromia*. It occurs when energy has been pushed too far in one direction, and suddenly switches into the resisting energy it has been struggling to overcome (like Paul's conversion on the road to Damascus). The "I" cannot surface to take control, and without the "I," the outcome is inevitable: they become the very thing they fight. By setting up a civil war in which each side hates the other and refuses to negotiate, they leave themselves open from behind. There the real enemy looms, waiting for the civil war to exhaust itself. Then it will take over uncontested.

Jung believed that religion (*religere*, to reflect) is one of man's instincts, a natural need that must, therefore, be satisfied.[6] In our world, where the institutionalized sacred is being increasingly profaned, compensation takes over. People begin to treasure their own personal objects and invest them with sacred power. They create their own rituals, but because they don't realize what they are doing they may invoke the wrong god, and be subject to that power whether they like it or not. Again they are trapped into becoming what they worship. If they reject the world as it is, they unconsciously create their own fiction and attempt to project their own "sacred" world onto the world outside. The resultant collision is increasingly destructive.

Repeatedly a woman may tell me how hurt she is by other people's boorish responses. Her battered sensibilities withdraw from the constant onslaught. What she does not realize is that she is trying to make everything around her sacred and that other people may not understand that they are treading on her sacred space or moving in her sacred time, and so they are unwittingly desecrating her sacred temple. The temptation is to withdraw into one's own Holy of Holies and build the retaining wall so strong that no one can get in. Again the danger is that the Holy of Holies becomes a witch's brew. Without the Church to mark out those strong boundaries between impersonal and personal, sacred and profane, God and Devil, we have to be extremely conscious in order to protect ourselves from the demonic within and without.

The projection of the Perfect was once on God. When God "died," that perfection was often projected onto the husband. And now the terrible truth is that in many lives that projection has been taken off the husband and put onto a muffin. It holds that much numinosity; its captive cannot break the spell. At the same time, however, some voice of sanity or some inner laughter mocks the whole idea of *participation mystique* with a holy muffin. The muffin is not sacred and the power it is releasing is not holy power even when flavored with blueberries.

Then what *is* going on? In a religious structure, ritual is recognized as a transformative fire through which an individual moves on the journey from one level of society to another or from one level of awareness to another. Whether the fire is real or symbolic, the initiate submits to it, allows the old life to be burned away and emerges as a new person.[7] At the center of the fire is an archetypal force, a god or goddess so to speak, which the participant invokes in order to participate in its life. By contacting that energy in a numinous experience of suffering, dying and then rising again, the ego sacrifices itself to a Higher Power, is enlarged and transformed so that it returns to ordinary life with a new outlook. But what happens when these innate spiritual longings are not structured within an impersonal framework such as the Church could offer? The muffin cannot replace the divine wafer, nor can alcohol replace the divine spirit, nor can starving replace a religious fast. When our animal and spiritual signals are confused, bizarre behavior results. The emptiness gnaws and the wolf prowls until some kind of ritual is performed. If it is a compulsive ritual, it can become nothing less than a hurricane swirling its victim headlong into unconsciousness. The natural, spiritual hunger, if it is not fed by the sacred, is trapped in the demonic.

In sacred ritual the participants are always careful to go clockwise around the church, the walled city, the sacred temenos. Moving in that direction they invoke the good gods, and having moved in and through and out of their gods they emerge into consciousness with a new awareness and sense of harmony. In a Black Mass, where the participants are invoking the Devil, they circle to the left, go through ritualized behavior in reverse and experience themselves charged with demonic power. The two patterns could be symbolized by the spiral movement of energy emanating from either the eye of Medusa or the eye of the Great Mother.[8] In diagram form it would look like this:

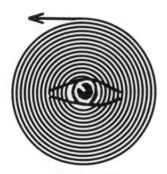 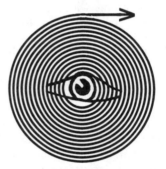

| | |
|:---:|:---:|
| **Medusa's eye**<br>Counterclockwise movement<br>of energy into the unconscious.<br>Depression<br>*Medusa petrifies* | **Great Mother's eye**<br>Clockwise movement of energy<br>toward consciousness.<br>New energy released<br>*Being feeds Doing* |

The inner monologue as the energy circles counterclockwise into a demonic binge sounds like a negative mantra:

I'm exhausted. I'm ravaged by all these people around me. I'm hungry. I can't hold myself together. I need food. There's no love in my life. I'm not lovable. It's not my fault. I need sweets. I've got to have sweets. I won't be deprived of everything. My life is all wrong, but I can't help it. It's not my fault. I can't deal with it. I can't do it. I can't do it. I can't do it.

Looked at psychologically, this woman is not taking responsibility for her shadow, nor is she taking into account the reality of her situation and then taking action to care for herself. In renouncing that responsibility, she also renounces her own guilt and her own self-destructive activity. Her infantile desire for instant gratification makes her indifferent to her own feeling, and thus she opens the door to negative emotional flooding (the full consequences of which are evident in the passage on page 38) when the binge reaches its nadir. (I should emphasize here Jung's distinction between feeling and affect: feeling is a rational function telling us what is of value to us; affect or emotion comes from an activated complex.)

In contrast, as a person's energy circles clockwise around the Great Mother, the inner monologue sounds like a positive mantra:

> I am tired. I love myself. I love my body. I give myself permission to be nourished. I love my inner woman. What food would be best for her? Is it food I really want? Is it music? Is it dancing? Yes, I am fat, but I am trying to release my true feminine body, whatever shape it is. What is the reality here? This is me happening to me. I need to relax, to be quiet. I need a bath. I want to affirm my own life. I can do it; I can do it; I can do it.

In this monologue, fat is being faced as fact, as is the bright side of the shadow which has probably never been fully lived. Instead of dieting while saying "I can't," which merely reinforces the negative thought pattern, it is dealt with positively, all the time building the ego. The stronger the ego the more the projections can be taken back from the food. If psychic health is patiently reconstructed in this way, then there may be no need for new symptoms to appear once the weight loss begins.

The drivenness in the professional world can be just as demonic as that of the binge. Marie-Louise von Franz speaking of the symbolism of the wolf says:

> In the dreams of modern women the wolf often represents the animus, or that strange devouring attitude women can have when possessed by the animus.... The wolf represents that strange indiscriminate desire to eat up everybody and everything.... which is visible in many neuroses where the main problem is that the person remains infantile because of an unhappy childhood.... It is not really that *they* want it, *it* wants it. Their "it" is never satisfied, so the wolf also creates in such people a constant, resentful dissatisfaction.... The wolf is called *lykos*, light. The greed when mastered or directed onto its right goal is *the* thing.[9]

The following diagram illustrates energy moving like a pendulum. The more the energy goes into one side, the more the compensation on the other; the faster and wider the pendulum swings, the more liable it is to go right over the top (enantiodromia). The secret is to find the ego position which can master the greed and direct that energy in the right way onto the right goal.

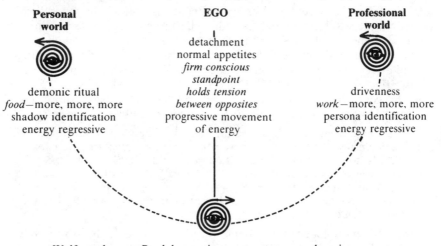

| **Personal world** | **EGO** | **Professional world** |
|---|---|---|
| | detachment | |
| | normal appetites | |
| | *firm conscious* | |
| | *standpoint* | |
| demonic ritual | *holds tension* | drivenness |
| *food*—more, more, more | *between opposites* | *work*—more, more, more |
| shadow identification | progressive movement | persona identification |
| energy regressive | of energy | energy regressive |

Wolf syndrome: Pendulum gains momentum as obsessive energy alternates between personal and professional activities.

In ritual binging, the negative mother is invoked by the very pattern leading up to the binge. The binger is riding home on the bus. She decides she won't get out at her usual stop because there's a muffin stand there and anyway a walk would do her good. She stays on; she *needs* the muffin; she becomes nervous. She stays on for two stops and then in spite of her best intentions she's out and racing back to buy those taboo, those holy, those hated objects. She is alone, of course. She would be ashamed if anyone were with her. She is already being walked, rather than walking of her own volition. She furtively hurries to her own flat, locks the door, unplugs the phone, puts on her ritual dress, takes her ritual position and begins to eat. At first she is overwhelmingly calm, a calm that moves into a sort of ecstasy, until muffin becomes MUFFIN. Her wolf is constellated: her body is bloated; her spirit is annihilated.

If she is obese, she will fall into bed in a stupor: if she is bulimic she will put her finger down her throat and vomit. She has betrayed herself but *she* feels betrayed, duped by some power within herself over which she has no control. The goddess which she unconsciously sought to incarnate, and momentarily believed in as she excitedly bought the food, did not appear. Or, if she did, she appeared in her demonic form. In her preparation for the binge, she thought she was invoking the positive mother; she felt loved, secure, protected, enthroned. But even as in childhood the *need* for the positive mother was all too often answered by the presence of the negative mother— or a confusion of the two—so in the binge the positive mother actually turns into a witch before the binger's very eyes and in her very stomach. The eucharist begins sacred and ends demonic, thus repeating the child's experience of the mother.

The mother, to be sure, may have felt trapped by her daughter's need. If she was locked into a loveless marriage, confined at home with children, desperate to get out, then her child's need would become her nightmare. Thus in relation to the child's yearning for a positive mother, the actual mother may in fact become negative no matter how much she "gives."

The childhood experience which one woman compulsively relived in every binge is described in the following passage written by her after three years of analysis:

> The whole structure of my existence has depended on one premise. I have to please others. I am incapable of thinking in any other way. No matter how hard I work to recognize what my own feelings are, however conscientiously I decide to hold onto the moment, I still fall into delayed reactions. Tomorrow or the next day I will know how I felt in the situation. Then it hits me like a bolt, sometimes anger, sometimes fear, sometimes joy but I can't get hold of the feelings until after the moment which should be spontaneous has passed. I spend one hour of analysis digesting the real feelings from the session before. Then it is too late to act on them. In the actual situation I am paralyzed because part of me is trying to please the analyst and part is trying to drop into my own feelings.
>
> I am incapable of interacting even with people I love the most—in fact, that is the most difficult. When I return to my aloneness I feel hungry and depleted because I cannot open myself to receive emotional nourishment, and I have not given of myself, so on my deepest levels I feel unexpressed, unfulfilled and self-betrayed. The flow of energy between people who love each other is short-circuited in me. I burble, I hear others burbling, but I am afraid to open up my own core. I have no idea what might come out. Intellectually I know that emotional and spiritual growth takes place through interaction, but I bury myself alive in a glass coffin sealed off from life. I'm withering in there. My body becomes more rigid; my soul becomes more hungry. I eat because I am, in fact, *starving*. It is self-destruction because I know I will eat till I fall into unconsciousness.
>
> It's all a replay of our family dinners—occasions with the best possible food my mother could prepare and my father presiding over the roast. The table groaned with goodness and love. What mother had spent her day preparing, we were expected to eat. To refuse was

to reject her. If I raised my voice to argue with my father, he said I didn't know what I was saying and quietly told me what I did think. And once when I cried and said that wasn't what I thought at all, my mother dismissed me from the table and said she wasn't raising any crybaby.

There was a plaque on our dining room wall—an ethereal head of Christ looking into heaven and underneath it said, "Christ is the head of this house—the unseen guest at every meal." There was an unseen guest all right, I was certainly aware of his presence. It was the devil himself. If I didn't eat what was offered—physically, emotionally, mentally—I knew he would materialize. He was a killer. I had no choice. I either swallowed what was crammed down my throat or I was killed. From the beginning, anything that came from my own little girl was mocked or silenced. The mess began before I was born. My mother hated her pregnancy, hoped to God she'd have a boy, went through hours of agonized labor, was finally anesthetized and I was dragged into the world, leaving her internally damaged. No wonder she couldn't cope with me. What she must have suffered trying to breast-feed me! And what I must have suffered trying to get the milk.

And that's the infantile pattern that still goes on—and I'm forty bloody years old. Every time I try to receive, I go through Hell. Outwardly it is the milk of human kindness overflowing from the bounteous breast, and I'm the dutiful infant forced by my overflowing mother and my own hunger to feed. Inwardly, I know I have to please Mommy and the only way I can please Mommy is to kill myself. Drink her poison and say thank you. The unseen guest is always there, that's for sure, telling me that everything I am is poison and the only way I can survive is to drink what I'm given, even if I know it is poison to me.

When I binge it is infant tyrant gobbling up witch mother and the terrible irony is that's exactly how I can best please her. Eat her poison and annihilate myself. When I starve it is infant tyrant rejecting witch mother. But the outcome is the same. Reject life and die. I am incapable of receiving into my own Being. I cannot trust the sweetness of the milk. I can't receive communion. I take the wafer but I do not receive it. Even springtime—I see, but I do not feel, how beautiful it is. I am in a death-trap, a constant contradiction. I want to survive. To survive I must please. To please, I must die—I, my feminine feelings, my sexuality, my needs, my desires. Instead of accepting, I escape. I live in my glass coffin—ugly as it is—and watch life pass me by.

The passage makes several points very clear. The binge is magnetic in that it seems to promise the presence of the Loving Mother. In anticipation it appears to be a sacred ritual governed by Eros, with a fixed center from which the starving spirit will go out satiated, released and secure, moving into a loving community. In fact it is merely a compulsive repetition governed by Thanatos, trapping the worshiper into deeper isolation, more profound hunger and no release. It is simply a mechanical act that must be gone through again and again until its meaning finally becomes clear. And the only way that meaning can be deciphered is for the person to become conscious enough to ask the question: "What does it mean about *me?*"

So long as the question isn't asked, the unseen guest is the witch mother masquerading as a sentimentalized Christ or other savior figure. Once consciousness takes hold of the problem and dialogues with the unconscious, the guest reveals himself in a very different form and what *seemed* sacred is recognized as demonic. So long as a woman doesn't know what she is doing, she is deluded. Unless she has the courage to ask, "What is going on here?" she does in fact fall into the unconsciousness she has prepared for herself. What she forgets as she buys her muffins is the panic involved in that darkness. What she in fact faces in the unconscious is the negative mother witch, and the greater the panic the closer she comes to the complex—to the negative mother she never dared face as a child. The fear and rage evoked in facing Medusa are swallowed down in the binge. (The binge and the blessed sleep may well be nature's way of protecting her from a psychotic corner she is not yet ready to face.)

Once a woman is ready to break her identification with the mother, once consciousness understands what has been going on unconsciously, she can understand that her real mother and therefore the mother within herself were simply not able to give food. So long as she is obedient to a mother—actual or internal—who unconsciously wishes to annihilate her, she is in a state of possession by the witch; she will have to differentiate herself out from that witch in order to live her own life. Only then will she be able to nourish herself, and thereby transform a demonic ritual into a sacred one. The time may come when eating may be simply mundane, but until food loses its numinosity, eating for her will have to be a sacred rite.

Obviously there is an unconscious, instinctive voice which refuses to be silenced. Something is refusing to adapt to ego demands. Unless it is heard and heeded, life itself may be in jeopardy. Spiritual longing either becomes the friend of the ego and goes with it into the richness of life or becomes more entrenched as an enemy and sets up a counterattack against life. The nature gods make their demands felt. Whether we like it or not, we are forced to listen to them. If we have any insight at all, at some point we *choose* whether we will join our demons and scream out against the gods who are trying to save us, or whether we will adjust our conscious values in harmony with their demands, even in such a basic issue as funda-

mental body nourishment. Whether, that is, we will digest what is
necessary to life or whether we will allow it to sit like a lump in the
belly where it manifests as vomit or bloat or blocked kidneys.

The following passage, reproduced here exactly as it came off the
typewriter, reveals the battle that goes on during a demonic binge. It
is an extraordinary piece of writing because rarely can a person keep
conscious enough to realize anything once the binge takes over. It
shows the ego attempting to hold its own ground against the demonic sarcasm and laughter of the complex. The two voices are at
first clear enough, but once the frenzy really begins then this very
cultured woman (and expert typist) cannot control typewriter, spell-
ing or punctuation. The frail ego attempts to confront, then tries to
escape, but gradually goes down under the ruthless onslaught, frustrated, enraged, pounding the keys. It ends with an "out-of-body"
experience—the witch flying on the wind.

SO WHY ARE YOU SCARED TO TRY BECAUSE I WILL FAIL
NO THAT S NOT IT WHERE ARE THE FORCES YOU HAVE
ALLIED WITH WHERE ARE THEY DO THEY HELP YOU YES
THEY GIVE ME SLEEP WHY DONT YOU WANT TO BE
AWAKE BECAUSE IT HURTS TO BE AWAKE TELL ME HOW
MUCH IT HURTS OK ARE YOU READY? ALL THE TIME.

EVERY ONE LOOKS AT YOU SNICKER SNICKER THEY
LOOK AT YOU THEY DONT LOOK AT YOU TO EBE POLITE.
TO BE POLITE IS NOT TO NOTICE THEY DONT NOTICE YOU
STINK TOO ESP IN SUMMER YOU ARE ALWAYS UGLY
BODY AND NOW FACE AGAIN HAHAHAHAHAHA-
HAHAHAHAHAHA YOU THOUGHT YOU HAD GOTTEN
RIDE OF PIMPLES HAHAHAHAHAHAHATHEY ARE BACK
WHO IS HAPPY. TELL MY YOUR NAME HAPPY ONE?????
TELL ME WHO YOU ARE WHAT DO YOU CARE I AM
DEMON HAHAHAH ARE YOU PRETENDING? NO IIAM
HAPPY WHY ARE YOU HAPPY EAT AND SHUT UP EAT AND
SHUT UP DONT PLAY MUSIC MUSIC AMAKES ME HIDE IF
YOU DO PLAY MUSIC YOU HIDE TOO YOU HIDE WHILE
YOU PLAY DONT THINK DREAM WHILE YOUR AWAKE
DONT WORK BUT DREAM DREAM OF WHEN YOUR THIN
WHILE YOU EAT HAHAHAHAH THAT WAY I CAN GO ON
WHY DO YOU WANT TO GO ON BECAUSE BECAUSE WHY
OTHERWISE NO ME YES I WILL GIVE YOU A BETTER HOME
IN THE NEW ME YOU WILL BE A STRONG PRINCE AND MY
KING NOT THIS SNEAKING PERSON W YOU WILL GROW
UP WITH ME NO RUN RUN RUN RUN RUN RUN RUN RUN
RUN RUN RUN RUN RUN RUN RUN RUNRUNRS

WHY DO YOU RUN WHY ARE SCARED WHERE HAVE YOU
RUN TO????? YOU ARE NOTHING YOU ARE LITTLE YOU

CANT GIVE ME ANYTHING HAHAHAHAHAHAHAHAHAHAH
DONT YOU LAUGH AT ME YOUR THE ONE WHOS SCARED
YOUR THE ONE WHOS RUNNING BUT YOUR THE ONE
WHOS FAT HAHAHAHAHAH DO YOU R FEED ME POISON
????NO GOOD FOOD GOOD FOOD EATS EATS CANDY UYU-
MYUM YUMYUMYUM. PIMPLES WIILL GO AWAY ITIS JUST
BECAUSE I AM PREMENSTRUAL THEY WILL GO AWAY BE-
CAUSE MY SKIN IS HEALTHY NOW AND I WILL LOSE
WEIGHT NO NEVER YES NO YOU WONT ITS TOO HARD
DONT TRY JUST WAIT TDO IT LATER NOT READY YET
WHY NOT READY SCARED ITS TOO HOT TOTRY TOO COLD
TOO TOTOTOTOTO DSHFKDSJKFLDKSJD FJDKSIEU-
WIEOFKDMCKAFJDKSLA FJDOIWSIFJDIS NAKSLDOFIUW
NAKSODIFUDNASKDOFKGHTIWOALSKDJFIAOSODOFIAUSI
ODJAKL FJDKSOAIWUEIROSIUDIFOSALWKEJR DJSKAOWI-
WHYSKDFOAKWEY ROSIUANEKAOGNAMEKSODKGNA,-
FLEKSNGKAL WIND BLOWING WIND YOU LIKE WIND
WIND MAKESYOU FLY WITH ITUPIN THE AIR OTHER PEO-
PLE DONT LIKE WIND THEY CRINGEIN WIND THEY HIDE
FROM WIND I LOVE WIND WEEEEEEEEEE FLY ON WIND.

The twenty-six-year-old obese woman who wrote this passage handed it to me at her next session, saying, "In a way I haven't been born. I carry mother." This unconscious remark (two minutes later she didn't recall having said it) and the following description of the drawing on page 41 (by an anorexic psychology student) suggest that the binge has something to do with swallowing the mother. In the above passage, mother is still the enemy, the power-driven negative mother, and the ego is not strong enough to stop "wolfing" her down. The results are volcanic. In the following passage the woman recognizes the transformed mother and chooses to assimilate what she formerly used to vomit out. The result is what she calls a "fiery flood of transformative release," bringing together the physical and the spiritual. Here is her description of the drawing (the fourth in a series of six) and her feelings as she worked on it:

Its direct inspiration was Goethe's *Faust*, the "Mothers" scene. The basic shape is an alchemical vessel that is also a womb of redemption. At the base are two caldrons, a black and a white one, for the opposites. As well, there are nearly hidden renditions of an ear and an eye, for the two most important senses. They represent Logos, the sound of the word, time, and Eros, the shape of creation, space. Around the base of the alembic are images of women. A wise old lady tosses a key down the opening. A spider lady is reminiscent of the Amazon, Wonder Woman. A trickster woman looks down smugly. A dancer stretches one arm up. A lady dressed in 1890's fashion indicates the end of millennia of women's roles as satellites and the emergence of the suffragette movement. One ghostly lady is flaming in transformation. Behind these women are fertility goddesses: Diana of Ephesus, Venus of Willendorf and Venus of Lespugue.

At the back, filling the entire vessel, is a powerful, primal Earth Mother. Her eyes seem wounds of blood tears. Everything is contained in her womb, the walls of which are the alembic. The shape is an alchemical vessel of transformation, a womb, a flame flower, all of which are open at the top for an influx and outflux of the energy of transpersonal mysteries. The final external shape of the drawing is reminiscent of a scarab beetle, the Egyptian symbol of the solar god. Both the feminine and the masculine principles, the lunar rites of "Formation, transformation / The eternal mind's eternal recreation" and the solar rites of Apollonian clarity are symbolized in the drawing.

The most important figure is the one not yet mentioned—the black lady in the center. It took longer to draw her, and come to terms with her, than did the rest of the drawing. She began as a German farm lady but I sought something chthonic, earthy. I inked in a black body through her garments, which became a transparent veil. Her body is bulbous, like a series of rubber tires. Over her breasts and stomach are egglike configurations. She wears a pointed hat, like both a clown and a wizard. Her arms are encased in the original material. It was a bit disconcerting to realize this accentuated a phallic shape. She is crude and motherly simultaneously. In active imagination, while working on the figure, I seemed to be climbing her, a huge mother of black soil, sinking into her fertile moistness, smelling the earth's rich humus. I climbed in tears, in pain and joy, because she was the mother of compassion, the earth itself, and I was attached to her primal, nourishing mud.

Then I saw, in my drawing, the shape of a public toilet seat. I saw the "Mothers" in the toilet bowl. In the dichotomous guilt-laden memory of my anorexic binges and purges, I saw I had been refusing the feminine. The food I ritualistically vomited was a rejection of the "Mothers" and, hence, of their transformative mysteries. What I threw up for seven years was a refusal to be a woman; the "refuse" of regurgitated food was a rejection of the Great Mother in toto.

Only after this drawing could I understand the communion of the body and blood, of the physical and spiritual, because I found here a communion of the profane and the sacred. It evoked a wall-shattering, fiery flood of transformative release. The Great Black Earth Mother proved to be my atonement and redemption into a new way of living life. In whatever way I personally understand her, I know she is there for everyone.

Once the rituals are "betrayed" to the analyst, or some other perceptive person, then they are open to change. Once the magic is taken out of the ritual, then the false fears can be separated out from the real fears. Then the real danger can be faced. Isolated and driven by the media, a woman can unconsciously be lured deeper

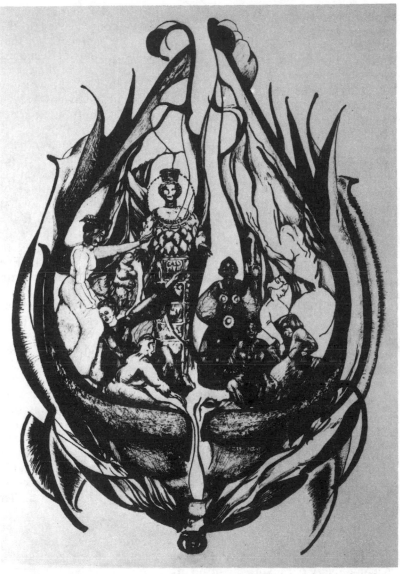

Analysand's drawing: "The most important figure is . . . the black lady in the center. . . . I found here a communion of the profane and the sacred." (text, page 40)

into a bewitched state in which she accepts that her fear of food is her fear of being fat. Once she brings her own consciousness to the situation a very different fear may loom at the center. Often that fear is related to loss of control. The overconscientious perfectionist knows she cannot control her obsession; she recognizes at the center of her whirlpool another power to which she is hostile. The whirling through daytime efficiency and nighttime compulsion avoids as long as it can the confrontation with the Eye. That confrontation demands surrender of the rigid, self-deceptive "I."

That surrender can only come in the fullness of time, and the resistances that arise must be respected. The AA program recognizes that it can do nothing until the alcoholic admits that she is powerless and can surrender to a Power greater than herself, The attitude of the ego toward the Eye is everything. If the ego is hostile, then it experiences itself as victim and sets itself up for self-murder. If the attitude is one of acceptance—not resignation, but open receptivity— then murder is transformed into conscious sacrifice. That change in attitude opens the heart to the power of love radiating from the Eye —the all-embracing, nourishing love that can support rather than destroy the "I." Psychologically speaking, so long as conscious and unconscious are enemies, the ego experiences itself in constant danger of death. Once they are in harmony the ego experiences itself open and supported by the maternal matrix of love.

In spite of popular belief, a binge does not depend on how much a person eats. For a person trapped in the negative mother, even one muffin eaten in her name is enough to produce painful bloating or a swollen allergic reaction. For those who have lived with a food complex most of their lives, great patience is required in the process of healing. The body may be suffering from hormonal imbalance due to prolonged periods of stress. The remnants of the neurosis may continue to trigger the original feelings of guilt and fear where certain foods are concerned. The body is crying out against the invasion of the witch, and the woman who can remain conscious enough to listen to her body is already on her way to discovering her own archetypal roots.

Ritual vomiting may be looked upon as a refusal to keep the mother in the stomach. The anorexic who refuses to eat, but ritualistically cuts her meat into sixteen pieces and eats one piece may be enacting a very old myth—the dismemberment of the mother. It may be a ritualistic act of defiance and power. In this case the unconscious is very calculated and dictates the behavior in a way that binging does not. (It is worth pointing out that in many myths the son creates the world out of the dismembered body of the mother which he himself has cut up.) The dismemberment becomes a process of transformation from the negative to the positive mother, a transformation which resides in the consciousness of a person who is finally able to separate herself from the negative mother and find a new meaning to food based upon her ability to listen to the needs of her own body. These needs she cannot hear as long as she is possessed by the witch.

The following dream may illustrate what I mean. An obese woman, in a double-edged effort both to lose weight and to gain spiritual insight, decided to fast for seven days. She dedicated herself to the feminine principle and this was her dream:

> I am driving through a heavy snowstorm on the freeway with my twelve-year-old daughter. The snow is so thick that I cannot see and I drive off the road. My daughter and I trudge through deep snow holding onto a fence for fear of becoming totally disoriented. An old gypsy woman takes us to her small tent, raises the skin-flap and we three sit together on the ground around the fire. She serves us a cup of tea. The cup she hands to me looks like a cup of my mother's which was my favorite. It is etched with delicate flowers. But this cup is very sturdy and heavy. I turn it over and find it is made of copper, and enameled to look exactly like my mother's china cup. The gypsy hands me an old piece of chamois. I am not sure what to do with it. She tells me to open it. I do so and find one earring. It is a stag's head with the antlers shaped so as to mold over my left ear. "That is your gift," she said.

The setting of the dream suggests a cold, unfeeling world in which the dreamer and her own young feminine side become so bewildered and confused that they are unable to proceed. They are forced to leave the collective highway, still clinging to some rational direction (holding onto the fence). They are met by the ancient gypsy, a feminine figure of ancient natural wisdom. She takes them through a natural skin-flap back into a uterine cave—the natural womb of the mother. Then around the transformative fire they share the most natural of female rituals, the drinking of tea. In this context the hearts of the three women are charged with the transformative fire of love, and what would have been a profane ritual becomes sacred as the dreamer is reconnected to her femininity. Here is sacred ground, a fixed point through which she can live, move and have her Being. Their shared silence vibrates with the mystery of the love that is being born between them, and none of the three desecrates that silence.

The cup that the old gypsy passes to the dreamer is her mother's cup, a cup that by association had caused considerable anguish between the dreamer and her mother. The child had been trained to give this cup to guests because it was the prettiest and best. The

mother had always admonished her not to break it when she dried
the dishes, and only her own feelings about the cup prevented her
from breaking it out of spite. Now in the dream the gypsy passes her
the cup from which she had not been allowed to drink. And the cup
is wrought of solid copper, metal of Venus, goddess of love. Her
female heritage, which her own mother had not been able to give
her because she herself could not receive it, is restored in the dream
through the archetypal image of the cup—as in the Grail legend—
from which she drinks.

That communion established, the gypsy puts into her hand a
more individual gift. The hesitation and reluctance to receive the gift
suggest the fear of life and the lack of spontaneity characteristic of
this dreamer. Most of her life she had, in fact, been living out her
shadow side because she was afraid to take responsibility for her
own gifts. Now she receives one earring, molded for the left ear.
Because of its perfect fit, it suggests her own individual capacity to
receive, reminiscent of an Annunciation picture in which the Virgin
receives her impregnation through her ear. "Left-handed thinking
relates to the primary process, the flow of things, and expresses itself
through unity and bonding to the earth."[10]

The cup refused to her as a child has been transformed into her
own cup of love. The gypsy and the fire are the transforming elements. The presence of her daughter suggests a new alignment with
the feminine. This theme is profoundly related to the preceding
week of fasting because she deliberately abstained from intercourse
with the negative mother, sacrificing to a higher feminine principle
identified in the dream with the gypsy, the fire and the daughter.
The chamois is the skin of an animal dressed with fish oil. The stag,
which in legend renews itself by eating a snake, is a symbol of the
integration of the instincts, that is, human nature does not rise above
animal nature but assimilates it as an integral part of itself.

Such a dream establishes fixed feminine ground—a firm feminine
love as a cosmos within which the feminine ego can resonate. Such a
dream is given because the dreamer had come to a point of confrontation with the complex, though this was by no means her final
encounter. Having swung back and forth on her obsession long
enough, she decided to end the swinging by a short fast. In refusing
to stuff down her negative feelings by eating, she did in fact make
the sacrifice required to release the absent goddess from her darkness. This she did in her own sacred ritual dedicated to her own
feminine principle. Her gift from the goddess was a new cosmos
which related her to the divine feminine and at the same time gave
her her own earthy reality. By drinking from the cup which had
never been allowed to her, her witch was transformed into a loving

mother; the witch's gall was transformed into milk. She was given ears to hear and eyes to see; she became more receptive to her inner maiden.

In Shakespeare's tragedy, Lady Macbeth as negative mother assumes the form of the three witches who upon the heath constellate Macbeth's destructive image of himself, the false image of Kingship that leads to his ruin. They are the negative side of his fate. In the above dream the three witches are replaced by three positive women, the triple image of the positive mother. Together they constellate the positive image of Queenship present in the stag's head, a medieval symbol of Christ.

Three is traditionally the number of fate. Fate, as all my anorexic and obese analysands recognize, is what pursues them. It can, as in Macbeth's case, drive them to a destruction which they see before them with terrifying clarity. At the same time, if they have been in analysis long enough, they begin to see their fate as another face— their own.

A famous Zen Master once said to his disciple, "Show me your face before you were born."

The Birth of Venus—Sandro Botticelli.

The more the feminine ideal is bent in the direction of the masculine, the more the woman loses her power to compensate the masculine striving for perfection, and a typically masculine ideal state arises which, as we shall see, is threatened with an enantiodromia. No path leads beyond perfection into the future—there is only a turning back, a collapse of the ideal, which would easily have been avoided by paying attention to the feminine ideal of completeness. Yahweh's perfectionism is carried over from the Old Testament into the New, and despite all the recognition and glorification of the feminine principle this never prevailed against the patriarchal supremacy. We have not, therefore, by any means heard the last of it.

—C.G. Jung, *Answer to Job.*


At that time [my mother] no longer wanted to see anyone, and always carried with her, even on a journey, the small, fine, silver sieve through which she filtered everything she drank. She no longer took any solid food, save some biscuits or bread, which, when she was alone, she broke into small pieces and ate bit by bit, as children do crumbs.

Her fear of needles at that time already dominated her completely. To others she simply said by way of excuse, "I really cannot digest anything any more; but don't let that trouble you; I feel very well indeed." But to me she would suddenly turn (for I was already a little bit grown-up) and say with a smile that cost her a severe effort, "What a lot of needles there are, Malte, and how they lie about everywhere, and when you think how easily they might fall out. . . . " She tried to say this playfully, but terror shook her at the thought of all the insecurely fastened needles which might at any instant, anywhere, fall into something.

—Rainer Maria Rilke, *The Notebook of Malte Laurids Brigge.*

# 3

# Addiction to Perfection

*Mirror, mirror, on the wall,*
*Who is the fairest of us all?*

My analysand sat down in the chair opposite me. She arranged her dream book and papers meticulously, almost oblivious of my eyes on her. We did not speak. I noticed the subtle pinks and mauves of her new blouse, and her new hairdo, cut to bring definition to her young face. There was a stillness around her, a kind of silent strength that too many had clung to. Too many had put their burdens on her and she had carried them. She had carried them so well that she was old beyond her twenty-five years and heavy beyond the weight her scales could bear. She smiled a slow, poignant smile that did not light her eyes. I smiled back, and thought of "the sad heart of Ruth, when, sick for home,/She stood in tears amid the alien corn."[1]

Since she had the courage and dignity of that name, let us call her Ruth. She was a university graduate, held a responsible, professional position, was psychic to an almost alarming degree, but her weight, now 325 pounds, had been her albatross all her life. Referring to her body she said, "If I have been playing this lovely instrument at all it has been a few heavy and hasty chords that no one, least of all myself, wants to hear. As Mother said about herself, 'I pretend it's an old fiddle, when I know it's a Stradivarius.'"

Ruth was the oldest child of a family of five. Her parents were both professionals. After eighteen years of a stormy marriage they had divorced. Her father had been a secret alcoholic for ten years. After a few months of analysis, she recognized her need for power, her longing for perfection, her desire for control not over others, but over life itself. She recognized too the radical contradictions in her habitual daydreams: the yearning for life, the rejection of life; the hope, the despair; the body, the spirit. The innuendoes of these attitudes are inherent in the following passage from her journal:

> I am not fooling myself. I know that eating sweets is consistently choosing death. They now give me indigestion and migraines. I give my energy to my illness instead of to my ego. I think I'm ready to lose weight and I thought my unconscious was ready to support me. But I'm still eating chocolates before the cottage cheese and the despair is

worse than it ever was. You're right, there is an emergency—a spiritual emergency, because I may choose not to be here at all. There is a physical emergency. Yes, there is a chronic despair in my body and I keep saying to myself, "One day I'll do something about that but meantime I have to take care of the emergency." Others don't understand the emergency. Others see my body as the emergency. They are repelled by my body. I am repelled by the world. I, God, refuse to enter the world, refuse to be incarnated. I choose the good and let the rest go. I take what I can get just standing at the door. I hate the evil. I hate the evil of myself. I know it's stupid. I want things to be true and yet the image of myself that I present is absolutely false. I do nothing to enter the world. If I can't do the whole thing, I'll do nothing.

Dieting is facing the real world. When I'm ready, I will do it. I fear the disasters to come if I enter life. I see the mess other people make of their lives, and I don't think mine is so bad. Still I pretend I'm not here. I know when I think about the real world I am full of fear, tension and hostility. Thinking about all the possible danger destroys my confidence, deflects my energy away from the main issue. I'm so afraid of failing, I try too hard. The rigidity and discipline go wrong. I am depressed out of all proportion by what's going on in the world. I can't even read *Time* magazine. *Hamlet* is heavy, but it isn't the same kind of weight as cheap weight in magazines. I feel prissy because of my withdrawal from the world as it is. I am trying to reach a spiritual plateau too soon—probably asking the right questions at the wrong time. I don't look at my body problem because I don't want to enter life. I am afraid to come out. And yet I am already out. If I succeed in losing weight, then to have to enter life.

I doubt my motives. In committing one crime, I am avoiding myriads of others and they are all the same. I know I am corrupting myself, but this is different from being corrupted by the world. Adults are false. I thought I might get to adulthood without being false. It is like putting on costumes to get to know yourself. I don't want to fail. I don't want to corrupt myself in the ways of the world. This is what I am and if they don't like it, tough! Sure it's false armor. I would fail more abysmally than they. No—I won't enter the world. I won't make tiny adjustments. Who cares whether carrots have more calories cooked or uncooked? The knights of the Grail weren't doing what was at hand. Big problems have to be dealt with in big ways. Big entries!

Everything is warped. That's true. But it is no excuse. I could enter in a big way, but meantime I could eat raw carrots. I tell the truth but I am playing games at the same time. One part of me says I'd like to be thin, and I answer "Liar." If only it were something I could stop outright! But you can't stop eating. They cut your leg off, you can learn to deal with it. You use crutches. But if it keeps pulling off every second minute, then you have real trouble.

Dad [her alcoholic father] was a flickering light. If there had been no electricity, if only he had gone away, we could have learned to live with candlelight. But we could never trust because we knew we'd be in darkness the next moment. Once you go into light, you can't go into darkness again. There is a terrible fear of that in me. I can't face suffering. The flesh is weak; don't feed its weakness. Stay out of this one. The body is too big; go and get another. Try spirit next time!

The rejection of life and the despair implicit in this last statement were characteristic conclusions in Ruth's journal entries. She would put down her pen, move into a death whorl, feel herself being sucked into the vortex, unconsciously binge on chocolate, muffins and milk, eat herself into a stupor and find herself afterward, at least breathing. The hated body persisted in its attempts to survive even when the spirit refused to inhabit it.

The body's wisdom is the thermostat that determines the appetite whether the ego likes it or not. Only as the conscious attitude changes, as the ego becomes strong enough to take responsibility for the woman as a human being, living in her body on the earth with human limitations, can the appestat find its natural "set point." Until the ego is strong enough to take that responsibility, the energy will come again and again to that rite of passage, fall into that whirlpool, experience the overwhelming conflict, regress back into the witch, and fail to make the resurrection or resolution. But each time it circles, it comes up or goes down (that is the crucial paradox) onto a new rung of the spiral, carrying new strength, provided, of course, the dialogue between ego and unconscious is still going on.

In that interchange the ego is being fed by the unconscious. The dreams are always full of images of food. The food that is attempting to broaden the ego's attitude will strengthen the firm standpoint if the ego is assimilating the food, in other words, acting on the new insight. This same food—be it physical or spiritual—will help the ego to be less rigid, allowing the flow, allowing things to happen. The obstacle, which before was avoided through fear, can then be looked at as a challenge with all its possibilities for richer experience. What appears as a contradiction to Ruth in the early stages of analysis eventually may become a paradox: the stronger the ego is, the more flexible it becomes.

Where a woman is able to participate in the rituals of a Church, Christian or otherwise, she is to some extent protected from the personal confrontation with the unconscious. Ritual provides a certain aesthetic distance. It also provides the certainty that the god who suffers and dies will rise again. But where the individual is going through the experience alone, without the orthodox ritual, she cannot know that the sacrifice of the old will lead to the birth of the new. All she experiences is the darkness of the birth canal without any real faith in the light at the end. If she loses her fat body (the only security she has ever known), if she sacrifices that, what will hold her on the earth? What will protect her from the terrors of a life she essentially rejects? To sacrifice her fat body before she accepts life would be to destroy the only bulwark standing between her and a psychotic break or death. The despised fat is, in fact, her anchor in life and its size may vary in direct proportion to her ego's acceptance or rejection of her own humanity. Nor is the fat so despised as on the surface it appears to be, for once the weight loss begins, the mourning for the lost body may have to be dealt with in order to prevent a sudden weight gain.

The religious ritual has always been a re-enactment of a myth: the god drinks from the cup, dies and rises again. It has been a way for human beings to participate vicariously in the life of the god. As St. Paul put it, "Not I, but Christ liveth in me" (Galatians 2:20). Now the divine rug has been pulled out from under us, or we have pulled it out from under ourselves. The rituals which were once vicarious are now being enacted *in us,* in everyday life. We have to take responsibility for our own lives. Ruth, I should point out, no longer had a religious affiliation. The sacraments of the Church played no part in her psychic life. The spirit she was attempting to build had to be constructed out of her own suffering and out of her own hopes. In order for suffering and hope to have meaning, however, they must be grounded in something or someone larger than the fragile ego. Call it Fate, God, Energy, Love, or Prana. The great danger in solitary rituals is that the ego becomes identified with the positive or negative side of the god.

That is precisely where women like Ruth run into trouble, as is hinted at in her writing. She wants to make her life into a fiction and identify with a spiritualized archetype. To identify with Hamlet is probably worth about 25 pounds; to identify with Christ must then be worth at least 120. Where the male authority in her psyche is a flickering candle, the god figure within cannot be trusted for light. Where the female authority in her psyche mocks her own feminine body, the goddess within cannot be trusted for love. The ritual does not work, because it perpetuates the alcoholic father who could not face life and the disembodied mother cut off from her own feminine instincts.

Rituals in that ungrounded world are games people play. Nobody really expects anything to happen. An ungrounded woman may work hard at analysis so long as it is an interesting game, but draws back in terror when the game becomes life and something may actually happen, actually change. What I am suggesting here is that for Ruth, as for so many modern men and women, the archetypes appear to lack the autonomy which in reality they have. Her archetypal image of God is, at the moment, tragically rooted in her

experience of her inadequate father. And she has no archetypal
image of a loving goddess. A theology of trust is at this point out of
the question, and recognition of a god who is independent of her
own experience of life is barely open to her consideration. Her
priorities, given her food complex, are of an entirely different order.

At this time the object of her trust must be the analyst. The
analyst, whether male or female, becomes for the time being a
positive mother providing the nourishing food she never had. The
ego can only become strong enough for the ritual to hold if the god
can be grounded in a life process from which the food addiction is
cutting it off. The psyche that has lived all its life in fear of not
being nourished by the mother, or of being snuffed out by the father
—in other words, the psyche that experienced fundamental rejection
—can cut the umbilical cord only when it stands on new ground.
Fear of abandonment is no different at twenty-five years than it is at
twenty-five days. Nothingness is always nothingness. The ego has to
come to realize that it is only insofar as it sees itself as an extension
of its old life—that is, possessed by the devouring witch—that it is
facing death. Once it realizes that the devouring pattern can be
changed, it realizes its potential for freedom. This is the creative
moment. If the ego decides in that moment to take possession of its
own reality, then it can move out of the complex into a celebration
of life. Christ puts it more succinctly: "Except a man be born again,
he cannot see the kingdom of God."[2]

From Ruth's journal, it is apparent that her life in the very midst
of her admitted defeats is nevertheless committed to perfection and
that there is an intimate link between her addiction to perfection
and her confessed defeats. Indeed, *perfection is defeat.* Jung makes
the distinction between perfection and completeness:

> One must bear in mind that there is a considerable difference between
> *perfection* and *completeness.* The Christ-image is as good as perfect (at
> least it is meant to be so), while the archetype (so far as is known)
> denotes completeness but is far from being perfect.... Natural as it is
> to seek perfection in one way or another, the archetype fulfills itself in
> completeness.... The individual may strive after perfection ... but
> must suffer from the opposite of his intentions for the sake of his
> completeness.[3]

The point here is that perfection belongs to the gods; completeness
or wholeness is the most a human being can hope for.

Any archetypal pattern is whole, complete in itself. But it is only
one aspect of the human. The archetype of the Wise Old Man, for
instance, denotes an aspect of wholeness, but striving single-mind-
edly for wisdom at the expense of, for example, irrational human
foolishness, is to miss many of the joys in living. Similarly, the

idealized Madonna is a certain perfect image of the feminine, but the real woman must also accept the whore in herself for the sake of her completeness. It is in seeking perfection by isolating and exaggerating parts of ourselves that we become neurotic.

The chief sign of the pursuit of perfection is obsession. Obsession occurs when all the psychic energy, which ought to be distributed among the various parts of the personality in an attempt to harmonize them, is focused on one area of the personality to the exclusion of everything else. Obsession is always a fixation—a freezing-over of the personality so that it becomes not a living being but something fixed, like a piece of sculpture, locked into a complex. There is always something catatonic about it, behind which is fear that can accelerate into blind terror so that the person may become like a wild animal caught in the glare of headlights, unable to move.

Perfection is something very like that when applied to human life. Certain types of people, movie stars for example, can be frozen into the glare of the camera lights and spend their whole career playing the same fixed type over and over again. Marilyn Monroe struggled to break out of the glare of the spotlights, but couldn't. Neither the film studios nor the audiences would let her. Addiction to perfection is at root a suicidal addiction. The addict is simulating not life but death. Almost inevitably a woman addicted to perfection will view herself as a work of art, and her real terror is that the work of art, being so absolutely precious, may in one instant be destroyed. She has to treat herself as a rare piece of Ming porcelain or what Keats described as a "still unravished bride of quietness," a "foster-child of silence and slow time" (above, page 7).

To move toward perfection is to move out of life, or what is worse, never to enter it. Addiction to perfection, which psychologically indicates enslavement by a complex, is equally apparent in the anorexic. Like the obese person, her food complex is rooted in the negative mother. Her binge takes the form of a fast, or what the alcoholic refers to as "a dry drunk."

\*

By the end of Ruth's session Eleanor was already waiting. She came in and sat in the same chair, sat tall and elegant like a piece of Copenhagen china, her white skin drawn taut over her fine bones. Her long blonde hair was like fine silk and her huge blue eyes alert, intelligent, but anxious. She was like a prize racehorse entering the gate.

Like Ruth, Eleanor was twenty-five, the oldest of five children. Her parents were both professionals, still married and highly respected in their social and professional circles. Like Ruth, Eleanor herself was a pillar of strength in school and in the community; both were locked into collective ideals. Like Ruth, too, Eleanor had acted as buffer in her family, carrying everyone's load, trying to keep constant harmony, trying to help one member to understand another. Throughout her life she had been an outstanding student, a good athlete and a good leader. At twenty-three she found herself eating nothing but popcorn, unable to make decisions, unable to speak to anyone for fear they would load her with one more thing that would break her. When she could no longer handle her work efficiently, she had to go into the hospital. Gradually her physical health improved and she came into therapy to try to adjust her attitude in order to make life possible. After some weeks she had the confidence to show me her book of lists—yearly lists of things to be done, monthly lists, weekly lists, daily lists, special daily lists—all meticulously organized. "I know it's crazy," she said, her eyes full of stress, "but I can't help it. If one thing is missing, what else might be missing?"

When I suggested that there had to be room for some spontaneity, she dutifully agreed. But a week later, she sadly assured me, "There's no point in making time for spontaneity, there simply isn't any in my life." And later in the session when I looked at her daily list I saw: "2:15-2:30 p.m.—Spontaneity." In that simple sentence lay the tragedy of her life.

Here is a passage from Eleanor's journal:

Many people shudder at the thought of anorexia and obesity. It is a small madness to keep the other madness at bay. During my worst period, I was both fat and thin. I ate enough to rank with the heftiest and yet due to ritual emptying I maintained an external slimness. It was a way to embody the paradox of the simultaneous empty and full. The idea of emptying myself wholly so that a divine presence could enter me, a purified receptacle, was important. This time it was an emotional, intellectual and experiential emptying. I followed Eastern yoga techniques. I sought death: the complete death of the personal ego and the clutter that had collected around it.

I entered blackness after blackness as I let go of everything I knew and understood. I lost "I" and became a void. Sometimes I dreamt I was being electrocuted painfully. Eventually the energy in those dreams transformed to pure, radiant light. The brilliance and power of the light is beyond description. I would wake in the middle of the night and literally see sunlight everywhere in the darkness as a radiant after-image. The extent of the illumination was only parallelled by an exuberant joy flowing everywhere within. Naturally I thought I had broken through to a source of divine beatitude and everything was synchronized. It wasn't. I had begun to learn, but had not begun to live creatively. God is the awakened creativity of every moment.

To get to the light was not easy. Matter exists on pure nothingness.

God is the unmanifest beyond the unmanifest. I had to accept the void. The rites of full and empty had been an escapist ritual that mocked the reality behind the symbolic meaning of my acts. My ego drowned in the binges; my body felt bloated. I had to unbloat. I didn't wish to float to the surface in dead buoyancy. I wanted to swim back up. I now realize I was looking for the sun but could never see it. What I craved was the sun to emerge in unburning, flaming, beautiful clarity from my mouth. Instead my belly seemed full of serpents, full of the chaos of *mater saeva cupidinum,* "unbridled and unbroken nature." I felt like the chaos before creation and sought to be the delineation of order after creation in universally alive, organized life. But organization begins at home.

Eleanor's analysis was more advanced than Ruth's, for there was a conscious recognition of the desire to empty herself and to enter the void. While there was a desire for the pure radiance of light separated from all darkness, there was also a movement toward creation, a dawning recognition of the need for a body. She was beginning to identify the creator god with a creation. Ruth, on the other hand, still preferred to keep the two separate. Eleanor was closer to becoming less of a god and more of a person.

In the obese/anorexic syndrome the original maternal matrix is demonically constellated. Unconsciously the child has been rejected by the mother; she is therefore not a person but a thing. One obese woman entering analysis dreamt of herself repeatedly, not as a person but as a golfball. The danger of being treated as a thing rather than a person is that it leads, ironically, to unlimited inflation. Such children experience themselves as God. Not the God of creation, the one who works on matter, breathing His life into the dust and declaring His creation good, but the God before creation whom James Joyce describes as "indifferent, paring his fingernails" in the void.[4]

The elation experienced in this syndrome is the belief that they can choose whether to enter life or not. "I am that I am," they declare. To share their "I am" in a life situation is, they persuade themselves, their own choice. Locked in the syndrome, they choose not to. To eat is not only to recognize matter, but to enter into it, or what is worse, to enter into it against their will which not only challenges but denies their omnipotence. That would be the recognition that "they are not that they are." Another force is present which is not them and that force is matter—the negative matter, the she-devil or witch. God is not alone and omnipotent. He has the devil to contend with. One bite of the muffin is Eve taking one bite of the apple. It brings death into her world. It brings about the loss of Eden, the loss, that is, of omnipotence. What such a woman does not see, as Jung so well describes it in *Memories, Dreams, Reflections* or

*Answer to Job,* is that the devil or matter or muffin is the *deus absconditus,* that part of the unconscious of God which has not been absorbed or digested.

The radicalness of Jung's position, though it has a long history within Christian tradition, involves what the Church calls a *felix culpa,* a fortunate fall. The first bite of the muffin launches the woman on the way to differentiation from her own deluded omnipotence and launches God on the path of incarnation. It is a first faltering step toward becoming human. In short, what is required before the individual can absorb that bite into her flesh is a radical evaluation of her one-sided theology. She must learn to make room for the shadow or the devil.

Most people locked in this syndrome are born Gnostics—they deny the incarnation. God remained God. He never degraded himself by becoming flesh. He was not born. He did not suffer. He did not die. He was not raised from the dead. Like them, God never lived on earth.

Eleanor, by rejecting food, was rejecting life. And the biggest problem to be overcome when she did begin to eat was that she lost the euphoric high caused by starvation. Life was no longer worth living without the intensity and drivenness of her tightrope resistance. She believed she was reducing herself to pure spirit, pure essence—a concept which may be related to shamanistic initiations, in which the shaman is literally reduced to skin and bone.[5]

What Ruth did not see was that her flesh was trying to save her, trying to force her to develop her own individual feminine identity. Rather than deal with the fat as fact, Ruth was trapped in unconscious identification with her large body. She had no ego with which to separate herself from whatever myth was being lived out through the fat. The reason she weighed 325 pounds was that she refused to accept the existential reality her body was forced louder and louder to proclaim. Between body and spirit there was a shouting match in which, like all shouting matches between two antagonists, neither one could hear the other. A body coming at the spirit with the full force of 325 pounds was countered by the spirit coming at the flesh with the full force of Bach, Mozart, Blake and Dostoevsky. A shouting match of such proportions would drown out God, though not necessarily the devil, who is used to such fights, because he is that part of God that has not yet entered consciousness. If you could but know how quiet Ruth was, you would see just how out of phase the inner and outer worlds can be.

In analysis the struggle for incarnation—God in flesh, spirit in/ matter—is repeating itself, not in theological terms but in psychological terms. It is not resolved until the muffaholic can understand that

what is in the muffin for her is what the Church calls the transub-
stantiated Christ, which means that the demonic ritual of binging
has to be replaced by the sacred ritual of receiving God's body as
the fruits of the earth which he declared to be good. Psychologically,
it means transforming the negative mother or witch into the Great
Mother.

It might be argued that in Christianity there has always been too
wide a gap between the spiritual and the psychological, between the
crucifixion and the resurrection. Instead of seeing them as one event
at the climax of a process they have been separated, and in that
separation is born a masochistic attitude toward suffering—or an
attitude toward it that would underestimate its importance. In the
obese/anorexic syndrome there is a very strong tendency toward a
masochistic attitude in which crucifixion or suffering tends more and
more to become an end in itself, as the individual is devalued in her
own perception by the evidence of continuous defeat. The desultory
omnipotence that may survive is so completely cut off from the
actual pain that it appears to have no relation to it. It is not the
resurrection within the crucifixion, but something unrelated to it
and, therefore, almost completely unreal. Both Ruth and Eleanor in
their journals continually turn to their tricks of mind which fortunately they cannot quite successfully perform upon themselves. *Consciousness of defeat remains their grip upon reality.* This, however, is
still a negative grip because the ego is unable to deal creatively with
it.

What must be established is a loving attitude of the ego toward
the body, so that the body's nourishment becomes the ego's concern.
The ego must learn to ask the questions which the body is ready to
answer in an unmistakably clear voice: "What are my real needs? I
betrayed myself in that meeting today. What did I really want to do?
What does my body want to eat? Does it want to exercise? What
would feed my spirit instead of my flesh? How can I make this heap
of flesh my body? Do I love my body? Do I want to live? Do I want
to enter life?" What the ego confronts is a degraded body image, an
image which strangely enough has little or nothing to do with the
reflection in the mirror. A woman possessed by the ugliness of her
body looks at her complex hour after hour and literally cannot see
it. It is a construction of mind which believes itself truly omnipotent,
saying to the body "BE," and it is.

Crucial to the healing process, therefore, is working creatively
with the rejected body. At least initially this must be attempted
outside the complex because the ego is not strong enough to deal
directly with the confrontation. Practical suggestions as to how a new
body-mind relationship can be developed will be discussed in depth

in chapter five. Suffice it to say here that a gradual shift from self-hatred to self-love *can* take place, and one day a woman can be "surprised by joy" when between her spirit and her body there is a mutual recognition.

This kind of aligning is an essential part of the healing process in which the movement from the psychic pole to the somatic pole is met by a countermovement from the somatic to the psychic. The body comes forward to meet the psychic process on the assumption that no matter how much work is done on the psyche, the body cannot absorb it unless it has been prepared. Keats speaks of bringing to the world of nature—a bird, a flower, a tree—a "greeting of the Spirit,"[6] as if the psyche recognizes something of itself in the matter of nature. *And the unconscious responds by becoming the perceived object.* What happens is in some sense a reciprocity in which conscious and unconscious, mind and matter, join to produce a third. That third is the meeting of body and spirit bringing with it an act of joyous recognition.

In "The Ecstasy," John Donne describes two lovers lying on a bank of flowers like "sepulchral statues." While their bodies are strongly attracted to each other, they refuse to intermingle until their souls have agreed. The souls have gone out of their bodies to negotiate above their heads as to whether the bodies are free to respond to each other or not. In their negotiations, the souls gradually recognize the importance of their bodies; without the bodies, there could have been no meeting of souls. The souls, like great princes, would have remained prisoners unknown to each other; therefore, out of gratitude to the bodies, they decide to re-enter them, bringing with them not only their approval of what the bodies desire, but a happy participation in it. Donne joyously concludes:

> To our bodies turn we then, that so
>    Weak men on love revealed may look,
> Love's mysteries in souls do grow,
>    But yet the body is his book.
> And if some lover, such as we,
>    Have heard this dialogue of one,
> Let him still mark us; he shall see
>    Small change when we are to bodies gone.[7]

If the woman who is trapped in the body/soul split can keep in touch with her own "dialogue of one," she too may look forward to the delicate negotiations open to Donne's ecstatic lovers.

From *The Book of Job*, 1825.—William Blake. (British Museum)

# 4

## Through Thick and Thin

*Without Contraries is no progression. Attraction and Repulsion,*
*Reason and Energy, Love and Hate, are necessary to human existence.*
　　　　　　　　—William Blake, *Marriage of Heaven and Hell.*

I have several times referred to Lady Macbeth's perverted conception of Kingship and while I have not used the term power complex,
certainly the omnipotence which preoccupies the compulsive personality suggests a voracious desire to control. The motivation behind
that desire, however, needs to be examined, for it is not simply a
matter of "I'm the king of the castle," thus reducing the rest of the
world to a "dirty rascal."

In murdering Duncan, the representative of God on earth, Macbeth breaks his oath to his king. In psychological terms, it is the ego
breaking its bonding to the Self. Lady Macbeth as accomplice to the
crime makes her prayers to the spirits that "tend on mortal
thoughts," asking them to "unsex" her and take away all "compunc-
tious visitings of nature," believing in that moment that she herself
would wield the knife, since Macbeth was "too full o' the milk of
human kindness/ To catch the nearest way."[1] But when she is about
to do it, she cannot because the sleeping Duncan resembles her
father.

This is the one spoken hint that Lady Macbeth is a father's
daughter, although all her choices reveal a woman who is more
dedicated to principles than to feelings. The moment she is out of
the actual presence of Duncan, she reverts to her ideals and manipu-
lates Macbeth into actually performing the murder. But it is she who
spins the web. While he is agonizing over the consequences and
coming to the conclusion that he will not destroy his "eternal jewel,"
she is preparing the potions and the knives. When he decides to
"proceed no further with this business,"[2] she is ready with the
master plan which he executes.

If Macbeth and Lady Macbeth are looked at as the masculine
and feminine principles, it is apparent that in the beginning both are
aware of the feeling values involved in their bonding to the king.
Both are threatened by the witchery spinning its confounding
threads of illusion and reality in the background. Macbeth, as the
masculine principle, rationally weighs the pros and cons and accepts
that if Fate would have him king, then Fate will crown him. Lady

Macbeth, personifying the feminine principle, is locked into a power
complex, hence betrays the true feminine principle of relatedness; to
please her, Macbeth commits the murder that cuts him off not only
from God but from everything, including her. The irony is that his
sensibilities foresaw the outcome of his betraying his own spiritual
values, but he failed to stand on his own ground. Instead he gave in
to her, who had already ravaged her own feeling values. Neither was
acting out of an inner sense of authenticity: consequently, once the
choice was made, he moved into the tragedy of his own conscious
self-destruction while she moved into the pathetic self-destruction of
unconscious nightmare.

Many 20th-century marriages and the children of those marriages
are in that situation, wearing the clothes of Kingship without the
inner grace to fill them. There can be no grace where the relationship to the Self is cut off, that is, where there is no love between the
human and the divine—in psychological terms, where there is no
conscious connection between ego and Self because the ego is too
frightened to receive from the unconscious. Without that communication, the ego tries to set up its own kingdom. But where parents
and grandparents and parents before them were not in contact with
their own feelings and instincts, their children in succeeding generations are increasingly undermined. Jung, speaking of the growing
fear which besets the person who shrinks from adapting to reality,
writes:

> The fear of life is not just an imaginary bogy, but a very real panic,
> which seems disproportionate only because its real source is uncon-
> scious and therefore projected: the young, growing part of the person-
> ality, if prevented from living or kept in check, generates fear and
> changes into fear. The fear seems to come from the mother, but
> actually it is the deadly fear of the instinctive, unconscious, inner man
> who is cut off from life by the continual shrinking back from reality.
> If the mother is felt as the obstacle, she then becomes the vengeful
> pursuer. Naturally it is not the real mother, although she too may
> seriously injure her child by the morbid tenderness with which she
> pursues it into adult life, thus prolonging the infantile attitude beyond
> the proper time. It is rather the mother-imago that has turned into a
> lamia. The mother-imago, however, represents the unconscious, and it
> is as much a vital necessity for the unconscious to be joined to the
> conscious as it is for the latter not to lose contact with the uncon-
> scious.[3]

Without the positive mother base, compulsive eating creates a
concrete base, with which the ego, in many cases, is identified. Thus
in dieting the loss of body weight releases genuine anxiety and grief,
for symbolically it is the loss of the mother. If the infant is basically
threatened from the beginning, it sets up a pseudo-ego which may
appear very strong but is essentially a defense mechanism which

reacts complaisantly or aggressively in an effort to survive. The real ego is not acting out of its own creative center, and therefore has to pretend to be strong, but its strength is in its rigidity and its concrete body base. The mother who is in this situation herself, because of her own heritage, cannot give her baby the strong bonding to the earth that the mother grounded in her own instincts can. Mother and daughter may have a close relationship, but both may share a negative mother complex, and both as a result are terrified of the "instinctive, unconscious inner man [and woman]...cut off from life." That terror of the instinctive unconscious bedevils daily living. It is that devil we are attempting to uncover in analysis, for so long as it exists, the psyche probably needs the security of the heavy body holding it to the earth. Even after the complex has been dealt with, any life-threatening situation may cause the body to take on weight without any change in caloric intake.

When "the best little girl in the world," who has always done everything mother wished and believed everything daddy said, reaches puberty she may suddenly rebel. She may turn herself into a baby monster or a boyish skeleton. Either way she has effectively destroyed her blossoming womanhood. What looks like rebellion may be inner collapse. What appears to be a power tantrum may be a disguised cry of defeat. She is called upon to be a woman, but she has no role model which she can accept. She may see her own mother as a woman who has never grown up, but who nevertheless has lots of backbone, lives by her higher principles and wears the pants in the family. Two options are open to her. Either she obeys and identifies with mother, or she disobeys because she will be anything that mother isn't. One option is not open: she cannot act on her own value system because she hasn't got one. Nor, at twelve, has she the strength to search in her own inner world. She senses that having a breast just big enough to hold a pencil underneath isn't exactly what womanhood is all about. Meanwhile the anxious mother, watching the magnified replay of her own girlhood, experiences herself as a total failure. Everything she has tried to do in terms of finding her own independence and living by her own principles echoes in her heart as failure.

Living by principles is not living your own life. It is easier to try to be better than you are than to *be* who you are. If you are trying to live by ideals, you are constantly plagued by a sense of unreality. Somewhere you think there must be some joy; it can't be all "must," "ought to," "have to." And when the crunch comes, you have to recognize the truth: you weren't there. Then the house of cards collapses. In trying to live out your principles and ideals, the part that matters the most was lost. The hideous irony then has to be faced. As one woman put it to me:

I have everything and nothing. By the world's standards, I have everything. By my own heart's standards, I have nothing. I won the battle for my precious independence and lost what was most precious to me. I want to love and be loved but something in me is sending love away. I do not understand.

For the person who is living by ideals, the essential problem in relationships usually involves the difference between love and power. If an individual is being fed and nourished emotionally by the mother—or a mother surrogate such as husband, company, Church, collective values—she is probably starving in relation to herself. She is dependent on the mother and therefore open to manipulation by the mother, vulnerable to her praise or rejection. She is not nourishing herself and her own feelings are being unrecognized or denied. She is starving. She has to perform perfectly in order to be loved. Her emotional stability is determined by another's reaction. On one hand she is being manipulated, on the other she is a manipulator because she has to be in order to be loved. She cannot depend on a love which accepts her for who she is. Whether the original manipulators are still in her life doesn't matter; they are alive in her psyche as complexes and if she isn't projecting them onto her "loved ones," she is turning them against herself.

In an effort to be mature and independent, such a woman tries to be more and more perfect because the only way she can alleviate her dependence on that judgmental voice is to be perfect enough to shut it up. But there is no shutting it up. It wants more and more and more. Thus the opposites meet in a terrifying contradiction. As she runs as fast as she can for independence via perfection, she runs into her own starving self, totally dependent and crying out for food. The overindulgent mother can be as negative as the too judgmental one because, if she is projecting onto the child out of her own ideals, her expectations may drive her daughter into a false set of values. Unconscious identity is involved in power: one person is expecting another to live out her expectations. The child picks up the unconsciousness of the parent and carries that weight with her.

One of my obese analysands, Rachel, has a very creative mother, once an outstanding performer who gave up her career for her family. Rachel tells the story of losing her mittens when she was a tiny child. She was frightened to tell her mother but she finally summoned the courage. Her mother reacted with hysterical weeping: "I knew I should never have gotten married," she cried. "I knew I should never have had children." "And I still feel my life depends on holding onto my mittens, literally," Rachel laughed sadly. "When I try to deprive myself of food, I feel I may be snuffed out."

The child sensed she was her mother's failure and the woman lived attempting to justify her very existence by being perfect in everything she did, or disappearing completely into chocolates. The thirty-year-old Rachel now rarely sees her mother, but the war resumes as soon as she attempts to discipline herself. "I don't want to be disciplined," she declares:

> Above all I don't want to be cultured. Culture is mother saying, "Do better." I look at the cultured world and I don't want it, but somehow my mother becomes responsible for the whole mess—my cat dying, the Falklands crisis, Lebanon. I have terrible anger. I can't get it through my head that the war is over. I still feel I have to fight to survive. I can hardly believe that people can love me.

So long as her energy is going into that war with the complex, she has no energy to put into finding out who she is and what nourishment she needs.

How the power principle may manifest is illustrated in the following comments of another woman:

> A big blob with two black eyes is always watching, always ready to eat me up. Everything falls on my shoulders and I have to do everything right. Nobody else can do it as I can. My mother acts totally incompetent. My sister does too. My man takes no initiative. I feel I have to do something. I put myself under incredible stress, yet I am convinced I am doing what is right. There is an addiction operating that makes me feel terrible emptiness, ultimate rage. No matter how much energy I bring to bear, I end up with nothing. That is despair. I decide to give up. I'll finish the commitments I've made and quit. Terrible depression follows that decision. I either level my rage at people at incredible personal cost, or I give up and take the consequences. I am addicted to trying to set things right.
>
> The adults in my life were not responsible. My mother's animus was destructive. Mine is creative so long as I'm getting my own way. If I go down, I'll take everything with me. I go like a freight train. I flatten everything as I go. I could put on the brakes but sometimes I decide I won't. If it happens to be a man, he goes too. Damn the torpedoes—full speed ahead! My rage comes from feeling I have no impact on my environment. I'm living out what my mother refused to push to do. I'm a fighter—my father by default.
>
> My man once decided to cut my fingernails. I resisted. We fought but he cut them. I felt I could commit suicide. I felt if I couldn't defend myself I would destroy myself. Cutting my nails was an invasion of my person. I cut off my hair. I felt powerless and dead. Then I had to feed myself, I felt so destroyed.

The fine line between power and Eros is very hard to find. If, for example, a little girl is making cookies with her mother, she is watching and trying to imitate. Her little hands pat the dough as hard as they can and the cookies are going to be tough. Does it matter? The mother can keep the child dependent by not giving her a recipe book to read by herself. She can protect the child from being burned by handling the hot pans herself, and she can avoid spills by putting in the ingredients herself without allowing the child to do the measuring. That seems innocent and sensible. But in order for the child's emotional needs to be satisfied, the cookies have to be the child's own creation. Otherwise, although she is praised for her excellent cookies, something in her knows they are not hers.

It seems a small issue, but if that pattern is the pattern of the relationship, the young woman will strive for praise, but the greater the praise she receives, the more she is denying herself. Nothing is connected to her. The more she achieves, the less she is related to herself. She sets up an unconscious masochistic pattern, manifested perhaps in eating or drinking too much, in that she strives more and more and receives less and less. The more perfect her performance, the less she is related to herself. The mother who does whatever is necessary and then praises her daughter for the result not only takes from her daughter any sense of her own accomplishment, but what is worse, persuades her that what the world may think is her accomplishment belongs to another. The more successful she is, the more inwardly she knows it is not her, but her mother in her. Her inner sense of failure is thus in direct proportion to her outer success.

This situation is graphically illustrated in the dream of a successful professional woman:

> I am going up a dark staircase into a stifling attic that I hadn't realized was in our house. . . . At the top of the stairs is a magnificent white Persian cat as big as a lion. On a Victorian settee in the middle of the room is a wraith of a woman too weak to lift her hand. I try to go to her, but every move I make the cat waves its plumed tail in my face as it stalks around her. He doesn't appear unfriendly, just noble and aloof, but I can't get near her. . . .

In their pioneer study of women writers and the 19th-century literary imagination, Sandra Gilbert and Susan Gubar analyze the split in the creative woman. Speaking of Charlotte Bronte's *Jane Eyre,* they write:

> Examining the psychosocial implications of a "haunted" ancestral mansion, such a tale explores the tension between parlor and attic, the psychic split between the lady who submits to male dicta and the lunatic who rebels. But in examining these matters the paradigmatic female story inevitably considers also the equally uncomfortable spatial options of expulsion into the cold outside or suffocation in the hot indoors, and in addition it often embodies an obsessive anxiety both about starvation to the point of disappearance and about monstrous inhabitation.[4]

The starving lunatic who rebelled in the above dream is tyrannized by the huge, perfectly groomed, perfectly fed white cat—an arrogant, spiritualized instinct. The dream also suggests the suffocation, "the obsessive anxiety about starvation and the monstrous inhabitation." The dream ego is being forced to recognize that part of herself which is dying in the attic, imprisoned by what is in effect an elegant animus. Fed with the dreamer's expectations of herself, he is the trickster who steals the food from the anorexic's mouth.

If that elegant, "noble" animus is projected, the woman may fall in love with a man who has tried all his life to please mother. He may connect feeling to the *idea* of being perfect. Thus he will try to be a perfect father, perfect husband, perfect son, but may at the same time be denying his own real feelings. He thinks he has to be better than he is and therefore rejects himself *as* he is. He sets out to please what he believes is the positive mother and looks forward to her rewards for his perfect behavior. He feeds her, but she turns negative and throws his gifts back. Her spirit cannot thank him. He is the man who says, "The more I try to satisfy her, the worse it is." That's being caught in the complex. The woman trying to relate to him may be saying, "What do I have to do to make him feel anything?" If he drops the image and says what he really feels, then the masochistic behavior and its symptoms can be dealt with. Instead of trying to please mother, wife, daughter, the world, he begins to think in terms of being himself. Until this point, he is not asking the real question, "What are *my* feelings?" and therefore not assuming the responsibility for who he is. He is living a masochistic psychology of denial, which often leads to rejecting other people before they reject him.

If the woman can take that projection back and, instead of blaming her man, recognize that she treats herself the same way, she may find that the elegant animus is a combination of her mother's animus and her father. (For better, for worse, partners do seem to deserve each other.) In an old Indian story, a woman cuts herself in two at the waist. The top half she attaches to her man so that everything that comes out of his mouth, she devours. Her entrails, hanging from her waist, hang out behind so that everything he does is obliterated by her excrement. The lower half she spreads at home to make sure he will return.

That's what the elegant animus (the wizard behind the witch) can do to a man or to a woman's own positive animus. When the negative mother is ready to devour every word that comes out of a person's mouth, that person will have very little to say unless it is perfectly considered for the occasion, because the "You're not good enough" is strangling what wants to come out. Spontaneity is destroyed. This can operate very subtly. A woman solicitously watching her husband or child working on something may mask her real attitude, "I know you can't do it. It will fall on my shoulders in the end." This is positive mothering that tries to take care of everything.

positive mothering is still mothering, with the assumption that there is a child to be supported. The personal feelings of the adult woman, the feminine ego, may still be locked in the mother. Women who as tiny children had to begin mothering younger siblings, or even their own "dear" mothers, may project this helpless child onto others. Beneath it is considerable resentment because they were never allowed their own childhood and, ironically, resent the responsibility they automatically assume in most situations.

Another area in which the negative mother combines with the perfectionist father to produce chaos is in attempting to write essays or prepare for examinations. The inner dialogue might go something like this: "I haven't read Kant; I should read Marx; Oh yes, there's an excellent passage in Nietzsche. I haven't done that, or this. I could handle it from this point of view—or that—or that." So the spinning begins, the thread becoming so twisted around itself that the woman may sit for hours drawing in more and more material without getting a clear perspective, and wind up at the end of the day with piles of books and notes but still no unified coherent approach to the material.

Such chaos can drive a woman to eat or drink in an attempt both to escape and to stay on the ground. She may have begun with a genuine interest in the paper, but when the complex takes over, mountains of material are accumulated under which the positive, creative animus suffocates. When the creative spirit is not breathing into the material, it dies. The essay becomes an overwhelming duty. One thing that complex hates is fun; it reduces everything to grim responsibility. Again the attitude toward it is crucial. If the ego is rigid, it is afraid of the overwhelming fertility of the positive side of the mother complex, for while she wants more, she also has a never-ending supply of seeds and possibilities. The ego can enjoy these, but must use its own considerable strength to decide what will grow and what will not. If it tries to hold onto everything, it will collapse. The only way to get out from underneath the weight is to bring the negative mother to consciousness, "Do I want to write this paper or do I not? I do. *I* do. I, selfish as I am, I want to do it. Yes, selfish as I am, I want to take the responsibility and I am going to enjoy it. I want to do it and I want to do it my way."

The negative mother does not want the individual to develop personally; she doesn't want joy, creative excitement or freedom around her. Repeatedly, dieting young women buy new clothes for a party with great anticipation, but go on a binge the night before and find themselves bloated and two sizes too large. The possibility of enjoying oneself—in work or play—is a danger zone which has to be foreseen and dealt with consciously; otherwise the complex takes over with its dark pall of duty.

If that woman happens to be married to a man who also has a negative mother complex, he too is in danger of being choked in the spider's web. He watches his wife agonizing over the indigestible pile of paper and, if he is unconscious, he goes crazier than she. Even if they are not talking about the material, her anxiety will constellate his, and either he is trapped and moves deeper into it with her or he pulls back threatened and angry. If he gives into the maw with her, they will both become mired in the miasma. If he can remain conscious and hold his own rational position, that in itself may constellate her ego strength. Both have to be very aware of the complex, talk it over when it isn't threatening, and discuss ways to outsmart it.

The Medusa complex in its extreme form does petrify in that it stops the flow of life, the natural giving and receiving of energy. The complex is happy so long as it is giving, because without the conscious ego making its own choices, the giving may be sheer manipulation. The child who has been manipulated by a negative mother's "unselfish giving" does not expect to be recognized for itself and is therefore very wary of receiving. In the first weeks of analysis, such a person might show a strong persona and talk as if everything were fine. Then one day the analyst says, "But how do *you* feel?" Then the dam is either reinforced or it collapses, or the woman may have to experience her own feeling through the response of the analyst. It is often experienced as a miracle when the "I" is finally recognized.

I once had an analysand whose life story was one shattering incident after another. For three months she told me her story with no emotional response. She seemed to be under a veil. Then one day she found an abandoned puppy and projected all her feelings about herself onto this quivering bit of life. She sat rigid and silent. I reached out and took her hand. She looked into my eyes as if seeing me for the first time and burst into body-wracking sobs. Then the analysis began. She told her whole story again as if she had no memory of having told it before, but this time her own feelings were in it. The complex that bewitched her could not turn my touch into a power play. It couldn't convince her that I was just an analyst doing my job. It might tell her I was just trying to exploit her and later on the hidden motive would emerge, but *she* knew it was a spontaneous, straightforward act of love and recognition. Her response was strong enough to crack the stone in which she had been living all her life. Of course, doubts and fears resurfaced periodically but in that moment she was able to know she was loved and she was able to receive that love without fear.

The tears that soften the stone, the ice, the glass, the concrete walls of dreams, are like the tears Viktor Frankl speaks of in his story of the concentration camp. "There was no need to be ashamed of tears, for tears bore witness that a man had the greatest courage, the courage to suffer." Of all the prisoners in the camp only one was able to put his boots on his swollen feet. When Frankl asked him how he had gotten over his edema he replied, "I have wept it out of me."[5] Keeping a stiff upper lip is one thing; being able to connect to our own reality in our own situation is another. The negative mother loves unconsciousness. So long as we are petrified in a static world there is no danger of us opening ourselves to weeping our own tears or singing our own song.

The witch mother has foolproof recipes for everything; if strictly followed (and to follow is to follow strictly) they guarantee success. She is impatient of error, having no room for it because there is no need for it. She is an efficiency expert. Anyone learning under her jurisdiction will be oriented from the start to clearly defined goals and objects. The real world is a world of things and the human job is to see that they work efficiently. Perfection does not allow for individual weakness or individual feeling. The daughter of such a mother comes to experience herself as a thing being manipulated toward a high level of efficiency. What she may not know is that her mother's knowledge is devoid of wisdom. It is without human meaning and personal love. The daughter thinks of herself as an object. However it is disguised—beautiful, intelligent, efficient, valuable, rare—it still remains dehumanized. Such a daughter has no inner standpoint of her own.

Here in essence is the tragedy of the obese and anorexic woman, as well as many another unhappy woman in our culture. Her spiritual striving and excessive discipline are undertaken in order to achieve a goal which has in reality nothing to do with her. It is a goal, when closely examined, which invokes the final obliteration of herself. Her goal involves her own death. Around such a goal creative forces cannot rally. Nothing in her real feminine nature can come to her support. The energy that is driving toward extinction is the demonic energy of the witch. So within the inevitable defeat of the woman there is the final cry of the abandoned child—Lady Macbeth's three anguished "Ooooh's" as she attempts to sweeten her little hand.

This can happen to such a degree that any attempt on the part of the daughter to introduce human meaning into her life arouses such deep anxiety that human meaning becomes in her mind a betrayal of the mother. For her to become human is to disappoint mother who has done everything in her power to turn her daughter into a successful woman. Since the daughter to humanly survive must overcome her mother's ideals, the real hope of resolving her problems resides in *understanding* the necessity of what she is doing. The evil lies in the nonhuman ideal. To be caught in that is to be ultimately

inaccessible to reality. She must see the reality from which she is
escaping in order to understand the meaning of her action. Once she
discovers what her mother never introduced her to—the deep, rich
love of being alive—her life becomes her possession. She is then free
to shape her own life. This radical shift from identification with the
mother to standing in her own shoes on her own ground is the
archetypal shift from the witch to Sophia. Medusa is human un-
meaning; Sophia is human meaning.

In the last part of chapter three I mentioned the coming together
of body and spirit. Where there has been a radical split, I believe a
somatic container must be prepared to receive the psychic labor.
There must be a greeting of the spirit, a chalice to receive the wine.
The dream of a woman who had been in analysis for three years
illustrates the harmony that can exist between body and spirit. The
spiritual energy is firmly rooted in the instinctual roots, at the same
time maintaining its relationship to the Self. The dream makes clear
the difference between the evil witch and Sophia:

> My friend and I are in a rugged stone country church. There are two
> side aisles, and one central aisle leading to the altar. The church is full
> of shepherds and simple folk. A woman in a long leather gown,
> wearing a primitive crown and carrying a scepter, which she uses as a
> pointer, is moving down the side aisle trying to make the shepherds
> sing. She persuades, scolds, and becomes very angry, but only while
> she is looking in their direction will they reluctantly sing. When she
> passes they mumble unhappily among themselves. She consults with a
> man who is dressed up as a king, who is also moving about, but he is
> even more angry.
> "That's no queen," I whisper to my friend.
> Then another woman enters from the same side door, tall and regal,
> dressed in a simple gown, without crown or scepter, but in herself a
> queen. She moves down the aisle and everyone sings. The peasants
> adore her and she loves them. Her radiance is connected to a genu-
> inely kingly man who now stands at the altar. Although her eyes
> never turn to his, her antennae seem to be guiding her inevitably
> toward him. She puts her hand into his outstretched hand, and the
> whole church bursts into a triumphant wedding song. I put my hand
> into my friend's hand. "She has Grace," he says.

The setting is a country church built of fieldstone, a sacred place
that rises straight out of the ground, and its occupants are simple
shepherds who live close to nature. In her analysis this woman had
tried to bring spiritual and instinctual together, as this setting veri-
fies, but the ego had not yet found its rightful relationship to either.

This dream illustrates that the dreamer has reached a crisis both
in her analysis and in her life. The dream clearly constellates her
choice between her false self and her real self and makes clear that

the reconciliation must come from the Self (Church) which is deeply rooted in nature. She watches two queens who symbolize two different attitudes. The one relies on her ego and the power principle, thus blocking the creative flow from the unconsious. The other has surrendered her ego to what the dream calls "Grace," thus opening herself to love, inner harmony and the energy from her own creative depths.

The dreamer realized she had to choose between going back to the collective, rigid world she had always known, or trusting herself to her inner spiritual guide, thus moving with her own destiny. She saw it as a choice between falling back into unconsciousness and surrendering to the Self. If she chose to go back, she feared being condemned by her own Reality. If she chose to surrender, she was terrified of losing her integrity in a world she did not understand. It is a crisis we all reach at least once in the individuation process. As the false queen, she is identified with the archetype and has endowed her man with an archetypal kingly costume. She is without Grace. She does what she does by ego strength for her own purposes. She tries to force the support of the people, but her motivation is power, and therefore there is a split between the conscious energy and the unconscious meaning. The dreamer related this image to her own attempts to use her will power against her feelings and her natural instincts, thereby forcing herself into masculine drivenness. Such an attitude precludes development, however, because the creative energy is not feeding consciousness; thus there can be no genuine growth in either feeling or insight.

As the real queen, she is a simple woman in a simple gown, without the accouterments of office, but with the inner grace of acceptance. She is not identified with the archetype; that is, her ego does not attempt to usurp power that does not rightfully belong to it, and thus she allows the god to make himself known. This attitude allows Eros to pour through her, allows for her unconsious emotions and images to flow into the personal dimension, so that she can build a personal relationship with her friend without transcending human limitations. Then all the disparate parts of the psyche automatically burst into harmonious song. The tuning note is the surrender of the ego to the gift of Grace, or in psychological language, the establishment of a nurturing connection between consiousness and unconscious.

The double image of offering hands—queen to king, dreamer to friend—suggests a mutual expression of trust, a recognition that each life is intrinsically changed by its interaction with the other. On a deeper level it symbolizes the dreamer's surrender to the masculine otherness. It is a tender recognition of vulnerability and a further surrender of ego because that vulnerability leaves her open to deep wounding. Trust, at this point in analysis, is most difficult, because by now one has seen one's own shadow and realizes one must trust that which is untrustworthy. But there is nothing to do but trust, and work, and wait. That's God's country. In this dream, it is the strong animus figure, standing confidently at the altar, who sustains her on her journey toward herself and him—that sustaining love which loves her real self and allows no self-deception. When she gives herself to him, far from reluctantly surrendering to his male ego, she steps into her own authenticity.

Many women today are searching for the authentic feminine, forced underground centuries ago by a patriarchal culture. Both Jung and Marie-Louise von Franz have discussed at length the significance of the dogma of the Assumption of the Virgin Mary, as it reflects a larger enantiodromia away from an exhausted and destructive patriarchy toward a new matriarchy in which matter is released. Here, for example, is Marie-Louise von Franz in her 1959 lectures on alchemy:

> In the whole Christian civilization [there is] . . . a secret unobtrusive return to matriarchy and materialism. This enantiodromia has to do with the fact that the Judaeo-Christian religion did not face the archetype of the mother consciously enough. It had to a certain extent excluded the question. It is well known, also, that when Pope Pius XII declared the *assumptio Maria* his conscious aim was to hit Communistic materialism by elevating, so to speak, a symbol of matter in the Catholic Church, so as to take the wind out of the Communists' sails. There is a much deeper implication, but that was his conscious idea, namely that the only way to fight the materialistic aspect would be by raising to a higher position the symbol of the feminine Godhead, and with it matter. Since it is the Virgin Mary's body which is raised to Heaven emphasis is on the physical material aspect.[6]

My interest in this book has not been with the political and religious implications of the Communist doctrine of dialectical materialism, though a moment's reflection would show, I think, that its embodiment in myth is the witch ending in the Russian Gulag. Rather I have concentrated on the psychic process related to the healing of the woman whose food complex is bound up with the mother. That her nightmare and its resolution are being acted out on a larger world stage, which the Church in its doctrine of the Assumption had in mind, strongly suggests the importance of these women, in terms of what they are struggling to achieve within themselves, for the future of our civilization.

Jung in his writings returned again and again to the conviction that the psychic illnesses of his patients, whether neurotic or psychotic, contained at their core the spirit of the age, the collective *Weltanschauung*. Women entering analysis, bloated with the sick affluence of one society or emaciated by the starvation of another, are enacting a Western end-of-the-world condition, in which, ironically, the starved and the bloated belong to the same society. Needless to say, a woman suffering from this syndrome is not concerned with the larger world issues; she simply wants to lose weight. She does not see any connection between her psychic condition and the Church's struggle with Communism. The present Pope does not appear in her dreams as the positive mother. As her analysis continues, however, and moves out of the necessary narcissistic phase of ego- and body-building, she begins to look out at the world around her. Her immediate response is to withdraw, to have nothing to do with it. It is brutish, deceptive and cruel, while she is pure. The point arrives, however, when between her and the world, as between her and her body, there is a greeting between body and spirit when she feels not only her interaction with the world, but takes some responsibility for it. And better still, she ceases to be what she was when she entered analysis—a Lady Macbeth washing her hands of invisible blood, knowing they can never be sweet.

I want now to describe a process of enantiodromia as it appears in analysis. My central image is a spiral, which can move two ways: out toward release or in toward destruction, with the crucial proviso that destruction and release, like crucifixion and resurrection, are one—with a long *and* in between. That realization is the feminine mystery, expressed by Christ in the paradox, "He that findeth his life shall lose it."[7] Though Ruth and Eleanor (in the previous chapter) were working with this paradox, it was not yet for them a paradox, but a contradiction. What we see in women's mysteries is the process by which *contradiction is transformed into paradox*. That transformation is the work of the feminine. To find the stillness at the center of the whirlpool, the eye of the hurricane, and not hold onto it with the rigidity born of fear, is what in analysis we struggle to reach. That center I call Sophia, the feminine Wisdom of God. It is not the masculine standpoint, the highly-principled "Here I stand." It is not Martin Luther hammering his ninety-five articles on the door. It is not a manifesto. It is an invisible center encountered only in a creative process, at first not consciously recognized, but gradually revealed as the process unfolds. That point, in other words, does not exist apart from the process; its being is always in the becoming, giving the process the assurance of its own reality.

When Matisse put to himself the question, "Do I believe in God?" he replied, "Yes, when I am working."[8] Nature is at once unchanging and in continuous change; one cannot be separated from the other. We can accept all the changes in nature—seasons, days, phases of the moon—because of our deeper awareness of the permanence residing within it. That continuous process within the eternal is what I think of as Sophia, Wisdom proper to the woman, the feminine Godhead.

As von Franz suggests in her lectures on alchemy, the feminine goddess, while present in Gnosticism, is not properly represented in the Judaeo-Christian tradition:

> There are a few obscure allusions to a dark chaotic mother-mass underneath, which is identical with matter, and a sublime feminine figure which is the Wisdom of God, but even she was eliminated in Christianity for God was declared to be identical with the Holy Ghost or the soul of Christ, and matter supposed to be ruled by the devil.[9]

Von Franz is describing the tendency in Christianity toward patriarchy: the masculine father God revealed in his son, with the feminine principle assigned to matter, supposedly ruled by the devil—in short, the feminine principle as Eve bound to the serpent, bringing to the world death and all our woes, the feminine principle as witch.

The obese or anorexic woman is, for very personal reasons having to do with her own parents, locked into this patriarchal situation. She is therefore intimately connected with the same problem as that involved in the redemption of Christianity from the one-sidedness of the masculine principle. This process, particularly in alchemical texts, is seen as the fallen woman, or Wisdom of God, sunk in matter, calling upon a human being of understanding to dig her up. In one text cited by von Franz, the feminine cries out: "He in whose embrace my whole body melts away, *to whom I will be father and he will be my son.*"[10] Here the lover and beloved, the feminine Wisdom of God and her male consort, replace the father and son of the old patriarchy. The Wisdom of God, von Franz writes, is "simply an *experience of God Himself, but in His feminine form.*"[11] The cry of the obese woman, her longing to be delivered from the matter in which she is buried, can archetypally be heard as the call of the Wisdom of God to be delivered from the gross or unredeemed matter to which, as the fallen Eve, a patriarchial Christianity has assigned her.

One of my analysands dreamt of Christ being born from her fat thighs, and another in her dream went to the washroom in the local theater, saw a filthy stable through the back window and a blinding light issuing from the straw. So Christ born in the stable because there was no room for him in the inn may serve as an image of the Self born from the rejected body of the obese woman.

What is involved here is an enantiodromia leading to the recognition that what Christ symbolizes is in everyone and he can be directly addressed, a view which led many a Joan of Arc to the stake to be burned as a witch. Her terror is unconsciously present in every woman suffering from the obese/anorexic syndrome, particularly since, in her struggle to survive, she increasingly adopts a masculine persona which is in fact destroying her feminine nature. The fire that consumes her is destructive and not transformative because it is the fire of the masculine principle, a fixed and rigid standpoint that destroys, rather than releases, the feminine process. It is the fire to which St. Joan was condemned when the Church turned her over to the English.

I would describe Sophia as an emerging archetypal pattern, not yet fully in consciousness, that is bringing to our Western culture a new understanding of the relationship between spirit and matter. The masculine Wisdom of God, as many of us have experienced it, resides in theology, dogma and moral philosophy. Because it is a knowable Wisdom it is accessible to reason, and being accessible it is codifiable. It can be and often is reduced to catechism. It is an institutionalized collective Wisdom. The Wisdom of Sophia, on the other hand, is the Wisdom of the unknowable. It is the nonrational, nonrepeatable and nonconsistent. It belongs to the here-and-now, the immediate moment. William Blake describes it as the moment in each day that Satan cannot find, as short as the pulsation of an artery.[12] It is the moment in which life is conceived not in some repeatable fashion, for it is unique and particular to the moment.

Just as there is a dark side to the Wisdom of the knowable God—the tyranny of the Church—so there is a dark side to the Wisdom of the unknowable God. It is utter chaos, the Void. The dark side of Sophia is the original Void before it was penetrated by Light, that is, the matrix in which the Light is first made manifest.

There is in von Franz' alchemy lectures an interesting interchange between a theologian and herself:

> *Dr. von Franz:* If you are with an analysand the only way you may perhaps help is by always saying: "I don't know, but let us ask God." By that you prevent the analysand from drawing rash conscious conclusions or seducing you into making them, and therefore every religious experience becomes a unique event. God in every experience is experienced in a specific and unique form and that includes even the red sulphur [sexuality], which means that if you put the question of the red sulphur before God, God will give His unique answer in each case.

> *Remark:* I think God has already given His unique answer in each case.

> *Dr. von Franz:* That is where we differ. You think God has published general rules which He keeps Himself, and we think He is a living spirit appearing in man's psyche who can always create something new.

> *Remark:* Within the framework of what He has already published.

*Dr. von Franz:* To a theologian God is bound to His own books and is incapable of further publications. That is where we lock horns.[13]

And that is the Wisdom of Sophia.

If you want to experience an instantaneous enantiodromia you need only get up from the table where you've spent an entire morning working through an enigmatic problem and go and jump into the icy waters of Georgian Bay. There is an instantaneous switch from mind to body. The result can be amazing. The shock to the body resolves the enigma of the mind. Things which were more and more opaque at the table are suddenly crystal clear, as clear as the crystal waters of Georgian Bay. Why does this occur? Jumping into the water releases the instincts: they swiftly rise to the surface to become the body's light. For the intuitive the question in the mind can often be answered by the instincts. To plunge into cold water after the heat of reflection is putting the question into the realm of the instincts, where it ceases to be rigid and begins to flow, as if in the depths of the waters of the unconscious the answer resides.

Sophia is the instantaneous illumination rising out of the icy waters. It is the mystery. In psychological language, it occurs when the ego has ceased to identify with either of the opposites, body or mind. Having once experienced their interaction, the ego can become their place of reconciliation, whereas to be identified with one is to be the enemy of the other: body and mind at war with each other. The ego that is grounded in reality can say, "Yes, those are a part of me, I am part body, I am part mind, but I am neither body nor mind; I am body *and* mind. I may be tossed about like a sailboat in a cyclone, but through thick and thin I am able to hold my standpoint here at the center; and here, because I now have eyes to see and ears to hear, I can surrender. Life can happen; life can pour through me. Whereas I was dead, I am alive again, was lost and am found."

It takes a very strong ego and a very long travail to surrender to Sophia. One can go on indefinitely swinging back and forth between the opposites. How much better to concentrate on that still point which is the ego's standpoint in surrender. Without that point there is no dance. Anyone who has worked patiently through the long hours of bringing consciousness to the muscles of the body, moment by moment, and guiding the energy from the solar plexus to each member of that microcosm, anyone who has labored to create that standpoint, and then one day suddenly experienced the *lift* of the dance, if only for a moment—in that moment has known all that matters:

> *O body swayed to music, O brightening glance,*
> *How can we know the dancer from the dance?*[14]

*Those masterful images because complete*
*Grew in pure mind, but out of what began?*
*A mound of refuse or the sweepings of a street,*
*Old kettles, old bottles, and a broken can,*
*Old iron, old bones, old rags, that raving slut*
*Who keeps the till. Now that my ladder's gone,*
*I must lie down where all the ladders start,*
*In the foul rag-and-bones shop of the heart.*
        —W.B. Yeats, "The Circus Animals' Desertion."

Deliverance is won through differentiation . . . when the spirit becomes "moist and gross" it sinks into the depths, i.e., gets entangled with the object, but when purged through pain it becomes "dry and hot" and rises up again, for it is just this fiery quality that differentiates it from the humid nature of its subterranean abode.
        —C.G. Jung, *Psychological Types.*

The first thing to be said of course is that Hagia Sophia is God Himself. God is not only Father but a Mother. He is both at the same time, and it is the "feminine aspect" or Feminine principle in the divinity that is the Hagia Sophia. But of course as soon as you say this the whole thing becomes misleading: a division of an "abstract" divinity into two abstract principles. Nevertheless, to ignore this distinction is to lose touch with the fullness of God. This is a very ancient intuition of reality which goes back to the oldest Oriental thought. . . . For the "masculine-feminine" relationship is basic in all reality— simply because all reality mirrors the reality of God. . . .

This feminine principle in the universe is the inexhaustible source of creative realizations of the Father's glory in the world and is in fact the manifestation of His glory. Pushing it further, Sophia in ourselves is the Mercy of God, the tenderness which by infinitely mysterious power of pardon turns the darkness of our sins into the light of God's love. Hence, Sophia is the feminine, dark, yielding, tender counterpart of the power, justice, creative dynamism of the Father.

        —Thomas Merton, in Monica Furlong, *Merton, A Biography.*

# 5

## Assent to the Goddess

*But O alas, so long, so far*
*Our bodies why do we forbear?*
*They are ours, though not we; we are*
*The intelligences, they the sphere.*
*We owe them thanks because they thus,*
*Did us to us at first convey,*
*Yielded their forces, sense, to us,*
*Nor are dross to us, but allay.*
— John Donne, "The Ecstasy."

Though this was not his intention, John Donne in "The Ecstasy" sets up the kind of situation that can occur when a woman in analysis lacks a genuine bonding with the mother, in other words, is not secure in the ground of her own body. When that bonding is absent, the woman tends to go into her head. However illuminating this may be in terms of new insights into the nature of her problems, the insights themselves remain disembodied; in Donne's words, the spheres are not connected to the intelligences. Analyst and analysand are then like Donne's two souls negotiating above the bodies of the two lovers.

In the intellectualizing of a problem, the body is cruelly abandoned. The shock that follows the analytic hour is the return to the body. As soon as the soul re-enters the body, as it were, it suddenly appears as if nothing has really changed. All that happened in the session is that the soul experienced a momentary release from its sepulcher, and was able to move about like the blessed in Paradise, before returning to its earthly grave to experience itself once more as buried alive. That sensation of being buried alive is a precise metaphor of the obese condition and the sensation of being released from the grave is the sensation of the "weightless" anorexic. The function of analysis is not to further encourage this body/soul split but to heal it until, finally, the soul in the body experiences itself as having undergone "small change," the body and the soul now being one. In the end, once the real limitations of the intellectual level have been recognized and overcome, the dialogue between the lovers negotiating their body/soul relationship becomes "a dialogue of one" (see above, page 57).

As the analysis progresses, especially where there is a deep psyche/soma split, neither analyst nor analysand dare assume that the body is merely a dumb animal encasing a very articulate, highly aspiring spirit. The language of the body, to shift the metaphor, is far more than the mutterings of a ten-month-old child sending out instinctual signals that identify certain animal needs but not much more. Once the analytic rapport is firmly established, pretending there is no body, or treating it with indifference, is pretending there is no shadow—a trickster's reversal of the emperor's new clothes, a game the obese trickster loves. At some point in each hour, even in the initial stages, the messages of the body must be recognized, if only for a moment. To allow the woman to leave the session joyous in her heady illumination, then face her shadow in the mirror as she puts on her coat, is a cruel reinforcement of the split. The bodies, as Donne says, must yield "their forces, sense, to us." Analyst and analysand must recognize those forces as not "dross to us, but allay."

Donne's image of bodily sense as allay (alloy) rather than dross is taken from metallurgy, which has behind it the history of alchemy. Dross is an impurity which weakens metal; allay is an impurity which strengthens it. The soul, like gold, if too refined or pure becomes soft and will not hold its shape. It needs to contain an impurity so that it can harden into an identifiable form. If the soul thinks it is above all identity, being too pure to have a form (as the anorexic and obese both feel), then it will experience the alloy of the body as dross. The woman's task is to persevere with the body until she recognizes that it is not dross but alloy. And the way to do this is to allow the body to play, to give it space and allow it to make whatever movements it wants to make.

The shift in perception from dross to allay comes when the ego begins to ground itself in the Great Mother, the body of creation itself; in terms of biblical mythology, it is when the virginal, disembodied Mary finally is able to seat herself on the lap of the wise Sophia. Then the atrophied instinct is able to make contact with the psyche's healing imagery which is reaching out to the wounded instincts in dreams. That imagery in its melted or softened condition, the condition of the dream, wishes to harden into the living world of the body until it experiences "small change" in the movement back and forth between the inner and outer worlds.

What is important to realize is that releasing the body into spontaneous movement or play constellates the unconscious in precisely the some way as does a dream. For this reason, I came to the conclusion that for many of my analysands a body workshop was as necessary as dream analysis. Since most of my analysands were suffering in one way or another from a deep psyche/soma split, I saw that the exclusion of the body in the exploration of the unconscious was at least as one-sided as would be the exclusion of dreams. Body movements, I realized, can be understood as a waking dream. In its spontaneous movements the body is like an infant crying out to be heard, understood, responded to, much as a dream is sending out signals from the unconscious.

The great advantage of body movement within a controlled workshop situation is that the individuals involved become participating agents in their own dreaming in ways that are far less apparent when they are asleep or when they are alone. It is therefore easier to work more directly with the waking dream (i.e., body movement) than with the all too easily forgotten sleeping dream, for which the only witness is the dreamer. A dream cannot be verified, cannot participate directly in the concrete waking world. Unlike the body, which does not lie, a dream can be forgotten, half-remembered, reduced to a fragment of itself, or even grossly distorted in the waking re-creation of it. The attempt to make prose sense of a dream subjects the dream to a grammatical logic that may be alien to the symbolic logic of the dreaming state, which is closer to poetry than prose. Although the dream is and will remain our richest source of information from the unconscious, body movement can bring us closer to the actuality of the dream, even as the dream may deepen our understanding of the psychic dimension of the musculature of the body. The two work together because they belong together. The body is the unconscious in its most immediate and continuous form; the dream is also the unconscious, though as a body of images it lacks both the immediacy and continuity of the physical body.

The unconscious per se is unknowable; it is a reality that is inferred from such things as spontaneous or involuntary body movement and dreams. Ultimately we may come to think of body movement or the dreaming state as a manifestation not of unconsciousness, but as a consciousness that operates upon us and within us. Certainly there are many who believe that what we now think of as the unconscious is equivalent to the traditional concept of God as an unsleeping Being within, an omniscient inner presence. Similarly, I speak of Sophia or of the Virgin because they are divine womanly beings associated with the feminine side of God. By locating them in the unconscious I am following the path of God from without to within, the path that characterizes the movement of consciousness itself. Moreover, I am suggesting that what we now call the unconscious is in psychological reality a consciousness that has simply been underground for too long. In alchemy there is the concept of the *deus absconditus* (male), the hidden god in matter.[1] But the unconscious also includes the *dea abscondita,* the Black Madonna, the goddess who has chosen to hide herself in order to protect humanity from the devastating consequences of killing her.

Modern society, far more than we realize, is the offspring of Nietzsche's declaration, "God is dead." He is not dead, nor is the Goddess. They are merely hiding. Their hiding place is the unconscious. When it is no longer necessary for them to hide in order to protect man from destroying himself by destroying them, they, God and Goddess together, will re-emerge. And when they do we will see the unconscious for what it is: God's consciousness of his creation which includes the body's consciousness of itself. That movement Nietzsche identified with Dionysus.

The return of God is one of the most ancient expectations of the human race. Every world religion has presented itself as preparing for his return. Every religion still awaits it. What does this expectation imply? We already know God in his outward manifestation, by his laws, his commands, his word. That is the Logos, the masculine side of God. What we await in the Second Coming is what we lack: God's inner dynamic or process. This—God in his creativeness rather than in his creation—is the essence of the feminine, traditionally enacted in the ancient Mysteries. The return is therefore the emergence of the feminine side of God, which has been gradually taking shape for centuries in what we call the unconscious. The time has now come when we can deal creatively with the concept of God as the union of opposites, and therefore see the feminine no longer darkly through a masculine glass, but face to androgynous face.

The Great Mother is the feminine side of God. In the Bible she is Wisdom (Sophia); in Leonardo da Vinci's drawing (below, page 128) she is St. Anne, on whose lap sits the Virgin—the feminine in both men and women, the receptive Being in whom divine and human meet. It is interesting to note that this powerful motif was portrayed by da Vinci in an extremely fragile pencil and charcoal drawing, so frail that it must be protected under glass in a small darkened room in the London National Gallery. If ordinary daylight were to enter, it would gradually disappear altogether. As a symbol of the role that the feminine has been allowed to play in the patriarchal world it is perhaps as exact an image as anything one could invent.

The word virgin requires clarification because it carries so many religious and social connotations. I am not using it in the sense of physical chastity, nor in any orthodox sense related to the dogma of the Christian Church. A study of the changing concepts surrounding the Virgin Mary, as Virgin, Queen, Bride, Mother, Intercessor, is eloquently developed by Marina Warner in her book *Alone of All Her Sex*. Having examined the contradictions inherent in this "ideal" woman, she concludes:

Black Madonna and Child (15th century).—Einsiedeln, Switzerland.

(See text, page 82)

The Virgin Mary has inspired some of the loftiest architecture, some of the most moving poetry, some of the most beautiful paintings in the world; she has filled men and women with deep joy and fervent trust; she has been an image of the ideal that has entranced and stirred men and women to the noblest emotions of love and pity and awe. But the reality her myth describes is over; the moral code she affirms has been exhausted. . . .

As an acknowledged creation of Christian mythology, the Virgin's legend will endure in its splendor and lyricism, but it will be emptied of moral significance, and thus lose its present real powers to heal and to harm.[2]

The Virgin Mary is certainly one archetypal pattern of femininity, albeit cluttered with the fears and ideals of twenty centuries. Warner points out, however, that as the cult of the Virgin developed, Mary usurped the qualities of the pagan goddesses, and she therefore embodies far more of the dark feminine than the patriarchy has allowed her.

For while Mary provides a focus for the steeliest asceticism, she is also the ultimate of fertility symbols. The mountain blossoms spontaneously; so does the mother maid. The old significance of the moon and the serpent as divine attributes survives in such sanctuaries as Montserrat, for there she is venerated as a source of fertility and delight. . . .

The image worshipped there is a Black Madonna. . . . When artists restored the images, they repainted the robes and jewels that clothed the Madonna and Child but out of awe left their faces black. Awe, however, did not arise only from simple veneration of their sacred image . . . but also probably because the mysterious and exotic darkness of the countenances had rapidly inspired a special cult. In Catholic countries, where blackness is the climate of the devils, not the angels, and is associated almost exclusively with magic and the occult, Black Madonnas are considered especially wonder-working, as the possessors of hermetic knowledge and power. . . .

In Sicily, the cult of the corn goddess Demeter flourished, and statuettes have been excavated showing her dandling her infant daughter Kore-Persephone in her arms, or supporting her, asleep on her shoulder—an image so close to the Madonna and child that at Enna . . . where Persephone was swallowed up into the underworld, the cathedral used to display a Greek statue of Demeter and her daughter on the altar. . . .

As guardian of cities and nations and peoples, as the bringer of peace or victory, her image the palladium of royal armies, the Virgin resembles Athene. She did indeed usurp the Greek goddess of peace in Athens.[3]

Our psychic roots are Judaeo-Christian roots that reach back through the centuries to absorb those early goddesses and moon worship. Our lives, however, have been lived with the literature, music and art of the great Christian tradition, and the archaic energy that resonates in us in experiencing the full moon dare not be cut off from the spiritual energy that resonates in experiencing a full choir and orchestra singing Handel's *Messiah* in St. Paul's Cathedral. That would be merely creating another split. If the concept of the virgin and the feminine side of God (or of Christ) can be experienced in a new way, then the trammels of orthodoxy can be removed; a new and living faith can resonate through our daily lives, bringing new dimensions to our physical and spiritual reality so that instead of being cut off from our heritage we are reunited with it. What seemed dead images and memorized verses can come alive, charged with profound inner truth and dynamic energy.

Esther Harding in *Woman's Mysteries* examines the original meaning of the word virgin. I quote her at length because one aspect without the other grossly distorts the unity of the image:

> To enter the boat of the goddess implies accepting the uprush of instinct in a religious spirit as a manifestation of the creative life force, itself. When such an attitude is attained, instinct can no longer be regarded as an asset to be exploited for the advantage of the personal life; instead it must be recognized that the personal I, the ego, must submit itself to the demands of the life force as to a divine being.
>
> The chief characteristic of the goddess in her crescent phase is that she is virgin. Her instinct is not used to capture or possess the man whom she attracts. She does not reserve herself for the chosen man who must repay her by his devotion, nor is her instinct used to gain for herself the security of husband, home and family. She remains virgin, even while being goddess of love. She is essentially one-in-herself. She is not merely the feminine counterpart of a male god with similar characteristics and functions, modified to suit her feminine form. On the contrary she has a role to play that is her own, her characteristics do not duplicate those of any of the gods, She is the Ancient and Eternal, the Mother of God. The god with whom she is associated is her son and him she necessarily precedes. Her divine power does not depend on her relation to a husband-god, and thus her actions are not dependent on the need to conciliate such a one or to accord with his qualities and attitudes. For she bears her divinity in her own right.
>
> In the same way the woman who is virgin, one-in-herself, does what she does—not because of any desire to please, not to be liked, or to be approved, even by herself; not because of any desire to gain power over another, to catch his interest or love, but because what she does is true.[4]

This passage is crucial to my understanding of the word virgin as it applies to this study. When the virgin, understood in this way as the feminine ego or identity, is firmly planted in her own wisdom—

which is traditionally imaged as the lap or throne of the Great Mother—the authentic woman emerges out of her own biological, cultural and spiritual heritage.

## Body as Sacred Vessel

Every archetype has its negative as well as positive side. The negative aspect of the virgin can perhaps best be seen in a paralyzing demand for perfection. In this paralytic condition she assumes the demonic guise of the negative mother or witch. Cut off from the wisdom of the body, the virgin is frozen. For the perfectionist who has trained herself *to do,* simply *being* sounds like a euphemism for nothingness, or ceasing to exist. When the energy that has gone into trying to justify her existence is redirected into discovering herself and loving herself, intense insecurities surface. Abysmal emptiness questions whether she is here at all. Her lifelong striving for perfection has created pockets of despair. These anxieties and resistances must be respected because they are masking deep-seated terror and rage which must be allowed to surface only when the time is right, that is, when the ego is strong enough to deal with them.

The first hurdle is the inner commitment. "Do I really believe that I am worthy of one hour a day for myself? I who have given my life to others, am I selfish enough to take one hour a day to find myself? Where can I find an hour? What has got to go?" This is a deeper problem than it may at first appear, because the negative mother hates joy and to do anything one enjoys produces guilt. So long as one's duty is being fulfilled, however compulsively, that is acceptable. To stop putting energy into duty, in order to release that energy for something creative for oneself, feels like being tossed in the washing machine, battered first on one side then the other. To cease to give is to cease to mother, and where the ego is identified with mothering it doesn't know at first what to do. It is so used to giving that it doesn't believe it is worthy to receive, or else thinks that receiving is demeaning or selfish.

Once the ego opens itself, however, once that forgotten energy begins to flow through dancing, painting, singing, joy is not experienced as selfish or luxurious, but as an absolute need. Then the negative virgin becomes positive. Then the danger is to want too much too soon. The important thing is to focus, not on the goal, but on the process. Be in the present. Let the unconscious play. Northrop Frye in a recent lecture quoted from Proverbs, where Wisdom proclaims that she was "set up from everlasting, from the beginning, or ever the earth was," and when God created heaven and earth, "Then I was by him, as one brought up with him: and I was daily his delight, rejoicing always before him."[5] Frye pointed out that "rejoicing" is translated from the root word for play and he preferred the connotations of "playing." For him, a little girl skipping is the image of wisdom. In that image, as I see it, body and spirit are one; Sophia is the love between them.

The fear of receiving resonates in the deepest levels of the pysche. To receive is to allow life to happen, to open oneself to love and delight, grief and loss. Sophia is the bridge, the love that opens the body to receive the spirit. There is a huge problem, however, where a person is not rooted in the body. Where the mother is not sufficiently in touch with her body she cannot give the child the bonding necessary to give it confidence in its own instincts. The child cannot relax into her body, nor later into its own. The underlying fear of life and fear of abandonment is only minimally concealed and the frightened ego is in constant danger of being swamped by the unknown forces that may sweep in from outside or from the unconscious. On that weak foundation is constructed a rigid superstructure based on collective values—discipline, efficiency, duty. The energy that wants to flow into creating, living, playing, is forced to find its outlet in blind compulsions.

Where the ego has no experience of concrete security, it lacks that image on which to build. If the creative imagination is given no time or space to create its own foundation, then the psyche does the only thing it can do: it concretizes the symbol. In the case of obesity this means that the absent positive mother is concretized in the body, and the fear of not staying on the earth is compensated by a body large enough to hold the spirit down. The greater the danger of disappearing into spirit, the greater the compulsion to put bread in the stomach. But bread can be experienced as stone when that process goes on too long. To persevere in that destructive behavior, to act out the compensation by feeding the instincts, merely widens the split.

The bread that becomes stone in the belly of the obese, the anorexic and the bulimic is a cruel parody of the spiritual bread which they cannot assimilate. Their condition is identical to believers whose faith resides in the literal rather than the symbolic word, those who are therefore, in St. Paul's terms, "killed by the letter" which, if spiritually discerned, gives life. These compulsives have a fatal attraction to the literal. It is evident, for example, in their propensity to conversion to Fundamentalist beliefs which reject symbolic interpretation of the Bible. The ultimate irony in their situation is that in their hunger for the mother, they deny the mother. The more they immerse themselves in matter, the less satisfied they are. The more they eat, the hungrier they are. They can, on some tragic level, eat their hearts out.

In order to heal the split, one has to bring conscious understanding to the destructive behavior and figure out what it is trying to say. Why do I need food? Why do I need a big body? Why do I need sweetness? What is this hole at the center? What is this fear? The answers will be different in each person, but the dialogue with the body is crucial to understanding. The problem is somewhere in the maternal matrix. I suggest that where the relationship to the body is even relatively secure, the symbols given in the dreams *do* bring the ego into relationship with that inner energy and transform the outer life. However, where the split between body and spirit is so deep that the instincts are damaged, the psyche may be producing the healing images, but the instinctual energy cannot connect to the image. The body that has not known security cannot imagine it; the terror of annihilation is trapped in the muscles, so that while the mind is letting things happen, the body is not. And the messages which should be going from the body to the brain, allowing for transformation of that negative energy, are not getting through. Even in the analytic hour the growing confidence may be evident in the dialogue, while the body is still writhing or stone still. And the voice, while it speaks what seems like honest feeling, is still coming from the head.

When the maternal matrix is damaged, the child cannot root itself in its own body, and no matter how hard it tries to find security through the mind, it is always, on some level, dependent on others and therefore in fear of abandonment. The psyche will do all it can to provide the solid base for healing, but if the messages from the body are experienced as contradicting the messages from the dreams, then healing does not take place. The shadow is in the body, too far from consciousness even to appear in dreams, and there is no Sophia conscious enough to make the link between body and psyche. Then Mater concretizes into matter and holds together with flesh what should be held together with love. The analytic hour or workshop sessions can provide space for that love to come into being and reverse the process from matter to Mater.

The workshops that have evolved out of my practice are a different experience for each participant, because each has had sufficient analysis to be well established on her own path; our primary purpose is simply to make space in which the body can speak to the individual. Undoubtedly a group dynamic does operate, but while the group is respected as a temenos, each individual is conscious of the need to maintain her own sacred space. The private symbols are respected as tiny seeds that need to germinate in their own dark ground before they are brought to the light of the sun, just as dreams need to be kept quiet while the process of transformation is taking place. To bring them to light too soon is to contaminate them with other people's material, or to scorch them with too much consciousness, or to release the tension so that no transformation takes place.

The goal of these workshops is neither weight loss nor body fitness, though these may be by-products. The goal is to integrate body and psyche: to take the healing symbols from the dreams, put them into the unconscious body areas and allow their energy to accomplish the healing work. One of the dangers in analysis is that we imagine we have done our work when we think we understand the dream images; we become fascinated by the interpretation. If the symbol is not contemplated, however, its healing power is lost. It has to go into the fire of the heart in order to be transformed. As von Franz points out, "Emotion is the carrier of consciousness."[6]

Each workshop begins with relaxation, to allow the body to find its own rhythms. The emphasis is on natural breathing and focused breathing in order to awaken and release emotions trapped in the muscles. Until the breathing is natural, the images too often remain bottled up in the brain. Fear and anxiety block our breathing. We learn very early in life that any display of archaic or primitive feeling is unacceptable, and we also learn (unconsciously) that the way to control intense emotion is to allow as little air as possible to go below the neck. The deep, full breaths that should nourish the vital organs, not only with oxygen but with awareness of emotion, are held tight in the top of the chest, and the round belly that goes with deep breathing is anathema in the fashion world. The full range of emotions is locked in below the neck and we hear constant complaints of stiff necks, sore shoulders and backs unable to carry their burdens. When the breath of the spirit (the masculine) is not allowed to penetrate the matter of the body (the feminine), *conception is not possible*. Our society tends to reject the conscious body, the natural container for the divine breath; what it celebrates instead is a flawless machine whose icon is a cadaver in Vogue Magazine. Our bodies have become so rigid and so plugged with unexpressed emotion that there is no room in them for creativity. If you doubt this, think of how many toilet dreams you have—plugged toilets, overflowing toilets, toilets you can't get to, toilets in the middle of the living room, toilets with outragous contents. In the New Testament this is expressed in a more refined way: "Neither do men put new wine into old bottles: else the bottles break."[7] Blocked expression leads to depression, and depression ultimately leads to collapse.

The following dream makes clear the power of the pneuma (from the Greek, meaning breath or spirit):

> I was in a large room with a dead woman on a bier. I was staying with her. People came in to pay their respects. Someone noticed she

moved a little. Later I turned to look at her and her clothes were disheveled. I soon sensed her movements even when my back was turned. I went to her and cradled her and talked to her. She revived. We walked through the door to the outside. She said: "Thank you for helping me over a bout of pneumonia."

That was the dream of a middle-aged woman whose emotions and feelings had been muted in childhood by a negative mother complex. Events in her life had become too painful to look at directly; concealing her distress, she continued as courageously as she could with her marriage and her job. She went through life by figuratively, and often literally, holding her breath, an automatic response to her fear; to let go, to simply let things happen, would be to surrender to the enemy. Her shallow breathing cut her off from the feminine principle deep within; hence she was suffering from heart pain. She was quick to accept the messages from the dreams, and she was also recognizing the growing gap between head and body—or more accurately between spirit and matter.

In an effort to reconnect insight and feeling, she did relaxation exercises and consciously took breath into unconscious areas of her body. Within days the love she invested in this ritual returned dividends in the form of the above dream and the renewed sense of life that came with it. The head recognizes; the body experiences. Surely, the opening statement of the dream, "I was in a large room with a dead woman," illustrates how crucial it is for all of us to find our own creative source, because nature presents her bill if we do not obey our instincts. And surely the last statement, "Thank you for helping me over a bout of pneumonia," identifies the pneuma, the creative spirit, as the connecting link. Whereas Medusa wants everything permanent and perfect, engraved in stone, Sophia wants things moving, breathing, creating.

Once the body is relaxed and the creative spirit is flowing between head and body, our workshops concentrate on the symbols that have been given in the dreams. Individuals work with their own energy circuits, attempting to recognize where the body is conscious and where it is unconscious, differentiating between habitual reactions and conscious body responses. Where a woman finds the body is "black"—that is, the energy refuses to move into that area—she experiments by taking a positive healing symbol from one of her own dreams, putting it into that area and concentrating until the energy begins to move and transform. This is a very different process from concretizing the symbol or taking it literally. Jung believed that the healing was in the symbol, for the symbol brings together body, mind and soul through the creative imagination. The poet in touch with the collective unconscious is given the exact symbol which, when read, brings goose flesh to our bodies, meaning to our minds, and tears to our eyes. Momentarily we are one. Thus when the abandoned little E.T., the extra-terrestrial in Stephen Spielberg's film, whispers, "Home, Elliott, home," millions of every age in every country weep. In our workshops we meditate on our own individual symbols to try to bring harmony between body, mind and soul.

One participant, Sylvia, has been in analysis and workshops for two years. Throughout her life she has had a very ambivalent relationship with her father. She was terrified of being close to him, but at the same time adored him and always tried to be "Daddy's little darling." When she was angry as a child, her mother always said, "You're mad as a hornet." She has always been prone to very bad colds and respiratory infections. At the time of the following dream she was attempting, for the first time in her life, to stand up for herself in her work. She recognized her own talents and was determined to have them acknowledged, but this sometimes involved being angry with her colleagues and Daddy's little girls aren't like that. This was her dream:

> I enter a room with my father. There are wasps flying about—big black ones. My father goes quickly through the room and into another room. I am supposed to follow but the wasps frighten me. I notice a hornet on my hand; I try to get it off but it won't leave. I feel I can't go into the other room with the hornet on my hand. I call to my father to come and help me but he doesn't come. I wake up terrified.

She awoke from the dream with "horrendous" fear, much more intense than in real life. The next day she felt a lot of tension in her shoulders and had a headache. Her head was blocked with cold. That night in the workshop she went through the following active imagination:

> The hornet is on my hand (as in the dream). I ask it if it wants to come into my body. It flies to the door my father went through, the door is closed—it comes back to my hand. I ask it again if it wants to come into my body. It crawls up my arm and across under my chin, up the right side of my face and onto my nose. There it sits. I ask it if it can talk to me. It buzzes. I ask it if it can explain its meaning. It buzzes. I ask if it belongs on my head and it buzzes a definite yes. It then crawls up my right nostril to the sinus cavity which is blocked. It comes out and up the left nostril. In between I ask it if it's looking for a home in there (it reminds me of the clay chambers that wasps make). It buzzes. It comes out of the left nostril carrying what looks like a piece of skin or tissue. It then flies away with the skin and lands on the palm of my left hand. It drops the skin and flies away. The skin turns into a small coiled snake. My fingers all have snake heads, my hand feels warm and alive with energy. The energy passes up my arm, across my shoulders and down my right arm where all the

fingers now have snake tails. My feet too start to tingle with the energy.

P.S. It's important to recognize my feelings toward the hornet, I awoke terrified because of it, I felt very apprehensive about conjuring it up again, but I just knew I had to. It took everything I had to allow it to crawl up my nose and I very nearly ended the sequence. It was only the genuine attempt of the hornet to communicate with me that reassured me that this would explain its meaning.

Sylvia said she saw the hornet as her "negative instinctual sides" which her father seemed to constellate:

I saw them as negative, but in fact they were positive. I always viewed anger as ugly—"animus" anger, like my mother's tearing people to pieces. But after this experience, I was able to go into the office and vent my anger, stamp my feet and pound my fist, which I had never done before. I was angry. Real masculine energy was discharged. It wasn't feminine anger. When my feminine is angry, my eyes grow wide, my nostrils flare, flame bursts out of me. No, this was masculine anger. I was standing up for myself professionally. And my head cleared and I've been able to smell things better ever since.

The hornet here was a symbol of the rage that needed to be released, rage associated with being Daddy's little darling. When the hornet removed the skin and opened the cavity, the skin that had acted as a block was transformed into the vital life force of a snake. All the fingers took on that energy, extending up the shoulders, down the other arm and eventually through the whole body. This energy was immediately available in Sylvia's life—rage transformed into professional and personal confidence.

One aspect of Sylvia's active imagination on the hornet dream is the incest motif. Jung, unlike Freud, believed that incest, symbolically speaking, is not necessarily regressive (see below, page 138). The taboo attached to actual incest does inhibit infantile regression, but the intention of the taboo is to redirect the energy to a higher end in which the father figure plays an important role in establishing a genuinely feminine ego. Incest in Sylvia's meditation is in the active service of the virgin. The transformation of the hornet into snakes activating her fingers indicates the transformation of her unconscious fear of incest into a positive affirmation of her love for her own feminine nature. The redirection of the incestuous energy remolds, as if with sculptor's hands, the feared father into a positive, beloved figure whose affirmation of her feminine nature, so strongly located by Sylvia in her body, becomes an affirmation of herself. What is apparent in Sylvia's meditation is her intimate contact with the feminine wisdom of the body. She has placed herself, in her newly discovered virginity, upon Sophia's lap.

Unconscious energy locked into the body releases itself or does not, autonomously. Like unconscious feeling it merely reacts like an animal. It is unredeemed in that it is not under conscious control. So long as that energy does what it wants to do, we will find ourselves acting out affects in pure animal fashion. The aim in analysis is to bring the magnificent energy of the wild horse under the control of the rider, without using a whip that will kill its spirit.

What we discover in body work (as in dream work) is how much energy has been caged. Once that energy is released (which happens very quickly), there is a great danger of accepting it without reservation as a saving grace. But it is shadow energy, and what the shadow wants has to be mediated by a civilized consciousness. The shadow dare not be simply embraced as a long lost sister. The ego has to maintain a healthy suspicion. To merely live out the shadow, the previously unconscious side of the personality, is not to integrate it. Integration requires chewing the primitive material in order to digest it. To bring consciousness to the instincts, to allow the ego to recognize them and yet not act them out impulsively, is to put the rider on the horse and let the rider make the decisions. That is putting civilized human nature in charge of the instincts, responsibly involved in where the energy wants to go.

The following dream illustrates the developing relationship between body and spirit in a mid-thirties woman who had professionally trained her body, but had only recently learned to love it:

> It is dawn on Sunday. The streets of the city are deserted. I am galloping on Leah [a magnificent horse] down the left-hand side of the street into the heart of the city. She responds immediately to the touch of my knee, or the pull of the reins. My cues are awkward, and I am amazed how precisely this great animal responds to my direction and compensates for my lack of horsemanship. I feel at home, in control. Or is Leah in control? She is confident, energetic. I feel at one with her.
>
> I put her in the pasture. I whisper in her ear, "You beauty!" She responds immediately, nuzzling my cheek, knowing and loving. Then her owner tells me, "Leah hasn't been exercised much lately. She's soft." She intends to give her a workout five times a day.

The love that goes into recognizing that energy and allowing it to live and be manifested in life is part of what is symbolized by the Wisdom of Sophia. Allowing that animal energy to transform into spiritual energy is another aspect of Sophia. The powerful instinctual drives are sacred but the ego has to ponder them in order to transform animal power into spiritual power. Mary sitting on the lap of the Great Mother is an image that recognizes that transformation. Out of that ground, through reflection, comes a woman's own individual feelings. Then and only then is she capable of relationship through empathy rather than dependence or power. Then she can displease mother, mother-husband, mother-Church, and know she is acting out of her own individuality. In the virgin the divine and the human meet.

Our workshops are in very experimental stages. Essentially we seem to be evolving in the same direction Joan Chodorow describes in her work:

> Although one's basic inclination may remain one or the other, self-directed movement tends to develop a relationship to both sensory and imaginal realms. When bodily felt sensation emerges as physical action, an image may appear which will give the movement meaning. Or, when an inner image emerges as physical action, the propriocep-tive kinesthetic experience may lead the mover toward connection to his or her instinctive body. The richest movement experiences seem to involve both sensation and image, fluctuating back and forth or oc-curring simultaneously.[8]

This is our basic philosophy in the workshops. It is a philosophy as ancient as Tantric yoga, but for those of us experiencing spirit being transformed into matter, and matter being transformed into spirit, the workshop is a place of the feminine Mysteries.

Throughout this study, I am focusing on the virgin as a feminine "way" toward consciousness. Jung, elucidating the Tao, writes:

> If we take the Tao to be the method or conscious way by which to unite what is separated, we have probably come close to the psycho-logical meaning of the concept.[9]

The virgin has two sides, and when the power of her dark side is contacted, it can erupt. If a woman has lived under the petrifying spell of an evil witch, she has almost no ego to contain that energy. In that case, the ego must be carefully prepared in order to avoid a psychotic episode or regression into a compulsion. The virgin is one "way" for the feminine ego to move toward consciousness.

One pattern that emerges in the workshop situation is the bipolar aspect of the Goddess. Sylvia Brinton Perera in *Descent to The Goddess* makes quite clear this dual relationship (individuals in the workshop are free to participate or not to participate, in order to allow space in which both aspects may be experienced):

> Psychologically, we see these two energy patterns in the empathetic and self-isolating modalities that are basic to feminine psychology, in relation to all inner and outer partners—children, creative projects, lovers, even to a woman's own autonomous emotions and perceptions and thoughts. The active engagement that wants another, that wraps the partnership in an active loving and warring embrace—that is Inanna; the circling back and down, disinterested in the other, alone, even cold—that is Ereshkigal. . . .

What is repressed for those who are intellectual, achieving daughters of the patriarchy is not always what is devalued and ignored by those who are caught in the roles of mother and wife.[10]

Our workshops almost always conclude with creative dance. The intense concentration has created sacred space and sacred time and in that world we reconnect with the ancient energies that are so ready to enter when the container is properly prepared. To dance is to enter the here-and-now and to know that Now is all there is. A movement in dance has no past, no future. It has only the instant of movement. When it is over, it is over. The movement cannot be repeated. That present-time Being in the body is the essence of play, the essence of dance. It is our workshop way of saying YES to the Goddess.

## Case Study of Bulimia

Bewitchment, the experience of being possessed, is the outcome of free-floating unconscious energy functioning outside of ego control. In the preceding chapters I have pointed out that the young child lives close to the unconscious of the parents, and therefore unconsciously carries the parents' unfulfilled dreams and ambitions, as well as their problems and unresolved conflicts. Jung expresses this unequivocally in his Introduction to Frances Wickes' *The Inner World of Childhood:*

> Parents should always be conscious of the fact that they themselves are the principal cause of neurosis in their children. . . .
> What usually has the strongest psychic effect on the child is the life which the parents (and ancestors too, for we are dealing here with the age-old psychological phenomenon of original sin) have not lived. This statement would be rather too perfunctory and superficial if we did not add by way of qualification: that part of their lives which *might have been* lived had not certain somewhat threadbare excuses prevented the parents from doing so. To put it bluntly, it is that part of life which they have always shirked, probably by means of a pious lie. That sows the most virulent germs.[11]

The unlived life of the parents may manifest in the daughter in some kind of eating disorder. In the case of a bulimic she is often unconsciously trying to swallow something she cannot or should not swallow, and her psyche, in an attempt to purify her, forces her to vomit. One brief example will illustrate how the psyche tries to free the woman to live her own life.

Elizabeth is twenty-six years old, a university graduate, the youngest daughter of a very artistic father and an intelligent sensitive mother. Throughout her childhood, Elizabeth lived happily with her family (parents, two brothers, one sister), did exceptionally well in school, was an outstanding athlete, and loved painting, music and writing. While she shared her father's artistic creativity, she was closer to her mother than to her father. Her intense intuitive nature made her vulnerable to unconscious shadow activity in her environment.

Throughout her childhood she had no trouble with her weight. At eighteen, with the loss of her first love, her weight problem began, greatly exaggerated in her own eyes. Her weight varied depending on whether she ate or refused to eat. She came into analysis because she wanted to take responsibility for her own body, but in spite of the best intentions had begun ritualistic vomiting. She would gorge and vomit sometimes four times a day. After eight months of analysis, a man whom she had loved as a child began to appear frequently in her dreams, so frequently that she had to ask herself what exactly he had meant to her. He had been no more than a close family friend. Her physical symptoms became more severe: the vomiting increased, the weight increased, colds would not respond to treatment. Over a period of eight months she had a series of dreams, beginning with this one describing her psychic situation:

> I am staying at a cottage with my mother. We are going to visit someone and I have nothing suitable to wear. Mom insists I borrow her green pantsuit. I try it on. It fits though I notice I am overweight. It is too tight at the neck.

The identification of mother and daughter is clear in the daughter's wearing of her mother's clothes. The suit is too tight at the neck, suggesting the sense of choking and suffocating that so often goes with being unable to be free of the mother.

Ten days later Elizabeth asked for a dream to help her "get a handle on" her weight. The following dream was her answer:

> I am a physical fitness instructor in a diet club. I am testing an out-of-shape friend. She came late and wasn't very cooperative. I decided to call the diet club "Confrontation."

That same night (also in answer to her question, and after seeing the movie *Resurrection*) she dreamed:

> There is a great tunnel of light as when a soul passes to the next sphere. Edward [the old family friend] appears walking from the light source toward me. We are in a large dark house. Mother is in the same room as Edward and me, and I am surprised to see her.

The subsequent dreams developed a deeper bonding between Elizabeth and Edward, with him pointing out to her that an error had been made, stressing that "it is not important who made the error, but that we know how to correct it." He encouraged her to swim, to do the back crawl. Then she dreamed:

There are two men. I am at a picnic with my Aunt Kate and some other woman. I am watching one of the men but I see only his young profile. Two children do something outrageous and this man stops them gently. I respect him. He leaves. Either I realize it myself or I am told that my Aunt Kate is having an affair with this young man and she is enormously vital and happy as a result.

Now I am in a house looking for Kate's mother so I can tell her about this marvelous affair. I tell my parents about my aunt and how happy I am to see her so enormously well. Mom is shocked. I say even my uncle seems happier and more reachable. Mom starts screaming at me, "What do you know about your aunt and uncle? An affair is wrong. Poor Uncle Jim! It's immoral." As I scream back at her, I realize she may be right about poor Uncle Jim and that I had just seen him blindly. Aunt Kate was so rosy he should be too. Mom and Dad walk out. I open the door and scream, "We're human beings; we're this amazing collection of cells and organisms and yet we're screaming about nothing. We're acting like primitive babies and we're missing the entire point. Morality isn't the issue. The wonder of Aunt Kate's transformation is."

I am totally exhausted. Mom and Dad return. The air has cleared and we can relate. I feel relief and gratitude.

The aftermath of this dream was headache, exhaustion, rash, gorging and vomiting. Three days later came the following dream:

I am at a restaurant. I see my mother with a male friend. I am seated near her though she can't see me. I can't decide whether to join her or not. She is partially hidden by a menu. She wants to be hidden.

Three weeks later Elizabeth painted her own "unborn child." This renewed her spirit and she decided to put her trust "in the void." Three weeks later she dreamed:

I am in the Yukon. I am standing on a frog in the water. I am not in the water because I have my period. The frog turns into a turtle while I am riding it. An Innuit or Indian woman is standing on the shore holding her baby out to me. She is showing me the baby.

This is an initiation dream prefiguring her own birth as a woman, but her body was not yet ready. She awoke the next morning feeling out of her body, "too huge, vast and ugly to return to—like a beached whale. Fear that I can't get back in, fear that I don't want to be in, fear that I do want to be in but don't know how to get back."

Two months later she had dinner with her parents. Both she and her mother were experiencing the same neck pain. In her journal she wrote:

I feel a definite growing apart from Mom. I feel I have to cut cold or be totally annihilated by her. I cannot figure it out, but I have put up a strong, impenetrable barrier. Mom is pained by my abandonment of her, but I know I have to save myself. I purposely underdress in order to separate myself from her values.

Accompanying this desperate need for separation came the following dream:

> I am watching a man walk along the street. He looks like my father. Instantly I am the man and yet I am still outside him. Across the street there is a crazed woman walking in the opposite direction. Conscious as the man, I calm myself inside trying not to create a vibration she can hook into. It does not work, I realize despairingly as she notices me and heads toward me. I am frightened but I remain calm, remain aware that I am an unemotional businessman. The woman has a gun and she is going to shoot me.
>
> She is very close now and the gun goes off. I have been shot in the heart—yet she still comes closer. I fall to the ground. My thoughts are still unemotional and analytical. I am fully conscious of the sensations in my body. I feel pain. I am sad and surprised that I feel so much pain and rather pissed off that my mind is still thinking logically, tabulating, while all this pain is inside. I want to stop thinking. I notice the crazy woman above my head. I can't believe what I see. She is aiming the gun just a little above and between my eyes, and moving it closer. I am terrified because I know she is going to place the muzzle right to my skin before she shoots. I feel the touch of the muzzle and a jerk to my whole body as she shoots. I awake at the same moment as the impact.

In an effort to save herself Elizabeth identifies with her "unemotional" father-animus, and attempts to stay clear of the witch. It does not work. Her Eros side—the heart—is shot through by the bullet. Still she is able to analyze her situation although she is full of pain. Then the killer animus of the witch (the phallic muzzle) comes right to her head (the analytical mind) and pulls the trigger. That awakens the dreamer to the realization that she must free herself or be annihilated. The witch's act here may also be seen positively (a *felix culpa*) in that she is forcing the girl to wake up. The old life has to die to make room for the new.

Two weeks later, after an unusual series of synchronistic events, her parents quarreled and Elizabeth mediated as usual. Her journal continues:

> Dad leaves. Mom says she has to talk to me because she feels I am growing apart from her—very coldly, clinically separating myself from her. I am relieved she has brought this up for we do communicate well and have lost this between us. Mother opens totally, asks me to try to explain to her about my life so she can perhaps understand. We talk. Mom drops a bomb. She had a lover for eighteen years. The affair started just after I was conceived. I guessed "Uncle Edward" and she nodded. The pieces fit.

She told me she had twice thought of deserting the family, but she couldn't leave her children so she concentrated her efforts on creating a close-knit family. I felt such love for her as she told me—such relief that passion had existed so intensely in her life. I had picked up all the pain, anger, and guilt that was my mother's. That is what I have been trying to unravel—what I needed to know to begin my own evolution.

Her mother's shadow—with all its pain, anger and guilt—had been unconsciously carried by Elizabeth all her life. Because it was not rightfully hers, she could not swallow it, and her psyche acted out through her body what it was attempting to tell her in her dreams. The bulimia did not cease at once. In fact there was a very acute period of readjustment, but she is now free to bring her inner child to birth.

This was a very painful but quite straightforward story of bewitchment. Everyone in one way or another carries the unconscious of the parents, and the psychological consequences of each situation require working out in their own time. The mother and daughter in this case were brought into a mature relationship because each was so sensitive to the other's needs and so able to love without judgment. Each looked into the other's eyes and saw Sophia.

The difference between looking into the eye of Medusa and into the eye of the dark Sophia (the Babylonian Ereshkigal or the Black Madonna) is clearly seen in Elizabeth's description of the depressions that overwhelmed her before and after she was released by her mother:

To approach my feminine self I was so ill-equipped I had to rely on "winging it," letting go of anything that did not fit. This left me with the feeling that I had nothing and I was nothing, and I could relate to no one. Separation from my friends and family was taking place, a cold-cut separation that only left me emptier. The night my mother told me the facts about her past started a warmth in my heart and an outlet for long held emotions. Once more I could feel, I could cry, I was alive. Rapid changes took place. From elation I would fall into depression, swinging back and forth. Yet underlying the tossing was a richness—a depth of soul-life that had been awakened and was struggling to make itself known. Prior to this, emotional changes, elation/ depression, would leave me fractured and empty when they subsided. It was as if there was nothing to salvage so I would just toss and turn with the flow. My body became my enemy, inflating and deflating with the tides in my head. My body too would fracture and become "the gang" which I would consciously take with me wherever I went. With the newly found depths, this previous pattern began to change. My depressions slowly became lessons to hold and nurture in my womb, to keep contained until they were ready for birth with the acknowledgment of the lesson and an awareness gained. Everything had meaning, a meaning I could relate back to myself and take responsibility for, whether positive or negative. I felt safe with myself.

Elizabeth had in effect been bewitched into carrying her mother's anxiety and guilt. Instead, therefore, of carrying her mother's genuine feminine feeling (the true virgin, expressed in her love for Edward), Elizabeth carried only her negative aspects, the virgin as witch. The closer she felt to her mother, the more she took on her mother's guilt. What she desired in her relationship to her mother (i.e., the Virgin on the lap of Sophia), she could not in reality digest. Opening herself to nourishment, she received poison. Hence her bulimia. When at last her mother confessed her eighteen-year affair, at a time when the negative aspects of that affair had been fully constellated in Elizabeth's dreams (which inevitably led to vomiting), she experienced immediate relief. This relief had also been constellated, because Elizabeth, in her dreams, had increasingly experienced her mother's genuine love for Edward. Not only did she have no reason to judge or condemn her mother, but on the contrary, she could feel only the deepest love and compassion because her mother's confession became for Elizabeth an affirmation of her own virgin identity. She was now at last able to take up her proper position on Sophia's lap.

Until the woman can assume that position she remains in a preexistent or unborn state. She is a soul in search of a body. For the woman, at least, her identity is indistinguishable from her body, and until she learns to look at it as the nourishing source of her feminine identity she will remain out of touch with herself, wandering about in a world alien to her feminine ego. Women like Elizabeth, in the first years of analysis, are virtually egoless and therefore pathetically susceptible to the invasions of the unconscious, their own as well as others. They are natural mediums subject to bewitchment. They live pseudo-lives which gather all their simulated strength from largely involuntary or compulsive acts of identification with others. Elizabeth's pseudo-identity resided almost entirely in her unconscious identification with her mother. Because that identification was with the negative rather than the positive mother, with the guilt rather than the love, she was forced to confront her own psychic condition if she was to live at all. Fortunately she was able to carry through with the confrontation, as her dream about the diet club had requested.

If the woman is anorexic in a situation like Elizabeth's, then analysis can become a race against death, for the daughter may be literally living out her mother's denial of her own life. When she finally confronts the cause or source of her own compulsive dying and is released from it, two things may occur: on the one hand, a feminine ego (the virgin) may finally be born from the womb of her own discovered wisdom; on the other, the external source of that dying (usually father or mother) may take back all the shadow material the daughter as medium has carried. Then the daughter is free of her unconscious death wish, and the parent must take responsibility for his or her own death wish. If the feminine identity has been truly born, then it can accept death in precisely the same way as it can accept its own life. The true measure of the virgin identity resides in that immemorial wisdom which recognizes and affirms that life and death are one. It is the wisdom which finally binds mother and daughter together on a level that transcends the masculine understanding of sacrifice. The true virgin accepts with love her own destiny. The gift of the mother to the daughter is the release of the daughter into life. The gift of the daughter to the mother is the release from her denied life into the authenticity of her own life or her own death.

## Journal as Silver Mirror

"Unreality was always 'the quintessence of horror' to him [Jung]."[12]

The daily journal is like a mirror. When we first look into it, the blank pages stare back with ominous emptiness. But if we keep looking and trusting in what Rilke calls "the possibility of being" (see page 100), gradually we begin to see the face that is looking back at us. If we stand naked, the mirror reflects things as they are. In its Latin roots, the word mirror suggests *wonder* and *curiosity*.[13] It is the bringer of secret mirth, helping us to disentangle the inner and outer worlds, giving us the objectivity to laugh at ourselves. There is more to the mirror than reflection. The long hours of sitting alone stripping off the self-deceptions, the artificial self-pity, the self-inflated maiming, build the Eros connection between the conscious and unconscious worlds in a way that connects both. With the mirror, we go through, we take our reality into another world, the world of the unconscious, and find a relationship to our own soul. Journal writing is a way of taking responsibility for finding out who *I AM*.

Facing our dark sides is painful. It is easier to know so much and no more. It is easier to turn away from our own swamp of anguish and aggression and say, "It doesn't matter. I've got friends. I'm well adjusted to my job. Everyone likes me." The mirror will not let us off the hook. It says, "It does matter. If you're not experiencing life, it does matter. Where was your own laughter today? Where are your

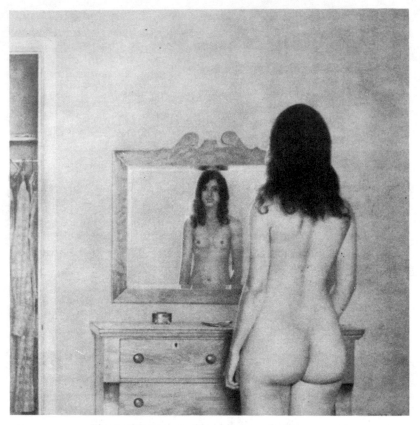

*This is the creature there has never been.*
*They never knew it, and yet, none the less*
*They loved the way it moved, its suppleness*
*Its neck, its very gaze, mild and serene.*
*Not there, because they loved it, it behaved*
*As though it were. They always left some space.*
*And in that clear, unpeopled space they saved*
*It lightly reared its head, with scarce a trace*
*Of not being there. They fed it, not with corn,*
*But only with the possibility*
*Of being. And that was able to confer*
*Such strength, its brow put forth a horn. One horn.*
*Whitely it stole up to the maid — to be*
*Within the silver mirror and in her.*

—Rainer Maria Rilke, *Sonnets to Orpheus.*

Nude No. 1, 1971-72.—Jack Chambers. (Courtesy Olga Chambers) tears? Why did you betray yourself? Haven't you got the guts to face your own truth? So long as you remain locked in that perfect image you're doomed to be a Grecian pot for the rest of your nonexistent life. You perfectly still, unravished bride!" That's the voice of the dark Goddess, goading us into being real.

At the age of thirty-two, married with children, Jane decided to burst her perfect pot. After four years of analysis and working on body awareness, the weight problem ceased to exist but the energy of the witch was transferred from food to sexuality, and later to spirituality. The journal excerpts here were written over a period of a year.

> All I could see was Picasso's fat, sad clown, heavy and full of grief. I prayed, "Please God, let me be light. Let me be happy." Then I said to myself, "I give you permission to be happy. Go ahead, Jane, love your body. It is beautiful. I give you permission to be sunlight." Then a child, beautiful, radiant, stepped out shyly. I said to her, "Okay, Little One, dance." And she danced. Spirit and body were housed in one beautiful form, inseparable and perfect. I wept with joy. She did not seem to be aware of having been prisoner all her life in the fat shell. She was not angry or bitter. She trusted me. I was like a mother. So I wept for her lost caged years. There was no anger or bitterness in me either. Just grief, consuming dark grief. But the Little One's radiance put light into the center of my darkness. I found my old body dancing the child's dance for the gods.

*Poem of Witch Passion*

to hell with all the symbols
no use trying to fool myself
i want to spread my legs
open my soft warm thighs
to you
i want to consume your masculinity
i will wrap my legs about you
entwine my being about your strength
my softness consuming your hardness.
do you not have the strength to take me?
are you that weak?
i become witch, i begin to hate you
i must cut off my feeling, me, to become prostitute
and having prostituted myself
i know that at my center
i have betrayed my god, my self.
in revenge i demand that you love me
you witnessed my soul,
i allowed you
now i want your blood

Beheading is a common motif in the imagery of witches. The following was written after dreaming of an attractive young man without a head (note the use of i, the complexed ego, and I, the conscious ego):

i seem to have solved my problem of our relationship
by cutting off your head
it doesn't seem to bother me
in fact i like it,
this way i don't have to admit
you exist
you are only a body
for me to do as i wish
(is this the witch speaking?)
i dare say it is
i see her,
I see her smile break across my face
my left shoulder comes slightly forward
the chin drops—eyes narrow—smiles of contempt wreathe my face

i want to control, you
with your head gone
i can be your brain
make you into whatever I wish
and service myself with your parts
"just get it up, my boy"

how i laugh!
as long as you remain the little boy
i have you by the balls
i will feed you, nurse you at my breast, fetch your coffee
i will make you dependent on me for survival
but, in return, i want your wealth
i shove you out the door to make it big in the world
Bring mommie home some riches, dearie,
keep me happy with furs and jewels
and this way i can stay at home
playing little girl taken care of by big man
Little boy, you fall for this act
you are no man
Get it up, boy,
i command you

> Goddamn it I want a man
> I want a man with a head
> and with a head
> comes a groin
> I want to be in relationship

> Oh i'll give you back your head
> but little boy with a head you must be responsible
> as long as i had it i was in power

you needed only to obey
if i give you back your head
and you choose to keep it
then you must take responsibility for your wisdom

and what of me?
I cannot be little girl with daddy to care for me
Game over!
I take responsibility for
Myself.

but what is that?

in search of the feminine self
where to begin
my god, this is terrifying
I know of no beginning
where are my feminine gods?
where is Woman?
where is your voice?

my passion, is it the demon lover?
that perfect man of power
masculine strength that knows no softness
a man that lets me bleed him of his manhood
and still has more
the more i take of him
the more he has to give
i always hope
yes, this is the man!
but how could he be?
a god
and in this life who wants a god anyway
I am no goddess,
it is human frailty
that redeems this energy
it is the compassion for what cannot be
because we are of matter and spirit
of two worlds, interacting
becoming one within me
knowing this
is my redemption
my humanness accepted
I can enter the reality
this world of matter
and be
woman
not goddess seeking god
but human
creating spirit in matter

can I take responsibility for this evil
that i witch have perpetuated?

my god, man, take back your head
I give you back your manhood
I let you go
out of my womb that turns to darkness
all light gone

I let you go, witch,
this evil can no longer go on
this is our life
that you would destroy
if you prevail all life will be destroyed
our adolescent stage is over
we must grow
in sunlight, together

we were locked together
you and i
i thought it was you who took away my feminine
i blamed you, raged at you, and yelled
NO LONGER! I AS WOMAN MUST BE HEARD!
but now I see
i was holding you in suspension
i held your head
and in the holding was such devotion
(oh how devious evil is)
that i could find no energy for me
and i blamed you
i thought you had put the knife into my back
i little knew
i was the one who held the knife.

In analysis it is crucial to hold the tension and keep the "crucible" sealed. It is equally crucial to try to bring to consciousness how the complexes affect our thinking and acting. When the mood grips us, that is the time to write—let it pour out of the unconscious. Journal writing fulfills the need to pour out the heart. Most people find intimacy very difficult, even intimacy with themselves. Since the whole point of analysis depends on that intimacy, journal writing is crucial to recognizing those parts of ourselves that we have shunned. Unconsciousness needs the eye of consciousness; consciousness needs the energy of the unconscious. Writing allows that interchange to take place.

If I am feeling "beside myself" or "three feet behind myself" or "in front of myself" then a complex has been activated. If I write while in the grip of that mood, pour out whatever comes through the pen, then later when my ego is again in control, I can return to that material; I can look at it and see how the complex affects my behavior. I may be able to recognize what constellates it and the point at which the ego "goes through the looking glass" into the unconscious. To merely pour out without reflection becomes sheer self-indulgence which merely feeds the complex. The less the ego is in control, the more florid the complex becomes. Any self-respecting artist is mindful of the difference between writing out of the creative center and writing out of the complex.

In Jane's journal entries, we can see her trying to hold the ego position (the "I"), then gradually slipping into the witch, waxing eloquent, then suddenly suspecting she is in the complex and continuing anyway. Again the ego struggles for control, and sees coming up on the other side Daddy's little girl. Archetypally speaking, she slips from Marlene Dietrich in trousers to Marilyn Munroe in baby dolls. The ego is not strong enough to relate to a man. Some evil force is interfering. She begins with a sexual fantasy, which would devour the masculine and destroy the feminine. Even as she writes she moves higher into her head, until her actual feeling and body responses are totally negated. She is cutting herself off from herself, winding herself tighter and tighter, alienating herself from the quiet relaxed center from which receptive femininity is born. Thus in the very act of writing, she is creating a masochistic fantasy which is denying her own femininity and setting up a sadistic response to the man. While projecting the beheading onto the man, she herself is cut off at the neck by the father and the negative animus of the mother.

In these passages, the ego is realizing its own inflation. The fantasy is sheer fantasy. No woman could do what Jane imagines. She begins to recognize the demonic element in her inflated femininity. This kind of "femininity" exists in the head; it has nothing to do with genuine eroticism because it is not coming from the body.

Jane's journal continues with the mother/child relationship. She dreamed a "Supermom" dream: "I look into the eyes of Judith [a supermom] and they are bleeding—bleeding bright red tears." Jane wrote:

Dear child i weep the blood tears
i weep them for you
i made you my garbage can
i put all my shit into it
and named it you
i have this great blackness in me
and instead of keeping it in my house
i put it into you, wee soul,
and then i hated you
for in you i saw myself
and took your little soul away from you
i devoured your being
oh dear child, forgive me,
I feel such grief such pain
instead of giving you life

i took it
and all in the name of supermom
i made you be what you are
for me
dear God, forgive me, for i did not know
i will weep the tears of red blood
and let her go
guiding that dear soul
and loving her for whoever she might be.

i am witch unconscious
she must only work in the darkness of the unconscious
once conscious, no woman could ever allow her to rule the house
she is driven by god the father
the father that sets standards
no mortal woman could ever fulfill
the rage is towards this man
this demon lover
whom the witch serves

it was mom/dad
that made me do what I did to my child
it was that god telling me
to be all things perfect

i tried to make my child satisfy your standards
dear child, merely a pawn to your evil
and it all came through me
the witch in her darkness served you
driving me to kill my child's Being
driving me to satisfy your god
your fucking bastard
taking the dearest soul, my daughter, and killing her spirit
I will stop this witch in me
I will put the witch in the fire
bring her to consciousness and let the true spirit of woman prevail
in sunlight love,
and giving life to all things anew.

The writing continues into the other side of the archetype (the "poor little me") and gradually the ego becomes more perceptive of its own position:

I suppose the tragedy for me
is that this is all fantasy
the witch was never given a real voice
no one heard
no one would believe that I wrote that
i was once described as
that shy little girl in the
latin class
terrified to speak.

i lived in terror of being found out
for what i do not know
but the terror still existed
and so, I tried to disappear
be whatever anyone wanted me to be
just don't ask me anything, i would beg
and this fantasy became my reality.

once strong in that reality
i found that people liked me
and so i got to be very good
and being a screen, a projection
living out their fantasies
and so i soon forgot that it was fantasy
it paid well, got me a man to marry
a job, a life on T.V.
the perfect myth complete
young prosperous professional couple
deliciously happy
we never fought no need to
i knew your script, acted the role
and we loved
in innocence.

it was wonderful
this play
but in dreams i knew it was play
i cried for the reality
but i could not shatter the myth
i was the myth
destroy the myth
and i destroy myself
that was too terrifying

And all the time she worked in my unconscious
eating away at my feminine self

dear witch
you are so devious and cruel
thank God you are balanced
with my fear
it was my fear of life
of failure
of survival
that kept you relatively impotent
but you took your toll on me
with your hatred of men
your prostituting my sexuality for your ends
my tension headaches
and my feeling that all this was somehow unreal

you made me say things that
sounded right

but had nothing to do with who I was
i didn't know who I was
i was too terrified to know
for i somehow felt
that what i was, at my core
was intrinsically evil

i could not find fault with anyone
i saw them . . . i told them they were perfect
because i had to be perfect

but in that lies the evil
I am not perfect
I am intrinsically good
it is the layer on top
that lies
in the lies lie the evil
i condone witchcraft
so that witch likes me
because i thought i needed witch to survive

when i looked into the mirror
the terror was that no one would be looking back
the soul was not there
i was an empty shell
in fear of facing that evil that blackness
i called on witch to give me power
over everyone . . . the ring leader
and in that way
I survived, and well
until I give that screaming child a voice, until I see her acting
consciously, and not turning witch passively,
I will be serving ego not God.
She makes my teeth ache and my jaw.

that is why my thighs are tight
my orgasms in tight muscles
for i refuse to trust
to meet and be caught
by those who love me

in fear lies the seedbed for the witch
so long as i cannot trust the earth mother
i am paralyzed with fear of falling
my muscles tighten in rage at the situation
and my inner being weeps at the cruelty of such a world
a world without unconditional love
my muscles tighten to brace themselves against the fall
in fear i rage
with a smile on my face
in disguise as supermom, queen bee

if I can learn to trust my dear ones

and then earth
and then god
for all are one
and at the core of all this
I trust in myself, the god within
if I can learn to trust
so that the touch of a man
might send me into the core of my feminine being
vibrating with the intensity of LIFE
with every living cell of my BEING
exploding into my passion

it is this passion i fear
it is the repressed passion for life
that all my life has lain dormant
and then comes the grief
so much grief for lost life, lost love, lost passion
I grieve for the lost child
the child that still lives in me
the child that cannot ask for life
for love,
for she knows it will not be given to her
so she withdraws in fear
praying for some sign of love
and at any point becoming inflated when a warm fuzzy comes her
        way
and so terrified when life does seem to go her way
when friends speak of her
give me love
i crave it so much that I become inflated
i start to think i am grand
but beneath all this
is the fear,
the child waiting for it all to be taken away
and i yell I WILL DO ANYTHING TO HAVE YOU WANT ME,
        ACCEPT ME
and i live in fear of being found out, that maybe i did something
        wrong
that if i do not live up to their expectations i will be rejected

and with that rejection comes death
i can not ask for love
i do not deserve it
i can not ask for help
i can not spend money on me for i am no good
and so the despair is there
that chronic despair
and then out from under
the shadow child appears
GOD DAMN IT I WILL NOT DIE
I WANT WHAT I WANT WHEN I WANT IT

in her full fury she rebels
without feeling, for in her feeling lies despair,
cut off from feeling, she rages
I want life

it is time to enter fear
the fear that lives
circling in my gut
turning round and round
the whirlpool of energy
it can't escape
it's locked

that scar on my heart speaks
it cries out in great pain
a huge incision from my neck to my diaphragm
carving out around my heart
the scar tissue locking the feeling in
so i only feel the pain of the old wound
the pain locks me in
it watches me
so I have no feelings

but my god
I want that passion
I am that passion
I want to be free of that cage
oh God let me trust in God
that I have now the wisdom
I know it is the passion of the instincts
that will connect me to life
yet it is those very instincts that i repressed
in order to survive
with mother i could have no instincts
for she was cut off from hers
and the scar, the wounded heart
that child that loved life with such passion
had her heart cut out
all feeling gone
she sewed up the heart
the hole
life was removed
she was removed from life
and could survive.

my left eye closes out of life
retreats from the vision of living
i am sure i wear glasses
for i could not see life

life was the enemy
and as long as i did not see it
i was safe from its evil, its madness, its passion
and with the temptation removed
i could live a life that was accepted

I want to see now
I want that passion
that despair must not rise and take over
the passion will rise
bringing me slowly into my feeling self
bringing me closer to wholeness
to life
to God.

The psychological issues involved in these journal excerpts will be discussed more fully in chapter seven. The passages illustrate the courage required to face this vale of soul-making. They illustrate too the value of the journal and the value of body awareness in recognizing fantasies, dispelling them and reconnecting to the ego. Like contact with the inner Sophia, whom Jane so earnestly seeks, the beloved journal grounds the ego in two directions, inner and outer reality.

*

If we look into the silver mirror and hate what we see, we are hating our own reality. We are setting up a split between our inner and outer worlds. Even worse, if we look into the mirror and cannot see what in fact is there, we are into a schizophrenic split. Somewhere in us there is a perfect image, a perfect work of art, a well-wrought mask that is cutting us off from our own flesh and blood. If we choose to move with our masculine principle, we move into the dead perfection of the "still unravished bride"; if we choose to move with our feminine principle we move into the living imperfection of the radiant ravished woman—the virgin with her unicorn.

The feminine mystery lives in the Now. Its energies are concentrated on what is happening in this moment—a forget-me-not sparkling with dew, the scent of wet pine, a hesitant hand—all uniquely coming together Now. It relaxes into total concentration and *is*. The feminine does not save itself for some glorious moment in the future, nor grieve over some lost moment in the past. It holds nothing back. Now is all there is.

Here too is the real mystery of the body in movement. Each

instant of movement is the instant of creation. To touch that instant, to bring consciousness into that movement, is to strike home to the very core of Being and to know it simultaneously in a gesture that is Being itself. Being resonates with YES to the Goddess.

Virgin taming the unicorn. — Castello di Grinzane, Italy.

**Practical Suggestions for Creating Positive Eating Rituals**

1. Recognize the difference between sacred and profane space. Recognize where I am unconsciously attempting to be at one with the gods, when in fact I need to focus on my own human needs and limitations.
2. Recognize chronic habits, and discipline the ego with love. Face the facts.
3. Diet toward life, instead of away from it. I want to take care of my body. I want to transform it from a heap of flesh into a conscious body. I want to listen to its wisdom. It knows how to heal itself if I give it the chance.
4. Rely on my sense of humor, especially in dealing with the animus. When he becomes nasty or self-righteous, take him for a dance or a nature walk.
5. Recognize the danger zones in each day. Change the rhythms creatively. Rather than rushing to the refrigerator for a 5 o'clock happy hour, have a luxurious bath, or dance, or listen to music.
6. Recognize the danger zones in changing the body image. Recognize how the new image is affecting me and my response to myself and others' response to me. Is there a different unconscious response to me? What are my sexual feelings? Who is this new me being born?
7. Recognize a time of mourning for the old body.
8. Recognize food as a symbol operating between the inner and outer world, and between the inner and spiritual world.
9. Recognize tricks in my own Pandora's box. Eating may be a diabolical plot on my own part against myself.
10. Recognize the difference between real hunger and acute emptiness. Find spiritual food for spiritual hunger.
11. Recognize decisions that have to be made now and act on them. Clean out all the old shadow material from my closet. Let go of the old attitudes and the old clothes and shoes that aren't me anymore.
12. Recognize my own responsibility for my own beautiful body whether it is big or small. This is my life.

*This is the time of tension between dying and birth*
*The place of solitude where three dreams cross*
*Between blue rocks*
*But when the voices shaken from the yew-tree drift away*
*Let the other yew be shaken and reply.*
*Blessed sister, holy mother, spirit of the fountain, spirit of the garden,*
*Suffer us not to mock ourselves with falsehood*
*Teach us to care and not to care*
*Teach us to sit still*
*Even among these rocks,*
*Our peace in His will*
*And even among these rocks*
*Sister, mother*
*And spirit of the river, spirit of the sea,*
*Suffer me not to be separated*

*And let my cry come unto Thee.*

—T.S. Eliot, "Ash-Wednesday."

When the soul deserts the wisdom (*sapientia*) of love, which is always unchanging and one, and desires knowledge (*scientia*) from the experience of temporal and changing things, it becomes puffed up rather than built up. And weighed down in this manner the soul falls away from blessedness as though by its own heaviness.

—St. Augustine, *De Trinitate.*

# 6

## The Myth of Ms

*I wanted to stop this,*
*this life flattened against the wall,*
*mute and devoid of colour,*
*built of pure light,*
*this life of vision only, split*
*and remote, a lucid impasse.*
*I confess: this is not a mirror,*
*it is a door*
*I am trapped behind.*
> —Margaret Atwood, "Tricks with Mirrors."

Once upon a time there lived a king in a beautiful castle called Casa Loma. Now the king was old and lonely, haunted by memories of the young bride he had once loved and their four children who were now scattered to the four corners of the earth. And he bethought himself, "I shall marry again. I shall find a new bride and have new children." And he sent his emissary into the provinces to search for the perfect bride.

When the emissary returned he brought with him a beautiful woman—elegant in body, educated in mind—whose sole longing in life had been to become queen, and whose sole phobia in life was dogs. Become queen she did, and bore her husband three daughters before his death.

The eldest, whom her parents treasured the most, was christened Electrica. She it was who inherited the best of her parents' beauty and intelligence. Her mother groomed her to queenhood, bending all her efforts to create Electrica the perfect queen. She acquainted her with Yves St. Laurent, Estée Lauder and the library at Harvard University; she opened the door to a post-graduate course at Oxford with the best princes academia could offer. And Electrica carried her regal crown on her regal head and performed meticulously. She smiled at the right times; she wept at the right times; she knew when to raise her long eyelashes and when to lower them in order to create her moment of mystery.

But Electrica did not prosper with her princely escorts. Instead she became queen of Wall Street, regal in her three-piece, pin-striped suit and electric-blue stiletto heels. Always she carried her

insignia of office, her black attaché case, full of important papers
and Anacin and Cascara and steroid salve for her headaches, consti-
pation and patches of psoriasis.

And before she went to bed in her chrome and glass apartment,
she turned off her microwave oven, she turned off her stereo, she
turned off her rheostat lights. She turned on her electric blanket and
heard her mother's voice crooning,

> *Old Mother Hubbard*
> *Went to the cupboard*
> *To get her poor dog a bone.*
> *But when she got there*
> *The cupboard was bare*
> *And so the poor dog had none.*

And as she slept Electrica dreamed of a computer monitoring
sound—the notes read out by a hole in the paper. She was fascinated
by the tangible measure of the sound. And in her dream she learned
to hear music by looking at the notes pushed out through the holes.

And in this wise Electrica prospered.

The second daughter was called Lesbia. And Lesbia was second,
always second. Her father rarely noticed her and her mother she
feared. Only one thing she knew for sure: what her mother was, she
wasn't. She swung into life in her red Capezios. She fell in love with
a handsome monk who of course, although he loved her, had to
reject her. Her heart stabbed with pain, she came to know herself
through the gentle love of a woman she could trust.

And Lesbia prospered as a poetess.

The king and queen had not wanted a third child, and when she
arrived, they had no idea what to call her. They named her simply
Dumbellina. No one paid much attention to fat little ugly Dumbellina. She wandered about in the castle kitchen hugging her Topsy
doll. She loved to talk to the gardener who taught her to listen to
flowers. And then one day she bolted out the front gate, down the
street and into the ravine. And as she ran, she fell through a hole.
She fell and fell and fell. And she was sure this must be what
grown-ups called dying. But she landed on dark earth, warm and
soft under her bare feet. And a very tall young man came to her.

"Who are you?" she asked.

"An altar boy," he said.

"You're too big to be an altar boy," she said.

"Depends on whose altar, doesn't it?" he said.

And he offered his hand to Dumbellina and led her through the
woods to a grotto covered with vineleaves. There he gave her crystals, snowflakes, teardrops and a rainbow.

"You must discover how these relate to each other," he said. And

Dumbellina many times wept as the rainbow vanished from the crystals, or the teardrops turned into snowflakes. She longed to go back to her mother, but there was no mother to go back to. She no longer knew whether she went to sleep to dream, or whether she awoke to dream.

But in the fullness of time, she grew tall. Her little face was no longer pressed against her puzzle. She could contemplate it with some distance and she discovered that by squinting her eyes a little shut, she could see more clearly. Then one day, quite by accident, she saw the green and yellow and pink of the rainbow emanating through the crystals, the teardrops and the snowflakes. It was the most exquisite tapestry she had ever seen. She felt taller and smaller, happier and sadder, richer and poorer than she had ever felt before. She felt herself in the presence of Someone. She turned her face and saw two great feet—white, soft, strong feet. She recognized where she was, where in fact she had been all along. She saw the great stone altar and the altar boy, not at all too tall for the high altar of the Goddess.

Now he wore a silver helmet and silver sandals. She looked up but she did not see the face of the Goddess. Instead she saw a vibrant blue light, shining like an intense full moon. Instinctively she needed to bow, and as she knelt the tapestry that she had been weaving fell upon her shoulders like a gossamer garment. It fell delicate as rain, a blessing from the Goddess. At last she had found the Mother she never had.

And as she knelt the voice of the Goddess said, "Lower." She lowered her body, but again the voice said, "Lower," until she felt the soft earth under her face and arms. And she knew she had to experience the love of that great body in order to carry the blue light back into the world.

How Dumbellina brings her new-found wisdom back to the kingdom of Casa Loma I'm not quite sure. Bringing the treasure safely back is always the most treacherous task in a fairytale. I'll be very modern and let you work out your own conclusion.

Now this tale has many inauthentic loopholes. It is woven together from the dreams and fantasies of my analysands. I am indebted to them for sharing their material, for it is only through dreams that we can observe the unconscious collective problem that is eating the heart out of our society. The story does reflect the skeleton of the issue we are discussing: how do driven, goal-oriented perfectionists find their way back to the lost relationship with their own heart?

In the psychological interpretation of fairytales we look at all the characters as part of one psyche striving for wholeness—and that one psyche is representative of a social culture. Here we have an old and dying king, symbol of the spiritual and political values that once held the culture together. His first queen is dead; in other words, the feeling values that made life with the old king meaningful and vital are no longer there. The children that the old culture produced are scattered to the four corners of the earth. In terms of our 20th-century culture, the collective myth that held it together for centuries is undermined. We are like that primitive Australian tribe which received their holy tree from the gods. They carried their pole with them wherever they went. Their communication between heaven and earth was through that pole. It was the center of their universe through which they established their value system, their love, their hopes, their sense of inner confidence and joy. The marked-out space around that pole was sacred space—the ordered cosmos. Outside that sacred circle was chaos. When their pole was broken, the whole tribe lay down and waited for death. Life had ceased to have meaning.[1]

In our culture the church steeples have ceased to be sacred poles. The cosmos that once surrounded them has vanished and chaos again is come. The center will not hold. In the absence of a collective myth, some of us are being forced for survival to try to establish our own sacred space in the midst of chaos, but in the hurly-burly of modern life we can't find our own myth. Thus faith, hope and love no longer abide.

In their place we have a false queen whose basic value system is rooted in power. Quick to take advantage of the king's waning virility, that virility that was once fed by its relationship to God, the false queen puts her ambition on the throne. Everything is twisted into feeding that ego-centered, materialistic craving for more and more and more of everything. But there is no satisfying a witch because her appetites are not grounded in the instincts and therefore have no natural satiation point. Meanwhile the real instincts are starving.

The witch begets three daughters, each one an aspect of the modern Ms, each looking for her own myth, without which life doesn't hold together. There are no modern institutions or rituals strong enough to contain her confusion until the conflict is either resolved, outlived or transcended. The modern Ms is swirling in limbo with no past to look to for models, no secure present and no known future. She is a pioneer and she has great courage. She is refusing to be Miss because she no longer accepts herself as the unmarried daughter of her mother and father. She rejects the identification with her family. She may refuse to be Mrs, except in private situations, because she no longer wishes to be identified with her husband. If she is experienced, she realizes that the men in her life are in a similar limbo because once their anima projections are rejected or withdrawn, the stereotyped patterns of relationship no longer work. And stereotype is the right word here because a stereotype carries no numinosity, no living energy, no intensity of feeling. A stereotype is a worn out vision, a dead archetype, or perhaps even worse, a parody of it.

Many of my generation were raised by Edwardian mothers in whom the feminine archetype was split. Consciously the woman attempted to live out the so-called Madonna role—perfect mother, loving, compassionate, dutiful and chaste. Unconsciously she carried the so-called whore in her body, with the result that her feminine ego was cut off from her feminine body. Unconsciously the children related to that dark side, the Black Madonna, and it is she who is now demanding attention in our society. The Black Madonna has always been present, of course, but not always recognized. In Victorian England a man had his wife and children at home, and his mistress in secret. In some societies she was accepted as fact. In more Puritan societies she was the slut, the delicacy on the side, the bunny plaything. Now we are throwing off our Puritan wraps and recognizing the energy of the Black Madonna. Collective dreams are forcing us into our own earth, our own bodies, forcing us to radically reorient our attitudes toward the feminine. The first release of that Black Madonna energy may result in the woman experiencing herself as a whore; men too may find themselves shocked or frightened by the release of that power. The integration of the shadow is dangerous work for the woman, and the integration of the anima is the masterpiece of analysis for the man. This is the treacherous no man's land which we must explore if we are to break our addiction to perfection.

Probably the most negative legacy mothers have passed onto their daughters for generations has been the repression of their sexuality and their bodies, with the result that women today are having to reunite their sense of themselves as emotional, thinking and spiritual beings with a sense of themselves as sexual, passionate creatures. They are trying to bring together their divine and animal attributes.

Erica is a typical example. She is thirty-five years old, beautiful, idealistic and highly respected in her profession. She has a golden persona, but she also has a "dark" side that she lives out in secret. She is putting up a heroic struggle to find out whether she belongs in this society or not. After her father left the family, her mother devoted her life to bringing up her children and repressed her own personal needs and feelings. Says Erica;

> At twenty I did not want to be a woman. If Canada had gone to war with the Moslems, I'd have been on the front lines with a machine-gun because that world represented the degradation of woman. I

wanted to gun down anything that represented the subservient re-
stricted role that I had grown up with. I hated that martyr role my
mother passed on to me. I wouldn't bow to any man. And I couldn't
pretend that I didn't have a body with needs and pleasures of its own.

When I was at university, I weighed 150 pounds because I was
hungry all the time. I'd buy a pound of cake and eat the whole thing.
Sex was very important to me, but I didn't understand why at the
time. Now I know it is my way of staying in my body. But the guilt! I
felt I was so guilty in relation to my mother. Every time I acted
outside her value system, I was guilty and I looked for a man who
would mother me, love me unconditionally, cuddle me, hold me — be
my MOTHER. And then my contempt would flare and I'd crush him
under my heel. I hated myself and I hated him. I hated him for
allowing me to be the little girl I wanted to be.

The contradiction at the center of Erica's psychology is clear. In
being what she wants to be, she experiences herself as a whore,
which isn't what she wants to be. She wants to break with mother;
she doesn't want to break with mother. She wants to be a woman;
she doesn't want to be a woman. To be a woman is to be like
mother, subservient to the man who has destroyed her. But she is
trapped by her own sexuality which, along with the daily pound of
cake, holds her in her body. The contradiction resolves itself into
this: by consciously breaking with her mother's values, she unconsciously affirms them. In emancipating herself she becomes in her
own eyes a whore. The pleasures of the body are canceled out by
guilt, until guilt and pleasure become identified. Here is the real
guilt! Happiness is feeling guilty, and only those pleasures which are
forbidden are carrying the magnetic energy — the numinosity of the
Black Madonna.

Erica's mother is unconscious of her femininity, but Lisa's mother
is a very conscious, professional 1950's woman. And Lisa's problem
is equally paralyzing:

> I love my mother. She is soft, understanding, intelligent, wants me to
> be whoever I am and she means it. She's my idea of exactly what a
> woman should be. If I find myself talking like her and dressing like
> her I feel guilty. I feel I've betrayed her by not fighting to find my
> own identity as she did.

In sharp contrast to Lisa is Judith:

> I tell you I will not be like my mother. Whatever she is, I am not.
> And you know the worst of it is she is now copying me. She tries to
> dress like me; she even wants me to help her with her make-up. She
> watches my reactions and imitates me.

These three young women all show signs of being trapped in
*participation mystique* with the mother, and their dreams, like the

dreams of many modern men and women, are pervaded with symbols which show how deeply they are ensnared in the mother complex.

There are countless women of the sixties and seventies who so deeply resented the patriarchy which had destroyed their femininity and that of their mothers that they lashed out against that patriarchy, but in doing so they identified with the masculine side of their own psyches.[2] In some cases they turned into the very thing they most feared—the witch side of their mothers, or in Jungian terms, the negative animus.

Appalling as that power principle is when it moves into destructive action, it may be psychologically necessary. Looking at the development of individual women, I see the little Persephone's come into my office, gentle maidens even at fifty, basically identified with their mothers, or on an archetypal level, with their own unconscious. In their dreams they are with mother, happily or unhappily picking flowers; they go further afield and are almost killed by a passing van, or a huge truck with two or three trailers in tow, such vehicles representing the depersonalized mother complex. Sometimes in their dreams the mother appears as a wicked witch holding them prisoner. Then it is important to remember the witch in Hansel and Gretel, who wicked as she was in keeping them caged, was at the same time forcing them to develop all their ingenuity in order to escape and survive. And it was the feminine principle, Gretel, who never gave up her faith in life, but continuously encouraged her despairing Hansel. When the right moment came, they were alert enough to throw their negativity in the fire and run. But that witch forced the development of their maturity and their recognition of what was of value to them (again, the *felix culpa* motif).

Similarly, in the story of Demeter and Perephone it is Gaia—Earth Mother, mother of Demeter—who arranges for Hades to capture the Kore, to rape her away from the loving care of her mother. Kore, as the myth says, found herself in bed with Hades, "much against her will, and yearning for her mother."[3] Having lost her home, her playmates and all the world she knew, Kore-Persephone found herself alone with the male principle in the underworld. That is the archetypal pattern: the woman has to be separated from the mother, and for that to happen she has to surrender to the masculine principle—externally or internally. Either the external man carries her off sexually or she identifies with her inner man; in either case she is in danger of animus possession.

The natural feminine way to feminine maturity is through the body. This is essentially what the ancient initiation rites were about. The rites grounded the girl in her own body which was then recognized as part of the feminine cosmos—a vehicle for fertility, the container which made her one with the Goddess, through whom life moved eternally.

In our society, however, we have no rites and there are few older women who can initiate us into our own femininity. Most of us, men and women, are unconsciously identified with the masculine principle (the conscious value system of our mothers), with little or no consciousness of our own feminine instincts. So we flounder. Some try to find validation for their femininity through a lesbian relationship; others try to find that validation through making their lovers into loving mothers; others unconsciously step into the constricting shoes of their mothers.

In such situations the genuine masculine principle is not present. The adolescent feminine, in both men and women, cannot relate to the masculine because the polarization is not there. There is no genuine masculine, no genuine feminine. Thus it is not "otherness" that the young feminine is surrendering to. Without that otherness the whole point of Kore being carried off by Hades and transformed into Persephone is lost. Miss is not transformed into Ms or Mrs. Where the masculine and feminine are undifferentiated, the act of union is merely an identification. In mythological terms she would be the neutered hermaphrodite. She may believe she is an androgyne, an independent woman, but in fact she has given up on ever being a woman, and unconsciously decided to be nothing instead. The true androgyne embodies the conscious union of the differentiated masculine and the differentiated feminine, something quite different from the neutered hermaphrodite, in which the opposites are symbiotically joined.

The great danger in our society is that a woman can believe that she has become the independent Ms when in fact she is merely *animus possessed.* In that case, she becomes a walking parody of a man. Trapped by the undifferentiated masculine, she is hoodwinked by a false myth. Far from being independent, she is polarized against her mother and ultimately against herself and her own feminine nature. She is likewise polarized against her man whom she herself has made into her mother. Such a woman may end up in despairing conflict, or in conflict which manifests as disease, or she may go on driving through life on her phallic broomstick hating or fearing every man she meets. Mothering in both its positive and negative forms is the aspect of femininity that has become a sacred cow in our culture. The hetaera has been the outcast. In order for the real Ms to emerge, the full feminine has to be differentiated and integrated in relation to the mature masculine.

To do that, to make that rite of passage, we have to pay in blood.

And we have to pay and pay and pay. Every rite of passage involves a death and a rebirth. The price is the sacrifice. Part of that sacrifice is the giving up of old securities and illusions. The danger in our time, however, is that in making that sacrifice we are playing fast and loose with the values that were won through centuries of heroic honing of consciousness and our culture may debouch into chaotic unconsciousness. The consciousness that was won in the past by heroes who fought their way out of the maw of the Great Mother by armoring themselves against the seductions of sensuality is in jeopardy. In Western society very little is sacred; connections between man and nature, man and God, are broken. We are without archetypal images, without sacred rituals, without a myth to hold our ego-orientation together. In giving up "Thou shalt nots" and "shoulds" and "oughts" we have released a storm of passion, and with it the rage and fear and guilt of our own shadows.

The anguish in the individual is no less than the anguish in the culture. Without the sacred rites to contain and help transform our fear and guilt, we as individuals tend to fall into aloneness, and when the isolation is too much we fall into unconsciousness. In earlier centuries, the hero (the courageous masculine spirit) exerted his strength to conquer his overwhelming instinctual drives. He was ashamed to surrender in war. He was afraid to surrender to loving arms, for fear of losing himself. Our civilization is the flower of his courage.

Now, however, that masculine principle (in both men and women) which was once so necessary has become not healthy ego strength but ruthless will power which has little respect for man, beast or God, let alone the feminine. Giving up that drivenness is part of our blood sacrifice. And it begins to feel like giving up life itself when an individual has lived life in a frenzied round of goal-oriented activity, leaving no room for loving. As Jung says, "Where love reigns, there is no will to power; and where the will to power is paramount, love is lacking."[4] One of my analysands put it this way:

> I try to stop making so many lists. I try to be less rigid. I am determined to let things happen. I go to my empty apartment at six o'clock, I open the door determined to write, to Be, just for myself. I take one look at that empty space. I hear that silence and I back out and slam the door. Isn't it terrible? I depend for my being on someone else. I have to be doing something or that terrible voice starts whispering in my ear, "You're not happy. You're not achieving anything. All that stuff you're writing couldn't matter less. Who are you anyway? You're not a woman. Men treat you like garbage. You're getting exactly what you deserve. You might as well be dead. And you know what they'll write on your tombstone?—'She was born, she died, she never lived.'"

Many a woman is feeling precisely that: she never lived. Now she is determined to find herself. But in her desire to sacrifice the old attitudes, she is experiencing a very real death. What begins with an attempt to change her relationships, may end with no husband, no home, no friends, even no children. The terror of her situation is often compounded by the realization that there is no possibility of immediate relationship—no man, no close woman friend. The energy has been spent getting out of the old relationship and trying to adjust to the outside world. Suddenly life becomes a vacuum. Fate seems to turn against her. The woman she was is dead; the new woman is not yet born. She is in a cocoon.

Instead of being terrorized by her aloneness and her feelings of abandonment and rejection, she can use this time to work on herself. One of the things she will surely face is her own inner killer—the overdeveloped masculine in herself that kills her femininity. During this withdrawal, she may release her own Black Madonna and do battle with her own negative animus until his sword is broken. If she doesn't work on herself she will inevitably repeat the same old patterns and end with the same raw agony. If she does work on herself, then, God willing, she may meet a Petruchio who has the guts to put a bullet right through the heart of her King Kong animus. Whether he does that with anger or with unrelenting courage and faith depends on his nature, her nature and the nature of their relationship.

The balance in relationships is exceedingly delicate where both parties are striving for consciousness. Very strange things happen. A woman who had been in analysis for some time had tried in vain to get her husband to see an analyst. Then one day, to her astonishment, he dressed up in suit and tie and went.

She awoke that night to find a dim light in the room, making strange movements across the ceiling. She opened her eyes just enough to catch a glimpse of her husband writing with a tiny flashlight pen, and he wrote and he wrote and he wrote.

"Why should he get such wonderful dreams?" she thought. "I only get two-liners."

She said nothing. She sighed loudly. He took the hint and went to finish his writing in the bathroom. But when he came back he got into bed with the bravado of one who had done his job well. He couldn't contain himself.

"Are you awake?" he whispered.

"Do you want me to be?" she asked.

"I've had a dream," he said.

She determined she would not listen. She would roll over and stay asleep.

"It was about you," he said.

"About me?...Oh...you're going to keep me awake, I suppose."

"Well if that's the way you feel about it, go back to sleep."

His sigh of self-satisfaction penetrated her like the two horns of the dilemma that had always disturbed their marriage. She wasn't sure if he was awake or if he had returned to sleep. She risked it anyway.

"I had a dream too," she said.

"Oh?"

"About china!"

"Really!" he said. "I dreamt I was in China too and you were leading a bunch of guerrilla warriors and you were doing a good job."

"Well," she said. "I dreamed you smashed my mother's Victorian china."

Dreaming each other's symbols, or what is going on unconsciously in the partner, is not uncommon, and learning to recognize the projections is the biggest problem in relationships. Withdrawing them, or having them withdrawn, is the most painful. But before going into the issues of relationship between men and women, we must move to another rung of the spiral and look again at the meaning of the feminine.

First, I believe that femininity is taking responsiblity for our bodies, so that the body becomes the tangible expression of the spirit within. For those of us who have lived life in the head, this is a long, difficult and agonizing process, because in attempting to release our muscles, we also release the pent-up fear and rage and grief that has been buried there, probably since or before birth. Within ourselves we find a stricken animal almost dead from starvation and mistreatment. Because it has been punished so long, it acts at first like a wild neurotic creature that hasn't known love. But gradually it becomes our friend, and because it understands the instincts better than we, it becomes our guide to a natural, spiritual way of life.

In *Border Crossings,* Don Williams describes Carlos Castaneda's don Juan entering sacred time and adapting himself to the magical deer, standing upside down and weeping:

> Thus he balances the joy of a man about to find his life with the sadness of a man rendered lonely, foolish and perhaps even fearsome by his vision. Both the sadness and the joy are genuine. And perhaps it is the soul that, like the radiant deer when no longer threatened, whispers, "Don't be sad."[5]

To find the natural rhythms of our bodies, to walk, to see, to hear, to feel with renewed sensitivity and perception, is to return to our birthright which is our gift from the Goddess. In my fairytale Dumbellina, through her love for her new-found Mother, touched her head to the ground, lower and again lower, realizing that she could never surrender to the beauty of the translucent light without the grounding of her body. Like the Moslems, she realized that prayer is putting your head on the earth, bringing your head down to the ground.

Secondly, femininity is taking responsibility for who I am—not what I do, not how I seem to be, not what I accomplish. When all the doing is done and I have to face myself in my naked reality, who am I? What are my values? What are my needs? Am I true to myself or do I betray myself? What are my feelings? Am I capable of love? Am I true to my love?

Working on these questions day after day is what I call differentiating the feminine. This is the process of becoming virgin—the woman who is what she is because that is what she is. She lives and moves and has her Being through some power within her.

And that power is based in the archetypal feminine, the Great Mother in both her dark and bright aspects. The Goddess, in my thinking, is the movement of the spiral. Like so many things in nature—plants, the seasons, the moon—the Goddess moves in her circular motion through dark and light, through death and resurrection, trusting in the darkness as much as in the light. She lives in the present and evaluates in the moment. What is right today may be wrong tomorrow. She lives by the spirit, not by the law. Therefore she demands constant awareness and spontaneity. She loves the potential in things: the possibilities in the growing plant, the growing child, the growing hopes and dreams. She trusts life, trusts change, trusts love and holds nothing static. She loves and lets go. She loves with her whole Being so that her vulnerability becomes her greatest strength. What for those who do not love her is contradiction, becomes for those who love her paradox.

If life is to be lived in a healthy, holy way, the archetypes that nourish the imagination must be pouring their energy into the ego. The dialogue must go on between consciousness and unconsciousness if we are to live creatively. It is therefore crucial to recognize when we have lost touch with our archetypal ground. When that happens we dream of crumbling foundations and flooded basements, collapsing underground parking lots, disintegrating retaining walls, cellars that have caved in. It is then our task to go down and do something about the chaos below. Women also dream of being taken to their grandmothers, the Grand Mother, in time of trouble.

If we watch our dreams long enough, themes are repeated, symbols reappear with variations. And if we contemplate these emerging patterns, gradually we begin to see some order in the chaos. We begin to see our own individual symbols weaving themselves, or being woven, into some greater pattern. We begin to recognize our individual identity in what was once confusion. Gradually we set up a dialogue between our ego and the Being who is weaving the pattern. In that dialogue is soul-making. The dialogue between the ego and the Self creates the soul. The crystals and the snowflakes and the teardrops, all manifestations of spirit in concrete form, are gradually woven into the rainbow's threads of heaven. And the gossamer garment falling on the shoulders of Dumbellina becomes the blessing of the Goddess. It is delicate as rain, but it changes life from a meaningless puzzle into an awesome journey.

Analysand's drawing of the Great Mother and herself.

Cartoon for St. Anne—Leonardo da Vinci.
(National Gallery, London)

Our culture has twenty centuries of Christianity behind it, and while the ancient myths are psychologically very valuable and interesting intellectually, they have lost the numinosity which could feed our souls. The old earth goddesses were not conscious, and those women who have won their way through to some awareness have done so through fiery hours of bringing the shadow into light. There are two thousand years between unconsciously letting things happen and consciously allowing things *to be*. We cannot go back.

Each one of us has to find the particular feminine archetype that makes our life meaningful. I can only tell you the one that has meaning for me. Last summer I was still waiting for the separated images to come into focus. I had had several powerful dreams. I had experienced the numinosity of the Goddess, and I knew Jung's view that the dogma of the Assumption of Mary is in fact an acceptance of matter, indeed a sanctification of matter.[6] But the overall pattern still eluded me. And then one day I walked into the National Gallery in London and looked at the da Vinci drawing of the Virgin sitting on the great lap of her mother Anne, holding the divine child in her outstretched arms, the child John standing beside.

Anne's face is accented with dark shadows and her eyes burn like two black coals. She looks like a majestic gypsy firmly seated on the earth, her outstretched finger pointing to heaven. The Virgin is radiant and serene, relaxed, absolutely confident. Her eyes are lowered as she ponders in her heart the beauty of her child. He, with his ancient face, echoes the gesture of his grandmother toward heaven. He looks into the receptive face of John and seems to bless him. They belong together, these two—the divine child and the human child, secure in their relationship through the transformative love of the Mother.[7]

This painting lives in me. There is the Great Mother, her face at once fierce and loving, her hand uniting earth and sky. On her ample knee sits the Virgin, her features like her mother's, but with a spiritual sensitivity, lit from inside with mysterious beauty. She accepts herself as part of the greater plan through which life eternally moves. Her vulnerability is her strength—gentle, loving, and just detached enough to let go. The child is hers, but not hers, as he reaches out to the other child. She accepts the power of the Great Mother on whose lap she sits, and dreams into the Mystery of the divine gift that has been given to her. The rest is silence.

That's my myth of Ms. It may not be yours. But if you travel far enough, one day you will recognize yourself coming down the road to meet yourself. And you will say—YES.

*Will the veiled sister pray for*
*Those who walk in darkness, who chose thee and oppose*
   *thee,*
*Those who are torn on the horn between season and*
*season, time and time, between*
*Hour and hour, word and word, power and power, those*
   *who wait*
*In darkness? Will the veiled sister pray*
*For children at the gate*
*Who will not go away and cannot pray:*
*Pray for those who chose and oppose*

   *O my people, what have I done unto thee.*

   *Will the veiled sister between the slender*
*Yew trees pray for those who offend her*
*And are terrified and cannot surrender*
*And affirm before the world and deny between the rocks*
*In the last desert between the last blue rocks*
*The desert in the garden the garden in the desert*
*Of drouth, spitting from the mouth the withered appleseed.*

   *O my people.*

                    —T.S. Eliot, "Ash-Wednesday."

*You stand at the blackboard, daddy,*
*In the picture I have of you,*
*A cleft in your chin instead of your foot*
*But no less a devil for that, no not*
*Any less the black man who*

*Bit my pretty heart in two.*
*I was ten when they buried you.*
*At twenty I tried to die*
*And get back, back, back to you.*
*I thought even the bones would do.*

                    —Sylvia Plath, "Daddy," *Ariel.*

# Rape and the Demon Lover

*I felt a Cleaving in my Mind—*
*As if my Brain had split—*
*I tried to match it—Seam by Seam—*
*But could not make them fit.*
                    —Emily Dickinson.

In the 20th century, the Christian idea of Hell has relocated itself in the public imagination. Now we fear the criminal underworld that operates as intricately organized hierarchical societies such as the Mafia or international terrorist organizations. More and more, as terrorists' bombs explode in parked Volkswagons, or as passengers of a 747 are held hostage, or as drugs are peddled in our own schoolyard, or as we find ourselves requiring triple locks on our own front doors, we sense that our society is gradually being penetrated by an underground life. This experience, both real and imagined, is a kind of rape. The rape of consciousness by subterranean energies over which we have little control threatens almost everyone's dreams with sinister and infecting fear. Our apparent helplessness before the onslaught of this eruptive world both within and without turns human society and the human psyche into a mine field.

Jung was very explicit on this point. His own first encounter with the unconscious took place prior to the outbreak of the First World War, and as he points out in *Memories, Dreams and Reflections,* he could not distinguish between what was coming up from his own unconscious and the forces at work in the outside world:

> Towards the autumn of 1913 the pressure which I had felt was in *me* seemed to be moving outwards, as though there were something in the air. The atmosphere actually seemed to me darker than it had been. It was as though the sense of oppression no longer sprang exclusively from a psychic situation, but from concrete reality. This feeling grew more and more intense. . . .
>
> I asked myself whether these visions [sea of blood covering all the northern and low-lying lands between the North Sea and the Alps] pointed to a revolution, but could not really imagine anything of the sort. And so I drew the conclusion that they had to do with me myself, and decided that I was menaced by a psychosis. The idea of war did not occur to me at all.[1]

At the end of July 1914, Jung delivered a lecture to the British

Medical Association, "On the Importance of the Unconscious in Psychopathology." On August 1, war broke out. In an effort to understand the extent to which his own experience coincided with that of mankind in general, he probed the depths of his own psyche. Writing down his fantasies was also writing the unconscious history of his own time. As Jung continued to develop his psychological insights, he increasingly experienced his work as a race against time. Finally he realized that he was searching for something which might stem the tide of human destruction that was now running out of control. He knew that in the past the Christian Church had performed this function, but now no longer could. What would replace it? What Jung saw on the horizon was a series of dictatorships governed by the exploitation of psychotic fear. He saw the world descending into a global reign of terror.

It is in this larger context that women's movements must be understood. Gradually, increasing numbers of women have seen in the events of this century a genuine image of their own condition as pawns in a patriarchal world. What this century has brought to light by acting it out in the most public and explicit ways is the psychological condition of the raped woman. Indeed, the raped woman has in some sense replaced the crucified Christ as the most powerful and meaningful of icons. D.M. Thomas's novel *The White Hotel* (1981) makes vividly clear the contemporary fate of the feminine.

For too long it was argued that Freud's psychology addressed itself only to affluent, hysterical, Jewish Viennese women. Equally it was claimed that Jung's coterie consisted largely of their Gentile counterparts. The element of truth in all of this is that the discoveries of both Freud and Jung were most often made through their own direct encounters with the feminine, whether in themselves or in others. The experience of the feminine is the psychological key to both the sickness of our time and its healing. While both men analyzed the sickness with a depth and precision that has not been exceeded, both, being products of their own culture, could not overcome their own fear of the feminine imposed upon them by that patriarchal tradition to which as Jew and Christian they belonged. This very patriarchal tradition is what finally drove them apart.

The feminine, which they only began to explore, can now be released into a creative and redemptive life. In this chapter and the next I am seeing in rape the ravishment that it can become. Rape in our culture is a fact which cannot be denied. When in the man the feminine is repressed, it becomes destructive; equally, when in a woman the masculine is repressed, it will inevitably take over. The contrasexual healing forces at work in the unconscious are only healing if they are actively sought out and supported without being allowed to take charge. We must build creatively on the fact that, historically and psychologically, rape has taken place in both men and women. Whether we know it or not, we are all the products or victims of it. My point is that we need no longer be victims.

The philosopher Hannah Arendt is a woman who consciously worked through this problem. Reading her essays, and feeling the generosity of her understanding heart, I thought of Jung's statement: "A part of life was lost, but the meaning of life has been salvaged for her"—referring to the woman who reflects on her life from the standpoint of conscious maturity, and "sees the world for the first time."[2]

Hannah Arendt was a refugee Jew fleeing from Nazi Germany. She pondered that experience until the reality of it became clear to her; gradually, through realizing what it meant to live in flight, she came to realize what it meant to live in life:

> We are contemporaries only so far as our understanding reaches. If we want to be at home on this earth, even at the price of being at home in this century, we must try to take part in the interminable dialogue with its essence.[3]

Hannah Arendt in her flight from Nazi totalitarianism personifies the unconscious life of many a modern woman, who in her dreams finds herself prisoner in a concentration camp, tortured by SS troopers, raped by Goering or Hitler. Again and again she throws some precious jewel over the barbed wire and attempts to retrieve it, only to be dragged back. Her boss can suddenly become Idi Ammin, her father Mussolini, her husband Dracula. Whether the men in her life are actually making these demands or whether she is projecting onto them, she is hearing these demands within herself and thus continually setting herself up for rape. Who *she* is and what *her* needs are have seldom in her life been the issue. The power animus has devastated her from infancy.

Taken collectively, such dreams add up to more than a few women's childhood experiences. Men too, in their dreams, are being attacked. If this is the world as our unconscious sees it, it is our responsibility to ponder that before it is too late. By looking at life from the vantage point of a refugee instead of running away, perhaps, like Hannah Arendt, we can learn to focus on our situation and then give ourselves to our own life. Nothing can change until we accept what is. Some of us have to recognize that we were forced to flee; some of us have to realize that we are in effect living in a concentration camp, that life has become a prison of renunciation in which, as our mothers used to say, "the thing that life misses helps more than the thing that it gets." If that is the reality that life has given to us, then that is the reality we have to ponder in order to transform it. To ponder is not to become bitter or resigned, but through the imagination to invest our situation with the possibilities of Being. If there is one thing that Hannah Arendt teaches us, it is that there is no health or redemption within the collective. The individual must walk her own perilous path:

> . . . be loyal to life, don't create fiction but accept what life is giving you, show yourself worthy of whatever it may be by recollecting and pondering over it, thus repeating it in imagination: "this is the way to remain alive."[4]

One reason people are suffering today to an almost intolerable degree is that their unmediated suffering has no conscious connection with its archetypal ground. Cut off from that ground they feel they are alone, and their suffering becomes meaningless. They do not realize that what they are suffering exists within creation itself, and that the gods and goddesses of religion and mythology have been there before. The agony of their suffering is caused by hubris, which Jung describes as "the overweening pride . . . of individual consciousness, which must necessarily collide with [the eternal truths] and lead to the catastrophic destruction of the individual."[5] The suffering itself can easily become gilt-edged, self-dramatized, when we lack the god or goddess at the center. To sympathize with that suffering in ourselves or in others beyond a certain point is to condone the arrogance, and to condone the arrogance is to paralyze the sufferer. The neurotic cut off from his archetypal roots is actually enamored of his pain and his gilt-edged guilt. Godless suffering is ironic, especially for those of us born into the Judaeo-Christian religion where a Father-God in his chthonic form made his way into a virginal garden and raped it, and for whom the rest of history is a working out of the Atonement. Seen from this perspective, we may acquire just enough detachment to enjoy a good laugh at our own role in the divine comedy.

The words rape and ravishment come from the same Latin root, *rapere,* meaning "to seize and carry off." The connotations of the two words, however, are very different. Rape suggests being seized and carried off by a masculine enemy through brutal sexual assault; ravishment suggests being seized and carried off by a masculine lover through ecstasy and rapture. Rape has to do with power; ravishment has to do with love. In this chapter I want to concentrate on the psychological symbolism of rape, and in the last chapter on the psychological symbolism of ravishment.

Thus far in this study I have placed very little emphasis on the father, although he has been omnipresent in the discussion of the masculine. The negative mother, as I have described her, is the mother who is herself a father's daughter, a woman who is not in touch with her own feminine feeling values, a woman more or less identified with the ideals of the patriarchy. Her partner will usually be a mother's son, closer to his feminine side than to the chthonic masculine, a man more related to his own inner world than to the world of outer reality. As such a marriage goes on, she tends to slip into the mother role, he into that of the son, so that when the baby daughter is born his inner beloved is projected onto her. There is the perfect seed-bed for the demon lover.

The girl most vulnerable to the demon lover is the one who adores or fears the idealized father. (If he is absent through divorce, alcoholism or death, her adoration may be even more intense.) Having accepted his anima projection from infancy, she has lived to please him, to share his intellectual pursuits and to meet his standards of perfection. In the dynamics of such a relationship, the mother is experienced either as absent or as a rival. While the daughter experiences herself as the beloved of the father, consciously she knows she dare not share his bed, yet instinctively her energies remain incestuous. Thus her love is split off from her sexuality. In fantasy she dreams of her spiritual lover; in reality, she remains unconscious of her sexuality, acts it out without love, or fears it as some explosive power that can destroy her. She tends to "fall helplessly in love" with a man who cannot marry her and around whom she creates an ideal world in which she is either adored or dramatically rejected. In life, she lives without her body; in dreams, she appears behind glass, or in a plastic bag or glass bottle.

Glass is an insulator that does not conduct heat, and the woman imprisoned in a glass coffin is not in touch with her passion for life. She stands outside looking in, yearning for what other people take for granted. From her prison, the tiniest details of living take on a mystical beauty. In her aloneness, she fantasizes her emotions, but she has no "I" with which to experience real feeling. Life does not flow through her. Having been filled with her father all her life, she has learned exactly how to mirror a man, but she remains a reflector. Jung calls her the "anima woman." She is Marilyn Monroe with parted lips and limpid eyes. She is her father's walking doll, yet sweet and erotic as she unconsciously may be, she has a pseudo-male psychology. Consciously she is a good buddy, a great friend for a man, and as a wife she is capable of sacrificing her life to serve her husband. If he matures, however, he will be bored with her lack of individuality and the ectoplasmic body that surrounds her. He can never quite reach her. While at first he may be flattered by being perceived as a god, he cannot sustain that projection and ultimately he will reject the denial of his own personality, knowing he cannot live up to her demands. She, meanwhile, is locked into a fantasy in which her true love is her father.

But father is both lover and jailer; the positive and negative aspects of his influence are close enough to be almost identical. Elizabeth Barrett paralyzed in her father's house was writing poetry that became even greater when she was released by Robert Browning.

The father's daughter walks a tightrope above an abyss, putting one foot carefully ahead of the other in a precarious balance between not living at all and living in a highly charged spiritual world. If she succumbs to her inner lover, he comes between her and genuine relationship, making a real man appear contemptible and sexuality seem like prostitution (as Jane describes in her journal; above, page 101). Her willing submission to her demon lover manifests in the outer world only by its effects—broken relationships, overly critical attitudes, drivenness, migraines and other symptoms of tension. If his power becomes magnetic, then the woman is in danger of death because she is unconsciously being lured into his trap, and without her feminine ground she is not sufficiently connected to her own instincts to stay in life. She is vulnerable to the suave manner, the eloquence with words, the perfectionism and ideals with which she endows him, and her own hold on life is so tenuous that she sets herself up for murder either by the man who is carrying the projection or by her own inner lover. The strength she projects onto her demon lover is no longer available to her. In fact, the projection drains her, leaving her fragile, physically and emotionally.

Ironically, at the core of that father-lover complex is the father-god whom she worships and at the same time hates because, on some level, she knows he is luring her away from her own life. Whether she worships him or hates him makes no difference, because in either case she is bound to him with no energy going into finding out who she herself is. So long as she can fantasize her love, she identifies with the positive side of the father-god; once the fantasy is crushed, however, she has no ego to sustain her and she swings to the opposite pole where she experiences annihilation in the arms of the god who has turned against her.

Female writers are particularly prone to the demon lover: Emily Bronte, Emily Dickinson, Virginia Woolf, Sylvia Plath. Women can still fall in love with Heathcliff and love him most when he stands with the dead Catherine in his arms rejoicing that now she is his. They do not see that it is a death-marriage. Women who sentimentalize over Emily Dickinson's love poems tend to overlook the poems of raw agony that were written in an heroic attempt to stay sane and alive. Where the demon lover is the controlling complex in the psyche, the counterbalancing poles of love and loss are both present. The perfection of death is at the center of each. When the "imperial Thunderbolt . . . scalps the naked Soul,"[6] it leaves "an Element of Blank"[7] that can lead to suicide. The thunderbolt becomes "imperial" because it defines the seemingly unbridgeable gap between the real and the imagined. The ego has undergone psychological rape, overpowered by the contents of the unconscious.

Psychologically, the most pernicious aspect of the demon lover is his trickster quality. He often appears as the perfect bridegroom, but for all his godlike perfection he is still a little boy looking for a mother, and continually demanding his victim's motherliness. Loneliness meets loneliness and they cling together in a symbiotic bond. But a child does not relate to mother as an individual; she is there to supply his needs. When the father's expectations of the girl have been combined with the negative animus needs of the mother, the woman's individual identity has not developed. That joint animus voice constantly whispers "You must, you have to, you ought to." In the vacuum left by her loss of feeling, the negative animus attacks, telling her she is unlovable, unworthy, ugly and forever his prisoner. So long as she falls under the spell of that voice, and projects that animus onto the outer man, the rejection she fears will begin to happen because in projecting her negative animus she instantly constellates the man's negative mother. Then she relates to him through logos, usually in a game of "judge and blame." She takes over the male role and both are left without feeling.

Through consciousness a woman may find she can protect herself from the rape of the masculine power principle. To do so she has to remain true to her own feelings, however insecure they may be. She may listen to his arguments (his logic is excellent) and then firmly respond, "Yes, that is true. You argue well, but you are without feelings. Those arguments have nothing to do with my essence. These are my feelings, even if you think I am making a fool of myself. These feelings are my truth." The feminine ego can be terrorized by the masculine invasion and its only defense is its authentic feeling.

Another psychological motif which can develop from the demon lover/negative mother combination is that of the orphan child. In this situation, a woman has experienced relationship with neither father nor mother. If the father has a very strong mother complex, his emotional stability will be dependent upon the reactions of others to him. His individual feeling will probably not have been developed and therefore he is incapable of relating out of personal feeling values—i.e., his anima. The daughter then becomes his anima, his bridge to his own unconscious. She becomes a walking archetype, a goddess—a goddess who has sacrificed her own humanity. She becomes responsible for his well-being, even for his creativity. The horror is that her own creative process is blocked: to create anything her father wants her to create, even to be anything her father wants her to be (whether it is natural to her or not) is to please Daddy, and the double horror is that to please Daddy is to move into incest. If she has married a creative man, she has probably recreated the same situation.

At some point she must recognize that she has been psychologically raped by the father. Where her spirit has been repeatedly taken over by him, she will have an overwhelming fear of opening herself to anything or anyone. In analysis, a rape dream involving the father is often crucial in getting the woman to recognize her situation. Face to face with the incest taboo, she may then go on to work through it consciously as a purposive aspect of her own process. "Incest," writes Jung, "symbolizes union with one's own being, it means individuation or becoming a self, and, because this is so vitally important, it exerts an unholy fascination."[8]

If a woman has unconsciously assumed the responsibility for the emotional well-being of her father, thereby identifying her own emotional welfare with his, her happiness is directly answerable to his happiness. She experiences herself as the source of his life. If the bond is close enough, she may, unconsciously, be her father's mother/mistress. As one woman told me, her boyfriends were always welcome in her home. Her charming father always said, "Let them come, Alice. We'll love them to death." Through their intellectual and spiritual pursuits father and daughter are bound by unconscious psychological incest. The instinct naturally wants to follow that love. But the incest taboo "forever intervenes."[9] Then instinct and love are split. Unconscious incest takes place at a spiritual level; the instincts are left floating autonomously in the unconscious, disconnected from the ego. The woman then is left unconsciously identified with her sexuality, and because her love and sexuality are split, sexuality goes into power. Speaking of the ego identified with power, Erich Neumann writes:

> The ego . . . remained . . . a victim of the unconscious forces. . . . It was subject to and dominated by these forces and instincts, which took possession of it in the form of sexuality, lust for power, cruelty, hunger, fear and superstition. The ego was their instrument and was totally unaware that it was in fact possessed, since it lived them out blindly and was unable to interpose any kind of distance between itself and the power which had taken possession of it. But for an ego which is required to accept responsibility, this stage of unconsciousness and possession amounts to a sin.[10]

While the love remains bound up with the father, in the sexual act the body can *only* autonomously give and receive, because the "I" is not connected to the instinct. Spiritually the woman may experience it as love, but the body is not in tune with the spirit. Eros is not related to the erotic. Eros is a feminine principle, but Eros is a masculine god. Whereas sex should be a symbol of union, it becomes a symbol of power. Total union is not possible when the ego is afraid to give up, and where the ego is not firmly grounded in the instincts it dare not surrender to the transpersonal power.

The problem is compounded because in the bonding of father and daughter, the mother is usually experienced as hostile. Whether that hostility is real or imagined, it breeds genuine conflict: to please father is to alienate mother. When she "falls in love," it will probably be with an "ideal" figure whose happiness she must mother, so that in the actual consummation of the marriage she is suddenly faced with the dynamism of incest and her rejection of her own mother in herself. If she has until then been promiscuous (i.e., living out her mother's unlived life), she cannot bring that sexuality into the "perfect" marriage.

The woman with a demon lover has an inflated view of the imaginal feminine and a deflated view of the actual feminine, and while she overendows the masculine, looking to men to save her, her undeveloped femininity is either terrified of the aggressive masculine or challenges it. Her insecure femininity meets a joyless Don Juan out to prove his masculinity—both essentially unrelated to their sexuality—and another scalp is on her belt. Sexual intercourse in that situation has nothing to do with relationship. The magnetic siren or femme fatale, who is cut off from her own inner woman, takes no responsibility for the men who fall under her spell. As one woman told me:

> In the past, I couldn't be sure of anything except food in my belly. My mother gave with one hand and took away with the other. Now I feel if I give to a man, he will disappear. I die without a man. He brings me into my body so I am dependent on him. But once he thinks I'm his, he's off to another conquest. I'm careful what I give. It's his conquest or mine.

Such a woman, in her "innocence," wonders why men call her cruel. The part of herself which she respects because it is carrying her soul, no ordinary man is allowed to come near. She waits for the man who can "ravish" her. In the opera *Lulu,* she finds him in Jack the Ripper; in *Othello,* she finds him in her husband who pontificates upon "the cause" even as he kills her. The woman who does not take responsibility for her own femininity may cause tragedies or find a tragic end herself, because her playful innocence is full of criminal ruthlessness. Speaking of the development of the ego, Eva Metman writes:

> When, however, a woman is aware of the right to be an anima without being possessed by it—that is, if she *enters* the confict between either being the totally incalculable anima or the fanatical rejector of that role—what she really wants is not to dazzle or to intimidate her man but to be freed from the power of the forces which rage through her. . . . This situation contains all the potentialities of the development of an animus-transference. If such a transference is fully lived through, it shows a rising and a falling curve: First the demand is made that a still more powerful magic shall be performed than that which keeps her imprisoned. In other words, the real man is expected to become a kind of super-animus and the positive quality of such a transference will first express itself in an attempt to make the man accept this role. In the later stage, when the curve falls, the transference will be withdrawn and if all goes well, the archetype will be depotentiated. In the bend of the curve the encounter with the shadow takes place, because this is the experience which alone can bring about the change.[11]

An example will make clear the three phases of that curve. Esther was married to Paul, a good, salt-of-the-earth man, but secretly she was in love with a flamboyant rebel, Jake. She decided to flee from her dull marriage into the arms of her macho lover. But Paul, instead of accepting his role as jailer, was willing to let her go. His amazing recognition of what was required in that moment overwhelmed her. Suddenly she was free. She decided to stay. Gradually she realized that her captor was not her husband but her own demon lover. Possessed by him, she had tried to manipulate Paul into the role of father-jailer keeping her prisoner in his concentration camp, thus projecting demon savior onto Jake. Paul's recognition of her real problem—her need for freedom—forced her to take responsibility for her own choice. *She* was going to have to abandon one of these two men. Paul made her confront her own shadow: the woman who was betraying both men. Out of that confrontation, she came to recognize that her real value was in her loyalty to Paul. The significance of the crisis for Esther was in the encounter with her shadow which forced her ego to take a standpoint. No longer could she identify with being Paul's ideal wife; in other words, she broke her identification with male psychology. In taking responsibility for herself, she freed herself from her own prison.

Commenting on the "mysterious charm" of the demon lover, Jung writes:

> It was Miss Miller's spirituality, which . . . was far too exalted for her ever to find a lover among mortal men. However reasonable and unexacting the conscious attitude may be in such a case, it will not

have the slightest effect on the patient's unconscious expectations. Even after the greatest difficulties and resistances have been over- come, and a so-called normal marriage is made, she will only discover later on what the unconscious wants, and this will assert itself either as a change of life style or as a neurosis or even a psychosis.[12]

What the woman is really projecting is her inner image of a god- man, and when she cannot find him or cannot hold him even in her imagination, her disillusionment turns into rage which constellates the demonic. If she identifies with that rage, she experiences it as Satan himself coming against her.

A case in point is Andrea, a woman in her thirties, divorced, with three children. She had no strong feminine principle operating in her life: her mother was dedicated to the masculine principles of order, efficiency and perfection; her father could never relate to her on any feeling level. In rebellion she chose not to pursue a promis- ing artistic career and instead became a flower child. Although she lived a "let it happen" kind of life, she was living it unconsciously, without ego direction. Although she became a mother herself, she had not sufficient femininity to relate to her own body, nor suffi- cient masculine strength to take responsibility for her considerable talents. When her husband left, she said to herself, "Now he's gone. I'll wear the pants in the family. I'll be the perfect mother, perfect father. I'll go to university and be the perfect student. I'll take a social worker's course and take on the whole world and heal it too." This pursuit of perfection was her Light.

In the last year of her university training, during the final exam- ination when she was striving to do her very best, Andrea had the following dream:

> I am in bed with the devil. He doesn't look like the devil but I know he is. We are both naked. A male baby is lying between us. The devil makes me masturbate the child. His penis falls off and blood spurts out. I am either told or I decide to put my mouth where the penis was. There is semen mixed with the blood. The baby is gone. The devil picks up a short pointed instrument like a compass. I want to leave. I beg him to let me go and he smiles and says, "You can't leave. I'll always be here." He stabs me in the mouth. I'm screaming. The pin sticks in my mouth. He pulls it out. I decide to spit the mouthful of blood in his face. But when I do he laughs and I realize he loves blood. This is what he wants me to do. He then stabs and stabs at my open mouth. I wake up screaming, "Oh God, Oh God."
>
> I have never been so terrified. I feel so helpless, but it is as if the dream is telling me that although I thought I was helpless I never knew what helplessness was until this.

The dream shows that Andrea's powerful energies have turned against her, and her life force, her very blood, is feeding back into the demonic. Having grown up without a real relationship to her actual father, she had created a perfect world in her imagination, a world in which the patriarchal values were idealized. In dedicating herself to that imaginary world, she was unaware of its opposite constellating in her own unconscious. Thus when the idealized projection onto her husband collapsed, and she undertook the realization of her own ideals, she desperately and blindly ran faster toward the Light, until the dark forces of rage and disillusionment gathered sufficient strength to smash through her obsessive behavior and appeared as Satan. The final examinations precipitated the confrontation.

What black irony—a woman believes she is running toward Light, and is unconsciously running straight into the arms of the demon lover! Mythologically it is a death-marriage, a mystical union with the dark side of God. The relationship is sado-masochistic; it fascinates because it has within it the elements of violent eroticism. In the dream the consummation is a hideous parody of the loving *coniunctio:* the head is attacked by a phallic instrument. The over-spiritualized, overintellectualized masculine turns in rage against the feminine and drinks its blood. The life force which was not able to find its proper channel into actual loving relationships is given over to feed the rage which, in turn, viciously stabs at its feminine victim.

The ravaging attitude with which she is attacked, she in turn enacts upon the child. The demonic *coniunctio* is precipitated by her being driven to masturbate the male child until its penis falls off. As she is ravaged, so she ravages, and the diabolical energy builds.

The reason for oral contact with the child is ambiguous in the dream. If she was told by the demon to suck the blood and semen, in other words, repeat the ravaging by sucking the life and creativity out of her own young masculine, then the result is disaster. If she chose to bring whatever healing she could through her loving relationship to his blood and semen, then she at least has that strength within her. In either case the vampire is against healing; he feeds on the blood of her femininity and her creative child, jeering at her attempts to fight back.

Shortly before this dream, Andrea had begun to have severe headaches, loss of sensation in her uro-genital area, and momentary blackouts. Then the attacks abated for three years, at which point her mother died. The link between mother and daughter had been very close, although the mother had been unable to give her daughter the bonding with the earth. "When my mother died," said Andrea, "I was born." The mother's death freed the daughter for new life.

As it happens, Andrea's "new life" has included being stricken with a crippling disease. The earlier inner ravaging had simply gone on too long. But she is neither bitter nor resentful, and her courageous spirit is living testimony to the psychological transformation. The Eros and creativity which she could not find in her early life she is finding now. Looking back at her dream of the devil, she sees enormous symbolic significance in her healing gesture toward the baby:

> I had to heal where I thought I could. Now I have neither hands nor feet. I can give with my mouth only. Giving my life's breath to the child, I stopped the blood. The wounding was in the masculine, the healing was in the feminine mouth. I can receive and give as I never could before. I am physically weaker and spiritually stronger. I was thrown out of the collective value system. It doesn't make any rational sense, but I know I am living my own destiny.

Many modern women are psychologically in the situation Andrea was in after the break-up of her marriage: with feminine consciousness almost nonexistent, the psychological feminine child remains unborn; the masculine consciousness unrelated to its feminine feeling lures her into a fantasy world of perfection totally unrelated to life or to her own body. The incapacity to deal with reality is experienced as helplessness. Raped from within by her own vampire-witch, and from without by that same attitude in the culture, such a woman dare not open herself to life. She tries to hold on as rigidly as she can to whatever frail structure she can manufacture for herself. If that structure is demolished—usually through loss of an important relationship—she is flooded by repressed unconscious contents. Raped by her demon lover, she yet remains "the still unravished bride."

Behind the rigidity is the fear of inevitable defeat. Then one day tragedy bisects her daily routine, and there is no logical reason why. Without the feminine principle to allow for a different kind of meaning, life becomes a constant battle against chaos and collapse. The demon lover lures and inflates the ego with pride, in defiance of the inner gods and goddesses, but unconsciously the individual knows the outcome must be defeat and escape from the struggle, whether in suicide, a terminal illness or a fatal accident. Sometimes the heart stops, not because Death overtakes it, but simply because it is broken.

When a woman goes out into the professional world, in an effort to take responsibility for her own animus (a responsibility which was previously projected onto a man) she often finds herself applying masculine standards of perfection to her entire life. She is exhausted. There is no time for a leisurely stroll in the woods, nor a long cup of tea with her husband, nor unplanned hours with her children. Organization and efficiency become gods. Periods of meditative silence are rare or nonexistent. The more refined the masculine principle becomes, the more it devastates the feminine. Locked into her incestuous love for masculine perfection, she feels secret scorn or pity for her partner. Her initiation into what must ultimately end in a death-marriage occurs when she becomes obsessed by her masculine drivenness, turns it against her own creativity and rapes it—as is illustrated in Andrea's dream.

Psychologically speaking, her power witch animus ravages her own creative spiritual animus. Far from allowing her positive animus to guide her into her own spiritual depths, she ravages and castrates him. She has broken out of the concentration camp, but she has not found the proper balance: she doesn't know how to channel the creative potential, nor how to bring the perfectionist ideals into a human dimension. This vampire energy is counterbalanced by rejected femininity and underscored by unconscious sexuality, because where the woman has no genuine relationship to her body, her sexuality will seep out unconsciously. Our culture thus becomes charged with a fierce masculine power drive, an outraged masculinity and an enraged femininity. Psychological rape is rife; actual rape is a growing peril both within the home and outside.

As a paradigm of the raped view of the human world, R.D. Laing in *The Voices of Experience* focuses upon the birth of a child. Childbirth, he argues, has been virtually abolished by technologically dominated obstetrics:

> We do not see childbirth in some obstetric units any more. What goes on there no more resembles birth than artificial insemination resembles sexual intercourse or a tube feeding resembles eating. . . . The obliteration of birth takes its place along with the obliteration of mind and death, as footnotes to the scientific abolition of our world and ourselves.[13]

By way of illustration, he describes a doctor's reaction to a home birth:

> She had her baby safely at home.
> "But why?" her obstetrician, counsellor and friend asks her. "You didn't have to go through all that! You could have come into my clinic and read a newspaper throughout. You wouldn't have needed to have known a thing until I presented you with the baby."
> "But," she replies in bewilderment, 'I *wanted* to go through all that!"
> He could not see how such a sentiment could have any value. He evidently sniffed some hysterical-masochistic heresy. Birth: abolished as an active personal experience. Woman: from active person to passive patient. Experience: dissolved into oblivion. She is translated from feeling subject to anaesthetic object.

> The physiological process is taken over by a chemico-surgical pro-
> gramme. End result: the act, the event and the coherent experience of
> birth has disappeared.
> Instead of the birth of a baby we have surgical extraction.[14]

The result of all this is that we are no longer born. We begin as
surgical extractions and we end as surgical extinctions. Between the
beginning and the end we are a chemically operated machine subject to more and more refined technology.

The Grimm fairytale "The Girl without Hands" suggests a possible way of healing for the wounded feminine. In that tale, a miller
in dire financial straits meets the devil in disguise. In return for
wealth, he promises whatever stands behind his mill, thinking it is
an old apple tree, never imagining that his most precious possession,
his daughter, is the pawn. Her tears, her own femininity, put sufficient energy around her to save her from total rape by the demon,
but her hands are cut off. According to Marie-Louise von Franz, she
chooses "to sacrifice participation in life, rather than fall into his
hands."[15] In other words, her father complex is so strong that as
soon as she takes up any activity she falls into pathological drivenness, and rather than succumb to that pitfall she chooses to remain
passive. The king's son finds her, gives her silver hands, marries her
and goes to war. She bears a son, Sorrowful, the fruit of her suffering that has mellowed into wisdom. Then the devil interferes again,
and through a series of misunderstandings she and her son are
driven into the woods where her king eventually finds his beloved
again. In one version of the story, it is only when her son is about to
drown that the handless maiden, in an outpouring of love and
prompted by an old man's encouragement, puts her arms in the
water and suddenly grows living hands in order to save her child.

Von Franz points out that the miller thinks he is just sacrificing
an old apple tree—nature—when in fact he is unwittingly sacrificing
his most precious possession. The whole realm of the feminine, as
represented by nature, is being handed over to the devil and the
price is the feminine soul. The daughter is so ravaged by the demonic father and the negative mother complex—their effects are
virtually the same—that she has to go back to "the unhurt virgin
ground in her soul," back through a healing regression into nature in
order to find her own life force.[16] The silver hands, which suggest an
artificial Eros relationship because the instinctive spontaneity is not
possible to her, can only be replaced by living hands when some
*miracle of love* intercedes.

In the language of this study, when a woman has been raped out
of participation in life by a masculine principle which unwittingly
hands her over to the devil, her only salvation is to go back into her

own instincts and work quietly and patiently in her introverted world until she connects with her own femininity—her own virgin firmly seated on the lap of Sophia. Then the real situation may arise which demands a love beyond any she has ever experienced. Then she as virgin is ready to surrender to the great life force that penetrates her. If she is strong enough to let go of her own rigid framework and allow love to pour through her, her own arms begin to grow, her own grasp on reality is born. She and her child are saved. It is nothing short of a miracle.

The story of the handless maiden has much relevance in the workshops discussed in chapter five, where many women discover how weak their hands are. After a period of months they often experience extreme pain as energy suddenly begins to flow back into their hands. Their dreams then are about their fathers, usually not father as he was but as one who can help them to relate to reality. In other words, a positive masculinity begins to constellate—strong, assertive energy that helps the receptive feminine to connect creatively to life. Generally, that assertive masculinity is not activated until the woman has discovered her own femininity; then an interaction begins to develop between the two. There is no one pattern of healing, however; each process goes its own individual way, and as in alchemy, one returns to the transformative fire many times to go through the process on another level.

The following dream illustrates how a new relationship may develop between the masculine and the feminine. Louise is in her early forties, has done intensive body work for several years and been in analysis for two. Her father died when she was three, leaving an ideal image of masculinity with which no ordinary man could compete. The dream shows a transformation taking place:

> We are in a gorgeous gold and glittering house and we are all playing parts that get more fantastical. A famous femme fatale [a Hollywood star] is the lady of the house. I have gone into the kitchen and look over the balcony. Below are two beds—one a double bed with David's mauve silk quilt on it, and the other a single bed. Bobby [a young puer type] comes in and I tell him that I have stayed in that apartment sometimes in the double bed, but the single bed was mine.
>
> Bobby walks back toward the living room, but turns to look back briefly. Our eyes connect and I think possibly the attraction has been acknowledged. Well maybe I'll get him.
>
> Then I am back in the living room which is all windows, gold velvet curtains, high ceilings. I'm in an armchair watching the charade and thinking how impressed our guests must be at our parties and then thinking they are not. Then Bobby comes over and sits on my lap and I'm wanting to take him to bed. Then he returns to the femme fatale. We had been concocting fantasies.

When Bobby leaves, suddenly behind me [an illustrious, old-school British actor] appears in the most fantastic costume, walking with great dignity in a black velvet suit with gold trim. It is 18th century, knickers to the knees with gold buttons, white frilly shirt, black jacket, black stockings, high-heeled black pumps with gold buckles and a hat of black velvet with gold and jewels woven through it. It is like a high turban perched high on his head. He steps with great dignity and is very erect. He carries a walking stick of black ebony with a silver tip which strangely has a horizontal bar on the bottom which makes it very difficult to use.

I look him up and down. He is imperious, gorgeous, and the stick is awkward. The femme fatale sees the game to be played and I think she'll never match him but she rushes over and with great style says, "Oh you've taken my most treasured possession (pause), my walking stick."

I think she is incredible. I thought she was going to say "hat," but no it's the walking stick.

He backs up into a beautiful glass and gold shelving display case full of the most priceless and exquisite dishes. The whole case goes over, as does he, and we realize in a split second—the game—and that it is over. Those dishes cannot ever be replaced. I can still see those dishes go.

The dream takes place in a glittering, artificial setting in which the assembled guests are playing charades. The game suggests that there is something unreal going on in the dreamer's life situation. When she looks down from the balcony she sees two beds, one double (which she has shared with David, her father-animus) and one single which is her own. The other side of her father is the puer Bobby, who constellates in her either the mother or the femme fatale. (Bobby sitting on her lap, both in the armchair, creates an interesting caricature of da Vinci's drawing of the Virgin and St. Anne; see page 128).

Seated in an armchair (from her own virgin position), the dreamer reveals that she has been trying to manipulate the guests, but then she's not sure they are impressed. The demon lover as he appears in the dream is the perfect trickster; dressed in an old-fashioned, elegant black costume, his exaggerated dignity suggests a performance. His extraordinary hat covered with jewels suggests the inflated importance that has been given to the head (intellectual and spiritual values) and a misplaced femininity. He is carrying the actress's most treasured possession, her black ebony stick with a silver bar on the bottom. The image makes clear the relationship between the witch and the demon lover: he carries her phallic broomstick, but in this case the silver bar (like the handless maiden's silver hands) does not allow the stick to touch the ground. There is a confusion of gender, both with the hat and with the stick. When she confronts him he falls back; in his fall he smashes the precious delicate dishes, and the game is over.

All the imagery in the dream suggests a feeling problem, but we need only focus on the ebony stick. It is not rightfully his. It belongs to the feminine witch. Its blackness suggests depression, but the depression is not grounded. The silver base blocks the black stick from the earth. Somewhere in Louise's psyche there is a depression masquerading as witch feeling, but it is not spontaneous—what is known psychologically as a "smiling depression." The demon lover, connected to the mauve silk bedspread, has usurped feminine feelings, but they are not real. The homosexual undertones in the demon lover are evident, as is the masculinity in the femme fatale. They manifest in a polished performance. The finale suggests that the dreamer is ready to end the charade, smash that artificial world. She sees through the performance of the witch and the demon lover. To smash that china world in the elegant display case of her traditional family values, the dreamer will have to differentiate her own feminine feelings. Commenting on the dream, Louise said:

> I'll never forget seeing those exquisite dishes shattering. He literally careened into them. It was awe-ful. I saw the trap that beauty is for me—beautiful objects, beautiful men, beautiful shows. I saw the paradox. By projecting all my own beauty out, I lost interest in myself. Now I am taking the projection off the perfect world. It was awe-ful to watch it go down. Destroying anything that is beautiful is terrible! But I feel its inevitability. Breakdown leads to breakthrough. I saw it go down. I don't want it anymore. I want my own life.

Feeling can be taken away from the demon lover in even small instances. If, for example, a woman is massaging her husband's feet and he goes to sleep, she may pinch his toes until he wakes up, demanding, "What's the point in my massaging your feet? You just go to sleep."

But if instead of getting angry or annoyed, she ponders his beatific peace, she may say to herself, "I enjoy massaging his feet. He enjoys his sleep. I enjoy caressing—hmmm—or is it manipulating? Who am I trying to please? What do I want out of this? To make love? No. I'm doing this for me. So dream on, my love." Then she is in touch with her own feeling; her hands are living hands, not silver ones.

The psychological situation is quite different where the woman is caught in unconscious identification with the mother. Then she has to be raped out of that identification before she can find her own individuality. This is the meaning of the Demeter-Persephone myth, where the Kore is carried off to the underworld by Hades. Commenting on this myth in the "The Psychological Aspects of the Kore," Jung writes:

The psyche pre-existent to consciousness (e.g., in the child) partici-
pates in the maternal psyche on the one hand, while on the other it
reaches across to the daughter psyche. We could therefore say that
every mother contains her daughter in herself and every daughter her
mother, and that every woman extends backwards into her mother
and forwards into her daughter.... The conscious experience of these
ties produces the feeling that her life is spread out over generations—
the first step towards the immediate experience and conviction of
being outside time, which brings with it a feeling of *immortality* ... An
experience of this kind gives the individual a place and a meaning in
the life of the generations, so that all unnecessary obstacles are
cleared out of the way of the life-stream that is to flow through her.
At the same time the individual is rescued from her isolation and
restored to wholeness. All ritual preoccupation with archetypes ultimately has this aim and this result.[17]

The supreme feminine principle, represented in the myth by
Gaia, knows that Demeter, the established mother, must bear the
ravishment of her daughter. In order for renewal to take place
within the feminine principle, the young girl (who might prefer to
stay with the mother) has to be carried into the underworld and
experience there the penetration and impregnation by the creative
masculine. Thus new life is born. This is the cycle of nature: summer
moves into autumn, the seeds of autumn lie in the ground during
the winter and sacrifice themselves to the new life in the spring. In
the individual woman's life, in a natural life cycle, the old value
system (Demeter) grieves, while the new value system (Persephone)
is ravished by the otherness that penetrates her and brings new life;
then old and new are reunited in a new way. Between mother and
daughter a similar transformation naturally takes place, if it is allowed to. The wise mother knows that the maiden must give herself
up to ravishment if new life is to be born and the life cycle continue.

It seems to me that what we are seeing in our culture is a
breakdown of that feminine mystery. Generations of women have
assimilated the patriarchal value system, each generation slightly
more removed from the feminine principle, until now Demeter and
Persephone are both raped by their masculine side. If a woman
cannot contact her own maiden, she cannot be ravished. She is not
present enough in her own being to receive the masculine. The
masculine power principle stands like a solid wall between her and
her own femininity. As one of my male analysands so bluntly told
me, "The cunt is the last stronghold of the negative animus." She
cannot give herself up to life; she cannot open herself to otherness
either on a human or divine level. She is afraid because "letting go"
means falling into an abyss, falling into blackness which is total
chaos, and the tragedy is that the harder she tries, the more she is
closing herself off. That masculine "trying" does not permit the

*There lives the dearest freshness deep down things;*
*And though the last lights off the black West went*
   *Oh, morning, at the brown brink eastward, springs—*
*Because the Holy Ghost over the bent*
   *World broods with warm breast and with ah! bright*
*wings.*
   —Gerard Manley Hopkins, "God's Grandeur."

feminine "letting go," letting life flow in, not only through the genitalia, but through every pore of the skin. She may have no idea what is wrong because her own Demeter mother was in the same situation—her Persephone too was raped, but never ravished, so that the feminine mode of relationship is either infantile or still in utero.

If Demeter is out of touch with her inner Persephone, she is out of touch with her own essence. Persephone is the maiden who looks in the looking glass and goes through to the other side, opens herself to the wealth of that inner world, experiences the ravishment and returns with a wealth of sensitivity and a sense of her own uniqueness—bearing new life. Without Persephone, Demeter is barren. In the myth, she turns her back on her own ground.

Modern Demeters are beginning to realize that their own earth has been ravaged and they are becoming so aware of the violation that they are trying to do something about it, not only for themselves but for their Persephones, their own biological daughters and psychological daughters. They realize they have been raped by the one-sidedness of the masculine principle that thrusts toward the goal without enjoying the pleasure of the journey. They realize that sexuality is far more than orgasm, and having a beautiful body more than fitting into a size ten dress. In my office I repeatedly hear comments such as the following:

"I can't subject myself to that again. I went to the hospital. They treated me like a machine. They put steel plates into me and around me as if I were part of the steel. I was raped. They didn't tell me why they were doing it. It was as if I didn't matter at all. My body just cried."

"Abortion is something more than getting rid of a foetus. My baby would have been three months old now, and I can't stop crying. I didn't know what I was doing. It seemed the sensible thing to do."

"I used to want to be raped. There was terrible hostility in it. I was daring the poor whimp to overcome me. I wanted my civilized, cultured man to suddenly revert to cave man and transport me to a sexual nirvana. I put it all on him. Now what a relief just to *be* there."

"My thesis director demands his kind of perfection. Every time we meet I feel I have been violated. My reality has been violently denied. But I can't stay with my own values. I identify with my animus and my own anger and self-criticism paralyze me. I can't write a word. I feel like the student in Ionesco's *The Lesson*."

"I don't understand the stone on my chest. I feel I can't breathe. I hear my mother saying, 'You shouldn't be tired,' but I'm exhausted. I am terrified that James will leave me. I hate myself for the dependence. And the truth is I'm not dependent, but the thought of him leaving kills me. All the time I am trying to let him go, I am desperately holding onto him. I know he feels that."

"I'm going to have my life. I can begin to feel it now. I think I was traumatized before I was born. My mother didn't want me. I've lived trying to be invisible. My body never cried out for anything. Now I'm dancing my own animal and is she happy!"

"So long as I can feel my hipbone I know I'm defined enough. The more direct I am, the less padding I need. When I'm muffled up with fat, I know I'm violating myself. I've lost my sword of discretion."

"I not only raped my whore. I tried to kill her. My eating was her passion for life gone crazy."

"My mother was like the English mother who wept as she said good-bye to her daughter going off to be married in the colonies. 'Never say *no* to your husband, my dear. Just lie back and open your legs and think of England.'"

The 1980's woman is realizing that her psyche has been raped as her mother's before her was raped. If she is conscious, she does not blame her parents, nor the men in her personal and professional life. She recognizes that both sexes are in the crisis together and she has to accept her own share of responsibility. Having carried the perfectionist standards of parents, teachers and society in general, her own world of inner uniqueness has been violated to the point where she fears even to look into the mirror, for fear she won't be there. Her husband, brothers and sons are in an equally precarious position. Moreover, perfectionist standards do not allow for failure. They do not even allow for life, and certainly not for death. Because life cannot be accepted and lived with the loving forgiveness of self and loved ones, death is perceived as the ultimate rape. Death perceived in that way precludes any possibility of vindication or resurrection.

I have said earlier that the feminine ego can be terrorized by the masculine and its only defense is its authentic feeling. The tragedy, however, is that in many cases the woman's feelings are so unrecognized that in a crisis they cannot be mobilized to protect her.

One example of a situation in which the feelings *were* mobilized may demonstrate both the kind of danger the demon lover complex can constellate and the feminine harnessing of strength that is required to break free of it. As will be apparent, the woman was sufficiently in touch with her feminine feeling to relax into it in order to immobilize the complex.

Ingrid was a woman in her mid-twenties. She had been traveling alone and arrived late one afternoon in a foreign city. She had to cross from one railway station to another. Suddenly she was accosted in the deserted street by a powerfully-built man who forced her into an alleyway, saying he was going to rape and kill her. Her initial reaction was panic, and she tried to fight back. But he was stronger. Then in a flash she saw the situation she was in; she saw the man; she saw herself. She accepted her death, her body relaxed and she looked straight into the man's eyes. Immediately, his fingers loosened on her throat.

"You don't even fight," he stammered. "You're no fun to kill."

"If I'm going to die, I'm going to die," she said quietly, never taking her eyes from his.

He became confused. She put her hands over his and gently took them from her throat. He began to cry, grabbed her by the wrist and yanked her into a nearby pub from which she escaped when he went to the washroom.

In the bar, he told her he had been watching her in the train coach in which they were both traveling. Immersed in a book, dreaming from time to time out the window, she was unaware of his presence. He, meanwhile, apparently thought that she was casting a spell on him. What *he* saw was a woman pretending to read while secretly concentrating on luring him into her feminine web. To break that spell, he would have to penetrate her. The rape and murder in the alleyway would be at once the gratification of the desire that her witchery had aroused in him and his release from it.

Although it seems likely that the man was psychopathic, the woman herself was not entirely blameless. She was in fact a dreamer who had blocked out the real world on the train and was lost in fantasies of her demon lover. She had undertaken the trip in an effort to overcome the pain of a broken relationship, and fasting had been part of her purifying plan. This city was her last stop on her homeward journey. Six weeks of near starvation had brought her to an almost bodiless state, detached from the world around her. Still enthralled by her "ideal" lover she was more ready to free herself into death than to move back into the reality of her responsibilities at home. What she was so "innocently" dreaming as she watched the world pass by, the man was picking up. She was willing to be sacrificed; he was willing to be sacrificer. Together, they were one. Unconsciously, at opposite ends of the coach, they constellated the wound and the sword.

When she was *actually* confronted with death, however, she experienced her humanness and fought for her life. Had the man been her lover, the complex might have carried her into death (like Othello's Desdemona). But the man was a stranger, and his very strangeness knocked her out of her fantasy world into reality. So long as he was "rapist" in her mind, and she was "victim," her violence mirrored his. Death was constellated. He wanted her to fight so he could kill. But when she suddenly saw herself as one human being strangling in another human being's clutches, her compassion for herself became at once compassion for him. She had accepted death; she saw him still in life, still fighting some ludicrous power battle. She was out of such conflicts and her visceral compassion transformed the demonic situation. Paradoxically, she became invulnerable through her very vulnerability. He could not kill what had already died. In that instant of surrender, she freed them both from the possession. She found herself and gave him back to himself. He was no longer "rapist"; he was simply human. In his tears, there may have been healing.

This incident had nothing to do with willing another person to do anything, nothing to do with manipulation or magic. There was no time to think, no time to understand. The young woman's experience of life could not possibly have helped her to understand how the rapist thought. Thinking in that moment would have meant death. What she was able to do was to concentrate her whole Being on that moment, open herself to its reality and receive what was flowing through her, exactly what was required in the situation. It is akin to what Joseph Chilton Pearce describes as *primary process* functioning.[18]

This experience turned Ingrid's life around. She had lived in a world of yearning for perfection, yearning for the perfect lover who would make all things right. She had believed that if she could be as perfect as possible, and love as perfectly as possible, and yearn as perfectly as possible—somehow that perfect yearning would magically be returned in perfectly possessing. In her fantasy world, "I want" was equated with "I get." Everything in that magic world depended on her to make it so. As long as she was manipulating, she could never relax into accepting it as hers. So long as she and her lover were trying to create a world out of their own projected desires, she could not be herself and her lover could not be himself. She was willing to put everything into making her fantasy become real. She had thus lived in a world of witchery, a world of magic. She now recognized that magic is delusion—that the world she was attempting to create she could not possess even if God answered her prayers. Something entirely new had penetrated her, something so vast that she had no choice but to surrender. In accepting that impersonal power, she saw how egocentric and manipulative her yearning had been. She set out on her journey a still unravished bride; she returned home unraped but ravished. She returned with a depth-experience of the feminine mysteries—the recognition that when what is inside naturally comes together with what is outside, that is a miracle—not magic. She inadvertently had opened herself to that greater Reality.

In mythological terms, we can see Ingrid as an innocent Persephone picking a narcissus in the Paradise of her imagination, when she was suddenly seized and carried off into what might have been a death-marriage. This Persephone, at twenty-five, had not developed a conscious enough ego to take responsibility for what was filtering out from her own unconscious into the world. In her professional life, she had developed a good persona and a good ego relationship to the outer world, but in this situation on the train, her unconscious was replacing the function of the absent ego. She was unaware of what was happening, namely the constellation of her demon lover. In the actual life and death situation, she momentarily died and in dying opened her material body to the Self, her inner Sophia. That spirit penetrated to the depths of the two human beings involved and transformed them. Thus the dark powers of the underworld, the unconscious, were broken, and a new woman was born out of that experience. By contacting her chthonic mother, she released her spiritual virgin.

In telling Ingrid's story, I am in no way minimizing the guilt of the rapist, nor am I blaming Ingrid, nor am I dealing with the legal and moral issues involved. I am suggesting, however, that we are as answerable to our own unconscious as we are to moral and legal codes, and I have considered this episode solely in terms of the unconscious factors involved. We are participants in our own destiny. Only by keeping in touch with our own feminine principle can we be aware of ourselves and others as human beings in the reality of the moment.

A woman can, out of her own biological nature, experience life as meaningful without knowing herself. In giving birth and nurturing, nature affirms her. But nature itself is unconscious. The woman, unlike the man who cannot give birth in the biological sense, has a natural fulfillment within nature, within unconsciousness. Psychological rape, therefore, is traumatic for a woman because to separate her out from her unconscious nature confronts her at first with extinction. This is the paradox of rape. It may be either destructive or creative. Before the woman can consciously confront the primal separation from the mother, which is the birth of her own identity, she must fully prepare herself. Her task is to bring nature into consciousness, including her own nature. Science attempts to understand nature but too often its methods are rape and exploitation. The feminine way is very different. Through the opening of the feminine, love can enter, thereby bringing with it awareness of what von Franz calls "the star"—the uniqueness of the individual in eternity.[19] Only through the feminine can creation complete itself in consciousness.

Somewhere at the center of this mystery is Reality. It has to do with the sanctification of matter. It is a mystery to be experienced; it cannot be verbalized, because it has to do with *knowing*. The pondering of that mystery is what I see as the task of the modern woman. It is an immediate and crucial task if our planet and our individual souls are to survive.

*A SUDDEN blow: the great wings beating still*
*Above the staggering girl, her thighs caressed*
*By the dark webs, her nape caught in his bill,*
*He holds her helpless breast upon his breast.*

*How can those terrified vague fingers push*
*The feathered glory from her loosening thighs?*
*And how can body, laid in that white rush,*
*But feel the strange heart beating where it lies?*

*A shudder in the loins engenders there*
*The broken wall, the burning roof and tower*
*And Agamemnon dead.*
                                    *Being so caught up,*
*So mastered by the brute blood of the air,*
*Did she put on his knowledge with his power*
*Before the indifferent beak could let her drop?*

—W.B. Yeats, "Leda and the Swan."

*When the god, needing something, decided to become a swan,*
*he was astounded how lovely the bird was;*
*he was dizzy as he disappeared into the swan.*
*But his deceiving act soon pulled him into the doing,*

*before he had a chance to test all the new feelings*
*inside the being. And the woman, open to him,*
*recognized the One Soon To Be in the swan*
*and she knew: what he asked for*

*was something which, confused in her defending, she*
*could no longer keep from him. He pressed closer*
*and pushing his neck through her less and less firm hand*

*let the god loose into the darling woman.*
*Then for the first time he found his feathers marvelous*
*and lying in her soft place he became a swan.*

—Rainer Maria Rilke, "Leda."

# 8

## The Ravished Bride

*Batter my heart, three-personed God, for you*
*As yet but knock, breathe, shine, and seek to mend.*
*That I may rise and stand, o'erthrow me and bend*
*Your force to break, blow, burn, and make me new.*
*I, like an usurped town to another due,*
*Labor to admit you, but oh, to no end!*
*Reason, your viceroy in me, me should defend,*
*But is captived, and proves weak or untrue.*
*Yet dearly I love you and would be loved fain,*
*But am betrothed unto your enemy.*
*Divorce me, untie, or break that knot again,*
*Take me to you, imprison me, for I,*
*Except you enthrall me, never shall be free,*
*Nor ever chaste except you ravish me.*

—John Donne, "Holy Sonnet."

In every creation myth a Divine Being creates a cosmos imaged as a container and a contained. Every culture moves toward the complete adjustment of the contained to its container. Culture assumes that we dwell within a universe that is our home. The loss of this home, for whatever reason, is the origin of neuroses: the contained has lost its container.

Images of disintegration flood the dreams of men and women when their individual, emotional and religious containers break down. The Earth, far from being a fixed center directed by an understanding Father God, becomes a desert of nothingness, whirling through endless space without a divine purpose. The dreamer, like King Lear on the heath, then experiences psychic exile, wandering from one place to another trying to find Home, and again and again sadly recognizing, "It wasn't really mine." Dreams of cyclones tearing out the inside of the house, and dreams of attempting to rebuild within the gutted framework, show the inner anguish and chaos. They show too how critical our individual and cultural homelessness is. For many of us, the Western world's containers are broken.

If it were possible simply to return to the Church, or to whatever our faith may have been, if it were possible to say this whole modern movement is a bad mistake, or even a nightmare from which we will awake, then my waiting-room would be virtually

157

empty. The institutions are still there. For many, however, their efficacy is gone. There seems to be no way to survive except to build an inner home out of the wreckage of our traditional structures.

I am very much aware of the irony of the medieval imagery that dominates this study. I know that the Madonna on the lap of the Great Mother, historically and culturally, belongs more to Chartres and the 12th century than to the woman who sits across from me at four o'clock in the afternoon in 1982. To believe that she, in the midst of her complicated life, can rebuild within herself the culture that reached its apex in the 13th century would be ludicrous. I am aware that there is almost nothing in our culture today that offers outward, tangible support to what we are trying to build within. But what we have that was not available to the 13th-century pilgrim to the throne of the Virgin is a more fully acknowledged consciousness of what that pilgrimage means symbolically. That consciousness is often the fruit of a neurosis, of a profound psychological experience of our own feminine nature, which, by a grace that cuts across the centuries, makes the 20th-century woman the true sister of the 13th-century pilgrim, even the sister of the pilgrims who journeyed to Eleusis. The archetypal patterns that connect us are eternal.

Each of us builds our inner container with the images that are most meaningful to us. As a child, the entire context of my life was shaped by the Church and the Bible. As I grew older I began to feel a lack of inner reality. I wanted to *know,* rather than to believe. After I entered analysis, I realized that the fabric of my dreams was woven with Biblical imagery, symbols that brought vibrant energy into my waking life. Thus I was reconnected to my archetypal roots. While the ancient myths bring invaluable psychological insights, I find my Home in the Christian imagery, albeit in an unorthodox way. I am neither a philosopher nor a theologian. I am a woman searching for the meaning of my life, and my dreams are filling in the feminine gaps left by my Christian heritage. Consequently the image of the Virgin, in terms of her relationship to the Great Mother, the Great Father and the Divine Child, is for me a crucial one. Each culture, of course, has its own mythology, as does each individual. But far from being separated by the differences, I find my analysands—Jewish, Buddhist, Christian, atheist—and I are joined through similar symbols that relate to the Grand Mother and the human woman who miraculously bears a male child. Our paths are somewhat different, but our goal is the same. It makes us realize that the collective unconscious is available to each of us in any given moment. Chartres, Jerusalem or Home is wherever we happen to be, even in a consulting room at four in the afternoon. The mystery of this psychic fact belongs to feminine consciousness.

This is the mystery pondered by many women in their dreams. The fear of invasion by the unconscious is so real that it often takes months, even years, to come to the point of trusting and letting go in the moment. If we have been the enemy of our inner Great Mother for most of our lives, she is not willing to let us go without some revenge. One woman, after three years of analysis and three days of experiencing autonomous rage welling up from inside her, recorded the following awesome encounter:

*Ego:* What is this rage?

*Great Mater:* You with your mewling humanness, your finite beingness! I accept that. It belongs to me. My matter rages. I am the matter, and matter rages.

*Ego:* My humanness isn't raging.

*Great Mater:* It is a matter of survival. It is My matter of survival. Too many times I trusted, too many times was I betrayed. You think I'll trust again—NEVER. While you were undifferentiated matter I wreaked my revenge so subtly that nobody realized what was happening. I destroyed by devouring the new babes, wrapped them in my embrace and suffocated them. They breathed from breath that I allowed them to breathe. Now you want to take that from me. You actually dare to trespass in my realm. I'll not have it! You dare to claim what I am! Claim it as your own? I gave and I can take away.

*Ego:* How can I appease your wrath? How can your rage be tempered?

*Great Mater:* Who says it can be?

*Ego:* We are trying, we are working to bring awareness to your plight.

*Great Mater:* Then don't call it yours!

*Ego:* But it is mine. If, as you say, I am of you, then your grief, your betrayal, your rage, are also mine. I can't let that rage destroy what we've worked at great risk and with great [conscious] humility to activate. You say so long as I was a blob of matter—a blob of you—without recognition, then you could have your way. But isn't this recognition of you and the acceptance of the responsibility what you've really wanted? Remember? When you nurtured the child of yourself, remember? When you infused your greatness into the child of your womb, remember? Perhaps everything did go sour, but you are giving birth now to a new type of being—a being who can and will honor you. Please don't rage at her. She's new and frightened at her huge responsibility. She needs you. She needs your nurturing. She needs to learn what you are truly about. You are part of her heritage. Help her. She is a new breed. She'll survive and her survival is your survival.

The passage suggests one cause for the unaccountable rage that many women feel.

As the woman begins to experience her own ego and actually confronts the complexes, an agonizing and confusing period ensues.

It is as if the complex (like Medusa) has been forever sitting like a great witch at the center of the psyche without manifesting its real strength, because being in control it did not have to fight. Once its power is genuinely threatened, however, it rears its full force against the ego, and the woman feels that all the hours of analysis have been for nothing. The situation is worse now than it ever was. There may be danger of suicide, for although a person enters analysis with the hope of change, when the possibility of radical transformation presents itself, it brings with it considerable fear. Once the door is opened, the bird who has lived in a cage all its life shrinks back from freedom and the terrors of the unknown.

It is the Self, the ordering center of the personality, that presents the ego with the challenge to move to a new level of consciousness. If the ego is afraid to make the passover, preferring to clutch at what it has always known, then psychological and physiological symptoms break out. These the ego has to deal with, for learning the meaning of these symptoms and situations is what leads to the new level of awareness and a new harmonious balance between consciousness and the unconscious. So long as consciousness is afraid to open itself to "the otherness" of the unconscious, it experiences itself as the victim. Once it is able to open itself to the new life flowing through, it becomes the beloved. To be a victim is to be raped; to be the beloved is to be ravished.

Ravishment, unlike rape, involves the integration of unconscious contents so that instead of being overpowered by "higher" or "greater" forces (i.e., archetypal contents), one enters into a loving relationship with them. Ravishment can only be experienced when the ego is a sufficiently strong container to receive the dynamic energy bursting through. Paradoxically, that point can only be reached when the ego is strong enough to be vulnerable enough to surrender. That, for the woman, is the point where her own feminine ego is so firmly planted in her biological roots that she is free to take on her own biological and spiritual identity. Then she is truly the virgin sitting on the lap of Sophia, ready to give birth to her own divine child.

At this stage of psychological development one must be most discriminating, because the witch mother has created a witch child and that tyrannical, ignorant child may attempt to control even a well-educated, disciplined, brilliantly creative adult. The witch child will be expressing all the repressed energy locked in the instinctual needs that were denied in childhood. Released from the oppressive silence by the dreams, the witch child is now in a position to have her revenge. The struggle with the negative mother, which could not be faced earlier, now has to be confronted. That child, in the guise of bladder, binging, begging, bragging, etc., now looks for a loving mother to care for her; in return for that loving, she will give back the life that stopped when the problem began. Being tyrannical, she will use the adult woman as the vehicle for her own unlived life. The woman dare not identify with this child. The danger of regression in analysis is that instead of exorcising the witch, the witch child is released. Some of her anger, hunger and grief has to be expressed, but to go through that cycle again and again can become self-indulgence. The dreams make clear where the energy wants to go—after the washing is done or the toilets are emptied. The negative energy, instead of being repeatedly recycled, will attempt to transform if the ego takes up the challenge. The witch child has to be sacrificed.

This is a period in analysis where I have found body work particularly helpful. Like the psyche, the body has lived its life holding on. Now the holding becomes conscious and manifests in pain. As loving mother to her own body, the woman can allow it to relax into her own love. Strong lesbian feelings often emerge because the feminine body needs the love of a woman in order to accept itself. Sometimes that need has to be projected in order to be recognized, in which case a lesbian relationship may happen. Often it is enacted in dreams. Physical cherishing by a woman, whether sexual or platonic, gives the feminine ego the grounding it requires. Body work is looking in the mirror-shield, gradually moving in, without facing Medusa directly.

Body awareness gradually dispels the seductive fantasy world. So long as a woman indulges in fantasy, she is like Andromeda in the Perseus myth (above, pages 8-10), chained to the rock of the mother, waiting to be sacrificed to the demon lover monster. Far from doing anything to save her, he demands her life as sacrifice. The inert mass of rock is the other side of the demon in the sea—both are contaminated with arrogance and inflation. By refusing to be caught in a web of fruitless fantasy, a woman opens herself to her own humanity, and having located herself in Now, she simultaneously opens herself to the divine (as did Ingrid, described in chapter seven). Armed with the sword of discretion, she then knows what the moment requires and releases herself into her own life.

Looking into the shield which bears the image of Medusa is taking guidance from the Self, recognizing the light and dark sides of the Goddess. Warring against Medusa is not warring against flesh and blood, though Medusa's snaky, grasping locks would suggest a sexual or food problem. Warring against Medusa is warring against evil. Reflecting on Medusa in the mirror prevents the direct confrontation which would actually constellate her; in confrontation she is

Perseus and Andromeda.—Titian. (Wallace Collection, London)

almost inevitably stronger than the ego. When it is clear from the
dreams and from the symptoms that a sacrifice must be made, then
the ego has to open itself to the supportive strength of the Self.

The woman's positive animus, symbolized in the myth by Perseus,
is her guide to the Self, and it is his sword of discretion which gives
her a true sense of who she is. Perseus carries the shield, the silver
mirror, the medium in which are revealed the healing symbols aris-
ing from the unconscious. The mirror is the stage on which creative
fantasy plays in the form of symbols. Watching the symbols is
dealing indirectly with Medusa; that is the only way to avoid identifying with her. Negative and positive symbols will appear in the
mirror. They cannot be united rationally, but in reflection something
new arises that partakes of both, and yet is neither. Energy plays
through the symbol without being trapped in it. The wind of the
Holy Spirit "bloweth where it listeth," from positive to negative with
the same ease that a sail turns with the shifting wind. The ego learns

to adjust moment by moment. The position of the sail in one moment is not its position in the next, and if we try to hold on in the new moment to what was appropriate in the old, the boat turns over. As soon as we lock the sail or the rudder into position, we are in a complex, the ego-Self axis is broken and we drown in unconsciousness. It is crucial that the right hand know what the left hand is doing because there must be synchronicity between rudder and sail, matter and spirit. This is not a crucified man hammered to the opposites, for it is neither one nor the other, but both. This is living the symbolic life, the life that comes about through reflection.

If we ask the right question, "Do I see what I am doing?"—then we are alive in the moment. If we ask the wrong question, then we paralyze ourselves because the right hand may not know what the left is doing. Consciousness has to be brought to its proper object, which is not the paralyzing awareness of separate parts (right and left) but consciousness of the whole. The wrong question is fatal. Medusa paralyzes because she drives consciousness to the wrong object. She forces us to isolate the muffin from the total body/spirit relationship, and by ruthlessly severing the muffin from its organic relation to the whole she renders it numinous and taboo. The muffin can be eaten, not as a thing but as an acceptance of the I AM, the union of body and spirit, only by accepting one's own wholeness and one's whole relationship to everything. The muffin then becomes part of our wholeness, released from Medusa's fixated consciousness. It becomes part of a synchronistic cosmos in which whatever is spirit is matter, and whatever is matter is spirit. Centered in that kind of wholeness, the ego becomes strong enough to give up its rigidity, strong enough to receive the Otherness of the Self.

At each stage of psychological development, the Self demands some sacrifice. It is no longer a case of "Thy will be done—my way." Sometimes we may rationally or idealistically decide to make a sacrifice, but unless the time is right, sacrifice is self-dramatization. The dreams make clear the real sacrifice that is demanded. Sometimes we are called upon to give up the part of our life that we hold most dear, and the fear and loneliness involved in that inner decision dare not be underestimated. At the same time as we are making the sacrifice, we are also required to meet the challenge of the new life. This is a time of darkness; it requires time and patience, space and meditation. So long as our psychological heritage is sound, we can trust that the Self will not demand more of us than we are able to give. We can't get away with offering the starving calf; it has to be the fatted one.

Sarah, middle-aged, with four years of analysis and several years of yoga and dance, was beginning to sense that a momentous change was coming into her life—the loss of a precious relationship. She was unable to make the sacrifice the Self was demanding. Just before events forced the sacrifice which she was still unable to endure, the following dream was given:

> I am falling through black space—falling, falling through the universe with terrible fear. Suddenly I land on what seems to be a beach. It is dark. I sit motionless. Then I touch the sand with my fingers. It's strange. I push my fingers through it, and realize it is not sand but feathers. They are soft, but strong. Then I see myself as a pinpoint resting on immense, outstretched wings with the sunrise etching the magnificent bird in gold. It is a dove. I wake up Knowing.

It was the power of the everlasting wings that emanated through the dreamer's soul and body. For the first time in her life she was able to allow her body to relax and open itself to whatever life would bring. She was able to give herself permission to play. *Being* became the exquisite beauty of plum blossoms in spring, the fragrance of wet grass, the crystal song of a robin at dawn. Having experienced and honored her body as never before, she was able to accept with certain equanimity what would otherwise have been a crushing blow. What sustained her was the "knowing," the shift from the personal, transitory empire, which she had tried so diligently to control, to the transpersonal, eternal Loving to which she surrendered. The experience of surrender was in her body when she awoke; her armor against the world was temporarily gone; her five senses were five portals through which life could flow into her, so that she could consciously experience the visible world and experience the Love that permeated it and her as part of that totality. Death was a part of that world, a dignified part of a greater scheme. The dove, the Holy Spirit, Sophia, the feminine side of Christ—by whatever name we call it, it is Love that opens body and soul to the eternal. In psychological language, it is the connection between the instincts and the archetypal images (the energy of the body that is released into the spirit, and the spirit illuminating the body) that brings about the harmony.

In the harrowing weeks that followed, Sarah did not ask the one question that had driven her all her life, "Why?" Instead she returned repeatedly to this dream, repeatedly surrendered her body, her actual muscles, to the grief and anger and love that assailed her. In the blackness of her despair, she found the dignity to walk consciously with her loss. She never betrayed her personal feeling. She loved enough to let go, and that love kept her connected to her own inner reality and the real values within her actual situation. She found a Home for her stricken heart.

It is extremely important to stress here that this experience of the

Goddess was given after years of commitment to that transpersonal power. The fear that men and women have of her bloody demands is quite warranted. Describing the rituals celebrated for the Great Mother, Erich Neumann writes:

> The womb of the earth clamors for fertilization, and blood sacrifices and corpses are the food she likes best. This is the terrible aspect, the deadly side of the earth's character. In the earliest fertility cults, the gory fragments of the sacrificial victim were handed round as precious gifts and offered up to the earth, in order to make her fruitful.[1]

The emergence of the feminine in our time carries with it all the primordial fear attributed to chthonic power. While women do not want to be deprived of the chthonic energy, neither do they wish to be reduced to it. In Picasso's powerful portrayal of the five women in *Les Demoiselles d'Avignon* (the title refers to a Barcelona red light district), they are reduced to fetish figures, two of whose faces are based on African ceremonial masks. Robert Rosenblum, commenting on this painting, says:

> The most immediate quality of *Les Demoiselles* is a barbaric, dissonant power whose excitement and savagery were paralleled not only by such eruptions of vital energy as Matisse's art of 1905-10, but by music of the following decade.... No masterpiece of Western painting has reverberated so far back in time as Picasso's five heroic nudes who carry across centuries and millenniums.[2]

Picasso is prophetic in his identification of the creativity of this century with feminine chthonic energy. Like so many artists who tapped the same source, he never differentiated real women from this archetypal image, but women themselves, rejecting their identification with it, have sought, and continue to seek, ways of bringing their own feminine energy out of the Barcelona brothel where Picasso located them.

The Goddess is demanding confrontation, and she is demanding it where it hurts most—through loss of families, loss of traditional faiths, weight problems, cancer, etc. If we turn our backs on that confrontation, we do pay in blood. If in the quietness of our own souls we go in to meet her, we find not a raving, bloodthirsty Archemaenad, but a Reality that turns life around. So long as we are afraid, so long as we ignore her, she is our enemy; when we turn to her with love, gradually she is vindicated. The ego has to surrender to the eye (see page 32): if unconscious, it surrenders to Medusa; if conscious, it surrenders to Sophia.

Maggie, after three years of analysis and body work, was ready to turn to the Goddess with love. She recorded the following active imagination:

I was drawn into the black. It was full of images. I sensed rather than saw them. They seemed more like voices than pictures. It was shown me that the black was necessary and what was within the blackness was the Light and the blackness was the protection. It was not yet time for that Light to be born. It was incubating, gaining strength in the blackness. It was like knowing the inside of a womb. I saw it all through the Knowing. It took me three days to do the painting [see opposite], three days to Know. I had no choice but to do it.

The singular thing it did for me was to clarify again at a level that could not be articulated that I was not alone. It was much broader, much more cosmic than my own aloneness. It was as though I had seen through a veil. It strengthened me unbelievably. I didn't do anything with it analytically. There was no need. I was part of it, but it was not unique to me. It was like the gestation of God.

It was a babe, but only in the sense that it was new. It was as if I had glimpsed a baby growing in the cosmic womb. I glimpsed Something in its borning. It was already born; it was just waiting for the right time. There was no feeling of any decision being made. It didn't resent my seeing. It seemed to be saying, "I have to wait until I am recognized. This is the new dispensation."

Four great serpents appeared, the loving guardians of Something so wonderful, like playmates. Everything in that circle was for and of that newness.

Then I had to concentrate on my own blackness and find out what was there. I had to look at my own reality. It was awesome, fearful and exciting. Had I a choice I don't know that I would have risked it. I'm not sorry I did. It was as if that was the beginning of my reality and I had to find my connectedness. Up to that point I didn't know what I was doing in analysis. Now I had to recognize that connectedness consciously.

The inestimable value of this experience to Maggie lies in its feeling tone, the sense of strength and commitment which it aroused in her, and the recognition that she is not alone, although her experience was unique. Having seen into the heart of darkness and glimpsed "the borning" of the God or Goddess, she recognizes that the fullness of time is not yet come, and she has work to do on her individual darkness. That work she immediately undertook in the painting which emerged over three days, bringing the symbol from the meditation into the reality of her life. At the heart of the painting is a child cradled on a crescent moon with the sun behind. Commenting on such an image, Esther Harding writes:

> The phallic god, Pallas, was not considered to be a rival deity but rather the associate of the Goddess. Each carried the symbol of fertility, but only when they were united in their functions was the "mystery" fulfilled.[3]

This same idea, that the divine power is manifested through the

union of male and female, is expressed in a symbol which is sometimes found representing the goddess Cybele, who was one aspect of
the Magna Dea. She is represented as a lunar crescent in perpetual
union with the sun.

The power of the four serpents is noteworthy in the painting, as
are the three animals in the lower half. The animals form the
instinctual foundation from which the spiritual energy (the serpents)
is rising.

To surrender to the Goddess is to plunge into paradox. Two years
after Maggie's active imagination she experienced herself being born
into a new reality. Afterward she wrote a poem she called "The
Lament," a part of which follows:

I am no more—now that I am!
I struggled—to learn not to struggle!

I fought so that I might lose!
I lived so that I might die!
I weep in joy!
I am joyous in suffering
I die so that I might live
I flow to stand still.

Extraordinary changes take place once the Goddess is accepted. Whereas before the body was a bulwark against the feminine, it now becomes the instrument through which the feminine plays. At first there is flooding of emotion, infantile regression and/or reinforcement of defenses. Those archaic contents have to be firmly channelled, otherwise Maenadic energy would take over. Sexuality previously centered in the genitalia begins to radiate through the entire body. Microcosm begins to reflect macrocosm.

Body awareness is especially important for fathers' daughters because their orientation to life has been through the mind; hence the body, whether they have been sexually active or not, is rarely in tune with the spirit.

Professional women in the fields of science and the arts are often Athenas, who have prospered through a close relationship with their father and their own masculine principle. The bright side of the father-daughter relationship is creativity and spirituality; the dark side is incest. In past generations, the problem was not so eruptive because a mature awareness of sexuality was lacking. Evidence for this is to be found in the moral outrage and outright rejection that greeted Freud's views of infantile sexuality and his recasting of original sin as the Oedipus complex. A father whose anima remains bound to the mother represses his sexuality. As a result he is not conscious of the incestuous bond with his daughter. The sexual dimension of the energy he puts into and receives from the relationship does not surface. Because the incest remains unconscious, no sacrifice takes place at any stage of the relationship. Because it does not take place, the daughter, when she reaches maturity, considers her creative ability to be the destiny her father bestowed upon her and affirms her positive relationship to him. That is, she commits herself to her positive animus and lives out as a creative person her childhood relationship to her father in a maturely creative way. Her sense of continuity—the child as mother of the woman—can be an enormous source of security and strength. Once she discovers her fate in her work she can live an extremely fulfilling life.

Now, however, these creative women who were initiated into their "calling" by their early relationship to their fathers are far more conscious of its sexual dimension. They cannot unconsciously repress their sexuality. Sexuality is the spirit of our age. When, therefore, the sexual dimension emerges at puberty, the daughter's sexuality splits off from the father and is denied the object toward which it has all along been moving. In the splitting-off of her personality, the very ground of her creativity undergoes an earth-shattering eruption. Sexually she feels abandoned or betrayed. She may even experience her creativity as her father's seduction of her, and reject it. She may, that is, experience her creativity as rape. The daughter is aware in a way that the father was not. What the father did unconsciously, she had to deal with consciously.

This era opens many options to her. The awakening of the sexual dimension in her relationship to the father may lead her to see all men as seducers or betrayers, rapists or tricksters. If she herself feels raped, she may express that feeling in the sexual revenge of the femme fatale, suffering within herself the full devastation of the body/soul split that seriously threatens her creativity. The extreme manifestation of this is prostitution.

For a woman whose sexual drive has been split off from her feelings through unconscious incest with the father, living out her sexuality will often bring the sexual issue to the kind of crisis out of which consciousness emerges. Sexuality for her is the dark side of the virgin. So long as she is spiritually impregnated by the father, her creativity is a virgin birth that has more to do with bringing forth fantasy than reality. If her fantasy creations are to become real (even as the divine becomes human), then she must be brought down from her ivory tower. She must confront and integrate the "dark side" of her creativity. She must confront the whore, the sexuality of the virgin, the whore she has been rejecting in the name of the father. She must look again at the mother. She will find in the mother what she now experiences herself to be in relation to the father: a betrayed virgin. A dynamic part of the bonding with the father may have been an unspoken alliance against the mother. Thus when the sexuality is split off it is Homeless. It has no positive feminine to settle into. The sexuality therefore goes into the negative mother. It is sexuality against the woman, against the receptive, against herself. If this negative sexuality is reinforced by a drive for revenge, the woman can be enormously destructive in almost every area of her life.

To prevent such behavior, she has to work through the negative relationship to the mother as the objective form of her own negative attitude toward herself. She arrives at the mother within herself. An old impasse has returned and this time she must deal with it consciously. She has to believe that things can change, that chronic despair is not her unalterable destiny. Sooner or later, in spite of what she thinks her mother did to her, or what her mother did to

her father, or her father allowed her mother to do to him, the
woman has to reconnect to her masculine spirit, for she needs his
sword of discrimination to cut her way through to Medusa in order
to allow her creative energy to be transformed. Then, instead of
projecting her own creativity onto men or expecting them to save
her, she takes the responsibility on herself for her own life. In short,
if a woman's creativity is threatened by the incest taboo, the problem can often be resolved through the mother. Creativity must be
grounded in the archetypal feminine. Only then can the virgin impregnated by the father seat herself on the lap of Sophia.

Julie is a father's daughter who has changed her relationship to
her body from enemy to friend through dance. The following is one
of her active imaginations:

Started with deep breathing, toning, sighing into singing.
Mind split: left side turned brilliant red, right side turned brilliant
   white.
Left side: voice was sexuality; rhythm was percussive, even beat;
   movement was jazz style, angular, playful, pulsating movements of hands, hips, shoulders, feet.
Right side: voice was pure, single, sustained note; movement in sustained curves high in the air, mostly arms. Felt very pure.
Suddenly I started to sing, "Holy, Holy, Holy, Lord God Almighty."
Sustained singing at first, gradually moving into the percussion
rhythm of the sexuality beat. "Holy, Holy, Holy" became more and
more absurd, empty-headed and meaningless. The dance movement
became percussive, sexually aggressive and as cold and mean as the
original red of the left side. My whole body went brilliant red and the
white left.
   I fell on my kness. I started to scoop up the earth. I kept saying, "I
am deep red. I am blood. I am pure red, rich blood! I am of the
earth, passionate, receptive, alive."
   I rolled over on my back to receive the life energy from above and
below. The dance became sustained, controlled, very powerful movement, very different to the empty float of the original "Holy, Holy"
dance. Then my brilliant red body with its pulsating heart filled with
consciousness and I became the heart.
   The energy of this heartbeat rooted to the earth suddenly spun off
into sheer white spiritual energy. As I breathed in, the air transformed
it into the red blood of my body; then I had that energy to send out
the white energy.
   I kept saying, "I am hot, red and white. Because I am so red I can
be white. Because I receive the energy from the earth, my red, receptive blood can give back and transform itself into the white."
   Then the pulsating action stopped. I took a kneeling prayer position, "I am because I AM. I know this. And God knows this and that
is all that matters."
   I became a pink, wild rose. My center is yellow, my leaves green. I

am merely here. No one sees me. No one needs to. I am rooted in the crevasse of the rock. The winds off the open water blow through me. My face faces the sun and the diamond reflections off the open water. I am beautiful because I am God's creation. I am safe though so delicate in this exposed landscape. And I know that I AM.

Through the bonding to Sophia, Julie has found the intimate link between body and soul. She describes it in the following vision:

I saw the Virgin Mary, sitting, holding a white water-lily in her crotch. The stem of the lily goes down between her legs and sinks deep into the depths of the water below her. She sits in peace, meditating on the open flower in her lap, but it takes all her energy to hold onto it. The lily does not sit on top of her head. She must look down into the open center of the flower, the center connected by the stem, to the center of the earth.

The vision recalls the sacred lotus flower, whose roots sink deep into the mud, whose stem rises through the water, and whose flower blossoms into the sun. The Virgin, focusing on her own creative center—not the head—makes a direct connection with the energy of the earth and has to concentrate to hold it there. The flower of the mud is spiritualized through her contemplation. Commenting on this vision, Julie wrote:

I am suddenly filled with grief and joy. The grief comes from knowing that I have never met a man, either within or without, who could see the Virgin as I saw her. It takes all the Virgin's energy and concentration to hold onto the image of the life force bursting into bloom. It is the divine sexual energy. The Virgin knows she must hold true to that moment—to hold that moment in her center of Beingness, for that is her true feminine sexual/spiritual nature. She must hold true to her knowing of the sanctification of matter, her matter mold of Being, and wait, wait for that to be brought to awareness, not knowing if that moment will ever come. Waiting with that intensity is the agony. The joy is having found the feminine purity—the moment of knowing that spirit and matter are one. But the waiting, and knowing that other women are waiting, only increases the awareness that this is how it must be for us in this culture.

When the passion for life of the whore side of the Virgin comes into harmony with the transformative spiritual side of Sophia, body and soul are one. The body is recognized as sacred space with a morality of its own which has to be honored or it will react with physical symptoms: vaginal disorders, cysts, frigidity, etc. That body morality has an extremely sensitive antenna. Matter is spiritually transformed through love. Matter becomes soul; soul becomes matter. One woman expressed it this way:

I always thought a woman could not separate her heart from her sexuality. I now believe it is the soul and the passion that cannot be

separated. A woman expresses her soul through her sexual passion.
Her passion for life is her soul and her sexuality manifests this. A
woman abandons herself in passion in the moment when soul and
body are one. This can only happen with a man she first trusts, and
secondly loves. Trusts first, because it is her soul she is abandoning
when she gives herself to passion. If she loves a man and he takes her
soul and leaves, she is left hollow. For when a woman makes love—
not genital love, but surrenders her total being—she becomes creator
and creation, and comes to know herself as a living soul. Trust is
therefore crucial to her essence. The sexual/spiritual energies woven
together through intercourse create a third. Not necessarily the birth
of a physical child, but the birth of a spiritual child, a relationship. It
is within this third that the man and woman come to know I AM.
This is the mystery—simple and profound.

The new woman, born of that sexual consciousness which was so
long denied her, is only now emerging. Finding a man who can
relate to her in her new realization of herself is becoming a huge
problem. If men are not psychologically prepared for a genuine
relationship with such a woman, they are likely to feel threatened.
This commonly manifests in rage, impotence or indifference. That is
another issue, one which our culture is just beginning to face. And
yet, in spite of the agony that may ensue in relationships, women are
being compelled to go through this psychic revolution.

In this book I have concentrated on women's experience, but this
new consciousness is manifesting also in the dreams of men. My
feeling is that because this energy is more natural to women, they
are more able to deal with it without overwhelming fear. In many
relationships the time has come to recognize the chthonic feminine
and accept it in a cherishing way that can redeem animal lust
through love. The unconscious femininity in men is as tied to the
mother as is the frail feminine ego of many modern women. That
femininity requires of men the same strength and love to release it
as does the feminine ego of women. Those women who are conscious of what the upheaval in themselves is about must take responsibility for the feeling-tone of their relationships. When their own
ego is in loving relationship with the Black Madonna, automatically
the feeling function of their male partners will change. It produces a
period of upheaval, and the result is not always positive. When it is,
however, the man experiences a new dimension to his masculinity.
One of my male analysands who had just encountered this energy in
his wife exclaimed, "I say to my friends, 'Go and get *yourself* ravished!'"

Once the woman has acknowledged her own madonna and whore
(i.e., Sophia) she finds herself pondering in a new place. There is
often a long, sometimes quiet, sometimes fiery, period of adjustment.

She is living in a body to which she is not quite accommodated. Her relationships and attitudes are confused or chaotic. Nothing is certain. Her masculine consciousness which tends to create either/or situations is being tempered by feminine consciousness which accepts paradox. She understands; she does not understand. She is learning to think with her heart. She is taken down to her bones and the questions are distilled from her lips. She stands to lose everything and she fears she has paid too much. Yet she knows she has no alternative.

One paradox which often emerges is crucial to this study. In the opening chapters, I stressed the striving for control, the need for a rigid framework in a psyche addicted to perfection. Once the feminine authority is brought to consciousness the truth can be looked at. The addiction to perfection can then be seen as a rejection of life and a denial of feminine consciousness; the striving for control is a fear of dependency—an infantile stark terror that the beloved object of that dependency cannot be depended upon for love, even for life itself.

Women today are reaping the harvest of generations of rape. Grandmothers and mothers have adjusted to patriarchal values to the point of extinguishing their own femininity. The mother who rejects her own feminine consciousness cannot see the child in its becoming; she cannot allow it to live its own imperfect humanity in its own imperfect world. Betrothed to her perfectionist standards and without her own feminine identity, consciously or unconsciously she longs for the ultimate way out of her prison. As a result, her daughter lives with a strong unconscious death wish. That very death wish may be what the young woman is attempting to redeem because, if the Great Mother rejected her birth, the feminine child has yet to be born. Her rigid routines are a framework in which she can at least survive. So long as the framework is intact, she may be dying within it without recognizing her own death.

In situations where an unconscious death wish is at work, the child will unconsciously give of its life to try to fill the need in the parent. Repeatedly, in symbiotic relationships, so long as the daughter is ill the mother is devoted to caring for her; if the daughter becomes well, the mother becomes ill. When this kind of bonding exists, the woman has to make a ruthless sacrifice of her own maternal instinct in order to release the child into its own life. That feels like suicide to the mother because she may be sacrificing the only identity she has ever known. But in losing her life, she may find it. This is the beginning of a woman's process of individuation. She finally asks, "Who am I?" Once the life force flows through her body, the woman (mother or daughter or both), because she is no longer dependent, can relinquish her need to control. The symbiotic relationship is severed. She no longer has *to try* to survive. She no longer has to die. She no longer fears an unpredictable fate. She and life are one and she is free to celebrate her own destiny.

The patriarchy that has become women's whipping post is based on an archetype of masculinity which is still in service to the Great Mother—sons who are not related in an individual way to themselves or to their feminine partners. Such men, like Macbeth, are the consorts of the Great Mother, adoring her and doing all in their power to please or appease her, at the same time fearing and hating her for usurping their masculinity. These are not heroes who have carved their way to individual freedom. Within such a situation, women for centuries have remained identified with their maternal instincts, ensconced in their biological function, fearful of being brought to consciousness. They relate in terms of mothering: to lose their children is to lose their identity. The only union mothers need is the union that will beget children. But there is another kind of union. In the Christian myth, God answered the prayers of St. Anne and she conceived Mary. Psychologically, the maternal instinct, in harmony with the Holy Spirit, gave birth to its own feminine consciousness, the Virgin. She, in the fullness of time, also opened herself to divine ravishment.

In order to grow, that is, the virgin has to be ravished out of identification with the Great Mother. As she begins to discover her own individuality through the penetration of otherness, what was formerly experienced as foreign and terrifying begins to feel like life itself flowing through her. That is the horn of the unicorn, which only a virgin can accept because she alone has the strength to open herself to his piercing awareness. So long as women remain locked in chastity belts that preclude the possibility of penetration by the phallus (physical or spiritual), they must take responsibility for the power-principled matriarchy that produces an adolescent patriarchy. Until women disidentify from the power of the Great Mother, neither they nor their masculine partners can be free.

My work with obese and anorexic women, especially if they are fathers' daughters, has made me very aware that women contending with an inner Medusa/demon lover have a different psychology from those contending with an Ereshkigal, the dark side of the Sumerian Goddess, whom Sylvia Perera so clearly describes in *Descent to the Goddess.* Their paths of healing are quite different. It becomes increasingly important to recognize which archetypal pattern is at the center of the neurosis, because if a woman is trying to contact her instincts through Ereshkigal, when in fact she should be trying to take the head off Medusa, she can find herself in paralyzing despair.

A ray from heaven illuminates the child (Mary) in St. Anne's womb.—
Hours of the Virgin, Bruges (?), *c.* 1515, by the Master of the Grimani
Breviary. (Pierpont Morgan Library, New York)

I had been pondering this difference for months, not quite satisfied with gentle Andromeda writhing on the rock as an image of
modern woman. Then Meagan, a professional woman, brought the
picture shown above. She had had a dream of blackness in which a
golden shaft of light appeared. The numinous light increased until
she was able to see herself and the man she loved bathed in golden
mist, making love within a ring of fire. A voice spoke clearly, saying,
"Yours is the spirit; his is the body. Ye two shall be one."

The dream was so powerful and authoritative that I did not tell
her it contradicted one of the basic principles of alchemy, according
to which "the male is the heaven [spirit] of the female, and the
female is the earth of the male."[4] On the other hand, it does accord
with Egyptian mythology, in which the vault of heaven is personified
as the goddess Nut and the earth as her consort Geb. In any case, as
Jung points out, even in alchemy body and spirit "are unrelated
without the soul."[5] In Meagan's dream the man had broken through
the ring of fire; the soul that unites them is their love for each other.
In their relationship, she, a father's daughter, was caught up in the
spirit until the man brought her to life—down to earth—by cherishing her body.

Further reflection brought me to Wagner's Ring Cycle. The plot
centers around the renunciation of love and the theft of the Rhine-

gold from the Rhinemaidens. The theme develops the conflict between love and power. Possession of the gold, including the ring, gives to its owner absolute power over the world. But there is a curse —he who touches the ring will be destroyed. In briefest outline, the part of the myth that amplifies the above dream has to do with Brunnhilde. She and her eight fiery sisters, the Valkyries, are spirits created by their father, Wotan, to fly through the heavens carrying the heroes to the paradise of Valhalla. Brunnhilde is an anima woman, armor-plated from head to foot by her father, riding on her winged horse, seducing men into sentimental feeling. She is their feeling relationship to perfection, a relationship that carries them off through the clouds to fight for "the cause" and ideal beauty. Wotan is the father, symbolic of greed for wealth and power, married to Fricka, the goddess of marriage and the status quo. She personifies the woman who lives by "the principle of the thing" at the cost of human relationship—impersonal relationship as opposed to personal. When Wotan is forced to choose between betraying the hero and betraying marriage, he allies himself with Fricka, because to destroy Fricka is to destroy Valhalla.

Meanwhile, Brunnhilde, his favorite daughter, has witnessed human love and chooses to disobey her father and fight on the side of the hero because her father will not allow him to bring his beloved to Valhalla. She values human love more than the ideal of perfection. Her father, wreaking revenge for the betrayal of his values, puts her on a rock and would keep her there forever. She,

The goddess Nut and her consort Geb.—Egyptian papyrus.
(British Museum)

however, persuades him to put a ring of fire, a ring of passion, around her, and if any man can break through that fire, he can release her. Wotan agrees, but there is a price: if a man dares to come through the fire and awakens her, she will no longer be a goddess. She will become a human being.

While she sleeps, the heroic Siegfried slays the dragon. After tasting of its blood, he can understand the birds, who tell him that a beautiful woman is imprisoned on a rock surrounded by a ring of fire. He journeys to the place, plunges through the magic circle of seething flames and sees before him an armed sleeper. Carefully he loosens the helmet, and gazes in amazement as Brunnhilde's long curls flow down over her bosom. Drawing his famous sword, he cuts off her coat of mail, and Brunnhilde in soft female drapery lies before him. For the first time he beholds a woman, and awakens her with a kiss. Brunnhilde rises in the full majesty of her womanhood. They sing together their song of ecstasy.

Meagan had been a Valkyrie, a goddess in her full armor of fat, fantasizing heavenly journeys with her lovers as she carried them off to Paradise. Like Brunnhilde, she had rebelled against her father when her own spirit cried out for life and love, but being his daughter, her body lay asleep in the fiery ring of her own passions. With the sword of her own masculinity, she dieted her armor away, but in spite of her yearning to be human, she could not contact her own sexuality. Her entire life had been lived in her head—studying, meditating, practicing her French horn. Her shadow whore was virtually unknown to her. Until her Siegfried plunged through the ring of passion, she could not connect body and spirit. His love awakened her to the full beauty of her own womanhood; body and spirit were joined. Then the power principle and the striving for perfection which had driven her in her scholarly world were mellowed by her love for a real man.

Observing this process in Meagan and other women whose necks simply did not make a bridge between head and body, I began to see many differences between Medusa-bound Brunnhildes and Ereshki gals (my term for Ereshkigal-type women). If a woman becomes her father's anima, and that anima is still trapped in the mother, she will live out his spiritualized, intellectualized world, but her Athena will throw her unconscious Medusa into the deepest cave in her body. In this situation, there is usually no mother to provide any feminine model. So long as her own creative masculinity is in thrall to the father, she becomes possessed by negative masculinity: collective values, opinions and judgments. Life becomes a routine of imitation carved in stone. Medusa's glance petrifies; it does not allow for spontaneity. Living becomes concretized by boyish masculinity that serves the Terrible Mother who wants more and more and more. Her worshipers become petrified in matter. Their imaginations concretize even the eternal so that the Virgin Birth, for example, becomes an historical fact. The Virgin thereby becomes an impossible ideal of purity that takes a tyrannical hold upon the feminine psyche, continually judging her "imperfection" by an impossible standard.

The effect of concretization is obvious in the body of the obese or anorexic woman. It is part of our culture's prevailing attempts to establish security with concrete objects until we are buried alive under our own piles of riches or junk, depending on the perspective. The mothers' sons who became Nazi murderers believed they could concretize Nietzsche's "superman" ideal, and threw this planet into a maelstrom of suffering attempting to do it. Negative masculinity cannot think in metaphor. Everything has to be concrete, serving the temporal rather than the eternal. Again the paradox surfaces. It tries to make the temporal as perfect as the eternal it rejects. The addiction to perfection is an addiction to unreality which leaves little room for the feminine.

This is the coat of male in which the Medusa-bound Brunnhilde is imprisoned. The authority in her life lies with her Medusa/demon lover, which takes its authority from collective consciousness. Her feminine spirit is in her head, while in her body is unconscious negative masculinity, separating her from her instinctual roots and leaving them susceptible to illness (e.g., cancer of the female organs). Her healing will come through taking hold of her masculine spirit in a creative way and severing Medusa's head so that her own creativity is released. The sword of discrimination is her greatest ally. In the Medusa myth, the dark twin born with Pegasus is Chrysaor, he of the Golden Sword. Harold Bayley, amplifying the sword in *The Lost Language of Symbolism,* writes:

> The Great Sword of Justice has at times been reverenced as the symbol of God Himself, and Henley thus treats it in his well-known *Song of the Sword:*

> ........................................
> *Thrust through the fatuous,*
> *Thrust through the fungus brood,*
>
> ........................................
> *Follow, O, follow me*
> *Till the waste places*
> *All the grey globe over*
> *Ooze, as the honeycomb*
> *Drips, with the sweetness*
> *Distilled of my strength.*[6]

That is what the sword in the hands of the positive animus does: it thrusts down into her body and allows her to experience intimations of her own feminine nature sexually and spiritually. In the Brunnhilde woman's dreams, snakes are often in trees, uncoiling downward toward the earth. So long as she is chained she carries the divine child in her head, an image which recalls the medieval idea of the Virgin impregnated by the Holy Ghost through the ear. If she is ever to contact her Black Madonna her snake has to move down before it can move up. She has to bring light into her concretized body and realize that it is a daily task to try to keep it there. (This may have something to do with psychological types. Certainly introverted intuitives have the most difficulty staying in their bodies, but the difficulty is by no means exclusively theirs.) Where the woman is not in her body, she is cut off from her natural, chthonic instincts; their affects are turned to stone.

A Brunnhilde, as an anima woman, has lived her life as a reactor, rather than an initiator. When the transformation begins, therefore, she has no problem with the concept of Eros as a masculine god. Because her savior is the connection between body and spirit, love is utterly numinous. As the light infiltrates her body she becomes flexible; her masculine spirit allows her to penetrate and be penetrated without fear, because the consciousness she is bringing into her body is not contaminated by the negative mother power principle. When she separates her own positive animus from the father, she can allow that spirit to penetrate to the depths of her own *materia* to transform it. She takes possession of her own body and discards the ectoplasmic barrier. Only when her animus is out of the father can a Brunnhilde accept ravishment. Then the incest is redeemed. She is open to the real world. In my experience, it is always a Brunnhilde's head that is attacked by the demon lover, but the instrument he uses is potentially positive. In Andrea's dream (see page 141), the compass is the instrument which, if used properly, outlines the mandala, the geometric image of God. Seen from this perspective, Lucifer becomes the morning star, the Light Bringer.

The Ereshki gal, on the other hand, is related to the collective unconscious whose representative is the Great Mother. She understands the laws of nature, which are not the laws of Eros but the laws of fertility. She too has the whore shadow, but is able to relate to it as a Brunnhilde is not. Her task is also to redeem the Terrible Mother, but in her the chthonic energy moves up from below and she relates to the masculine as son, who from the lofty position of enthronement (where she has placed him) is subject to her wishes and will do anything to placate her. She holds the masculine principle in her womb and will not let it move into her head, will not let it be spiritualized. Mother and son are in the body in a state of natural incest. So long as she identifies with the Great Mother, she cannot allow him to be born, nor, paradoxically, can she allow her own virgin birth.

For the Ereshki gal sexuality is part of life, part of nature. She cannot be devastated by it. She *is* it, she is one with nature. She has nature's raw power, and that she will protect from ravishment: if it is penetrated, her experience is earth-shattering because she is separated from her unconscious grounding. Such a woman must make the journey down through her undifferentiated identification with matter, recognize her individuality and separate. She can then relate to her natural chthonic nature. Once the mother surrenders to penetration, the daughter is born and the mother is redeemed—through relationship to the daughter.

The Ereshki gal has difficulty comprehending that Eros is a masculine god. As she matures, if she chooses not to become a Molly Bloom, she builds a wall to keep herself in, rather than to keep the masculine out. It serves the same purpose, but it is her fear of not being able to control the raw power that creates the wall. She has a certain inflexibility because the mother in her does not know how to surrender. Men appear in her dreams in chains, imprisoned in cellars or as bus-loads of cripples. Eventually they turn the chains on the woman because the dynamic behind sexuality is power. Sexuality is power; love is not. The Ereshki gal has to learn to love other women rather than see them as competitors. For her, Venus is the Light Bringer.

This is a very different psychology from that of a Brunnhilde, who has no contact with that raw natural power and therefore no reason to put up a wall. She relates to men platonically and wonders why they do not make sexual advances. Men in her dreams are gods or devils and any contact is through the head. Once she contacts her own raw power she may go through the Ereshkigal journey, but more likely her hold on her sexuality will be so tenuous that she will have to consciously focus on trying to keep in touch with it. Her natural inclination is toward her own creative work, and she has to discipline herself to hold the balance between her masculinity and her femininity. The Ereshki gal has also to learn the balance but from the opposite direction. She has to claim her creative masculinity in order to allow Venus, her conscious femininity, to redeem the Terrible Mother. In either case, the woman who experiences ravishment need no longer seek mother or father because they are sacramentally united in the inner union which is the Self.

By whichever route women take, feminine consciousness is making itself felt in our culture. The intimate connection between rape and ravishment has to be clear as we move on our separate paths toward individual freedom. In certain Christian traditions, so devastating are the consequences of original sin that Christians themselves are virtually paralyzed by what they take to be evil. Full of despair, they throw themselves upon the mercy of God in a pathetic affirmation of their own helplessness. If rape is brutal severance from a previous state of being, ravishment is a restoration of that previous state on a higher plane of consciousness. Without psychological rape mankind would have remained in a state of unconscious identification with the Great Mother—at one with nature. We would still be picking flowers with Persephone, blissfully unaware. Where this state of unconsciousness—life in the oceanic world of the womb—remains the ideal to which we yearn to return, the intimate connection between rape and ravishment does not exist. Neurotics long to return to an unconscious vision of a sunken Atlantis. This strong regressive pull unconsciously frustrates their efforts to wake up. They do not want to enter the world; they want to re-enter the womb. They are traumatized by rape because they cannot find its connection to ravishment.

Rape destroys a lower innocence; ravishment brings a higher innocence. The difference between the lower and the higher is consciousness and the wisdom peculiar to consciousness where it is grounded in innocence. Rape and ravishment can ultimately be seen as the same event separated by time, waiting to be brought together in consciousness when we are able to see from the timeless world of the I AM. Higher innocence is being armed in a world that previously had the power to destroy us. The armed virgin is different from the unconscious virgin. Armed in herself, the virgin can make her own choices; she can be who she is because that is who she is, ready for ravishment.

So long as the world outside is foreign to our inner world we cannot trust life. We fear whatever can invade our little space either from the Great Mother or the Great Father. Once ravished, twice chaste; subjective and objective worlds become one and we can learn to trust. Confrontation forces us into awareness. We are still vulnerable, but because we have consciousness to fall back on, we don't fall into a pit. The armor is consciousness; we are no longer the victims of blind unconscious reactions. The person who comes toward me from outside is the same person I have met inside. If that person happens to be a demon lover, I know him from inside myself. He is no longer magic. Fantasy becomes reality. He is a man, and the more to be loved in his human imperfection and individuality.

The virgin needs a male bridegroom, whether actual or spiritual, to complete her. Three different degrees of ravishment are quite distinguishable in the following excerpts. The first is from Molly Bloom's forty-six-page sentence on the trials and glories of being an Earth Mother. The second is from a meditation of St. Teresa of Avila (1515-1582), which shows a spiritual surrender to a transpersonal power. The third is from the journal of a woman who was beginning to bring together her sexuality and spirituality, experiencing herself as a human woman transfigured by love. Ravishment requires sacrifice, the conscious sacrifice of ego demands (unconscious power), being clean of ego desire, being spiritually chaste. Sacrificing ego demands is saying YES to life. That's ravishment!

I had that white blouse on open at the front to encourage him as much as I could without too openly they were just beginning to be plump I said I was tired we lay over the firtree cove a wild place I suppose it must be the highest rock in existence . . . you could do what you liked lie there for ever he caressed them outside they love doing that its the roundness there I was leaning over him with my white ricestraw hat to take the newness out of it the left side of my face the best my blouse open for his last day transparent kind of shirt he had I could see his chest pink he wanted to touch mine with his for a moment but I wouldn't let him he was awfully put out first for fear you never know consumption or leave me with a child embarazada.[7]

I saw in his hand a long spear of gold, and at the iron's point there seemed to be a little fire. He appeared to me to be thrusting it at times into my heart, and to pierce my very entrails; when he drew it out, he seemed to draw them out also, and to leave me all on fire with a great love of God. The pain was so great that it made me moan; and yet so surpassing was the sweetness of this excessive pain that I could not wish to be rid of it. The soul is satisfied now with nothing less than God. The pain is not bodily, but spiritual; though the body has its share in it, even a large one. It is a caressing of love so sweet which now takes place between the soul and God, that I pray God of His goodness to make him experience it who may think that I am lying.[8] [See page 184]

You are the synapse that makes me smile the smile I never knew till you, the sundrenched, blood-warm smile that sings *I am* and *you are* and the world *is*. Your fingers set my flesh afire in the night, and yes it burns, it burns all day long down the deep corridors of my bones. . . . I am carried on the wave, the great wave gathering momentum as it rolls, the new Yes to your uncompromising Be. I am de-atomized. I am Love. I am Light. Yes, I say yes and I am lifted into the source of Light. I am splayed from vagina to crown. . . . Your living seed sings within me. Your heart beats its quiet miracle next to mine and we are the translation of all the tunes the interstellar spaces ever sang.

The Ecstasy of St. Teresa.—Bernini. (S. Maria della Vittoria, Rome)
(See page 183)

So long as we honor the transpersonal power of the God and Goddess and recognize that power as coming through us, we are safe from the fatal inflation of imagining that their power is ours. Unless there is genuine giving and receiving in the coming-together, their power is not released. There is an explosion, but nothing significant has happened. The man goes back to his anima unchanged, the woman to her animus. The genuine *coniunctio* is a glimpse of the profound mystery of the spiritual life.

One young woman after several years of analysis began to experience profound changes in her attitude toward her sexuality:

> This is the beginning. I am in a period of natural celibacy. I relate to me. I see my lover; his boyishness no longer attracts me. How does a woman relate to a boy? I have to admit I am afraid to give up the numinosity of my mothering power. How do I relate to a man? Even now I sometimes want an unconscious man who will yield to me. Our connection was magically incestuous. I feel nostalgic because that is gone. I don't know how to hold onto that numinosity in consciousness.
>
> I have come to a realization of my aloneness. How do I connect to another individual? My sexuality is changed. This is beyond lust, beyond anything superficial. The urge comes from deep inside me. I have known what love-making is—to surrender spiritually to the thing between us, to surrender to the body, to the process. It's completely I-am, We-are space. The yearning is so primordial; it's like getting back into the origin of things on a conscious level. Growth can only happen with a conscious man, or perhaps a genuinely spiritual man, because they have yang, the yang that can give a woman the proper nourishment for her yin. It gives the balance, the complete wholeness, the complete interchange between yang and yin. If I can't have that, I'd rather not have any sex. Anything else is like making love to a corpse. In real loving you feel the blood, the bones, the beating heart. Once you've had it, you don't want anything less. To accept less is to betray yourself.
>
> Working at it doesn't make it right. I tried to develop my sexuality by developing good muscle control, but it didn't work. Men fear the meat-chopper. Naturally! Women have taken on men's competitiveness, without recognizing that competing creates further separation. A woman has to go into her own Being. Because she is giving all the time, she is receiving, and the man must also receive and by receiving he is giving because he is letting go. Both are the container, containing both. The crown of the penis floats in the vagina in its own rhythm. The body is surrendered. The cervix floats in its primordial rhythm like the ocean. *I am that I am.* It is a meditation. It's the space of the great primordial beat.

There are many women in analysis fearful of the period of "natural celibacy." They fear losing their sexuality. It is not a period of coldness, nor a period of power in which the woman withholds from her partner. Rather it is a period of purification in which the old habits of relating are purged. It is a period in which a woman is finding new roots for relationship within the security of her own feminine grounding. If the morality of the body demands a temporary cessation of sexual activity, it is not a period to be feared. It is a phase; the fuller relationship will come.

Masculinity and femininity are dormant until they come into consciousness. Unconscious femininity is a power principle that is transformed by the true masculine spirit into conscious passivity, action receiving action. If the woman waits, stops trying, and in response to the masculine allows the feminine energy to come in, then the mystery happens to her. Then having experienced masculinity, she redirects that into action. Sexual intercourse is like conversation. The feminine listens and responds; the masculine translates what is heard. The process requires the full recognition of one by the other. When the masculine penetrates and knows it is penetrating, and the feminine receives and knows it is receiving, then yin and yang are functioning in both partners. That is how Tao manifests in relationship.

Consciousness viewed in this way is Eros. The greater the capacity to receive and to give, the greater the consciousness of the essence of everything. That interplay is creativity; in the moment we are constantly creating. I in my Being give a muffin—or an orange or a black-eyed Susan—to you in your Being. Something has happened between us.

Essentially that is the message of Christ, the message we cannot hear so long as we are sidetracked by unpalatable dogma. We forget that Christ was crucified because he ostensibly broke the laws established by Yahweh—the Ten Commandments carved in stone. But Christ himself said, "I am not come to destroy, but to fulfill."[9] Fulfillment, for him, meant breaking the stone and transcending it through the spirit. When he found himself in a position where he had to choose between obeying the letter of the law and recognizing an individual soul, he acted in the spirit. When, for example, he came upon the woman taken in adultery, instead of upholding the law-abiding citizens who were about to stone her to death, he said, "He that is without sin among you, let him first cast a stone at her."[10] He lived in the moment, recognizing the essence of those around him. That is the feminine side of Christ, now forcing itself into our culture and breaking down the old rigid codes.

For the first time in history, men and women are seriously exploring the possibilities of relationship based on separateness rather than togetherness. Instead of clinging to Yahweh, to a rigid set of laws established by a jealous Father-God who will rant in fury if he is disobeyed, they are simply ignoring that ranting, walking away from it, and attempting to put their trust in the irrational. In other words, they are trying to live by the spirit. In recognizing individual lives, they are compelled to take human imperfection into account. Those who have broken with the rigid codes, faced their own breakdown and strengthened their own ego, find new life through relationship. So long as one does not cling to another, nor try to possess another, mutual love is the bond, and new depths of personality are released. What gradually emerges is an individual morality in which the inner laws are absolute.

If, for example, a woman is genuinely in her body so that spirit and matter are one, she cannot separate her sexuality from her love. Sexual union with a man she does not love is self-betrayal, and therefore rape. Individuals who have become conscious of certain laws within themselves, laws about food, alcohol, tobacco, etc., laws that become more refined as consciousness develops, discover that persisting in the old ways leads to physical illness in which the illness mirrors the psychological problem. This body/spirit relationship is another example of the sword exactly fitting the wound. Often the wisdom of the body clarifies the despair of the spirit. Breaking the stone does not give us licence to do as we please. Rather it opens us to our own inner laws and the fulfillment of our own destiny.

Living in the spirit, the Now, demands an acceptance of the feminine principle of death and resurrection. In the Christian myth, matter dies, crucified by the letter of the law, but after three days rises again, transformed into spirit. The upheaval in our culture may be seen as the emergence of the spirit, and while it is imperfect and chaotic, it can lead toward the feminine, the irrational side of God. For those of us in transition, the chaos feels like the three-day descent into Hell. Having sacrificed our old attitudes and traditional structures, we are not at all sure that Yahweh won't destroy us. We stumble along, walking as proudly as we dare, trusting in the love of others who are walking their parallel paths, mustering the same kind of courage, trusting that there is meaning in the irrational. What we are finding is not a dead god, but the divine child born of the virgin whore.

If we allow ourselves to receive, to be ravished by the irrational, we are compelled to face our own evil. Trust takes on a new dimension, for in knowing our own darkness, we know only too well what another's darkness can release. We learn to forgive and to love our "crooked neighbor" with our own "crooked heart."[11] That is God's country. There we don't know from moment to moment what can happen next. Each new situation is filled with new energies, new demands. Living energy is interacting with living energy and transformation happens because we recognize each other and in that recognition is the love that brings us and others to our full stature. We see with new eyes. We look into a beloved face, we see new lines, new shadows in the eyes. We love, and that love goes with us into the daisies we are arranging, the omelette we are cooking, the new prospectus we are preparing. Sexuality is no longer limited to the genitalia. It becomes our total response to the whole world. Love engenders soul.

So long as we are concretizing, love is lost. We are trying to make something happen our way to satisfy our own ego desires. If, for example, I invite you to my home for dinner, hoping to impress you with my Chippendale furniture, my succulent chicken Kiev, my perfectly landscaped garden, then I am concretizing my Self. My ideal of perfection is projected; in effect, I identify with God when I believe I am in control in my little kingdom. If, on the other hand, I am in my own Being, then I invite you to my home because I love you and choose to share these beautiful objects that I love with you. They are a manifestation of my inner Reality, but my Reality is not projected into them. When the ego is conscious enough to recognize the Self—the kingdom of God within—it does not project the perfection outside. It is the dead god that is projected into the concretized perfection; the ego, caught in a massive inflation, is denying the inner Reality. Happening cannot happen. So long as we project onto the collective world—institutions, media, society—an authority it does not rightfully possess, we are allowing ourselves to be contaminated by alien elements. If we allow the Self to come to consciousness, the authority is inside. Happening happens. We make the space, we unlock the door, and wait. We surrender to ravishment.

To be true to the soul is to value the soul, to express it as uniquely as possible. It is loving from inside, rather than accepting a foreign standard that does not take our essence into consideration. To strive for perfection is to kill love because perfection does not recognize humanity. However driven it becomes, the ego cannot achieve its perfectionist ideals because another Reality is within. Nor can it accomplish the task of loving. Only by opening ourselves to the inner Reality do we open ourselves to the possibility of the gift of love. Action and ego choice are involved: we can accept; we can reject; we can withdraw at any point. But we cannot make it happen. Love chooses us.

The true feminine is the receptacle of love. The true masculine is the spirit that goes into the eternal unknown in search of meaning. The great container, the Self, is paradoxically both male and female and contains both. If these are projected onto the outside world, transcendence ceases to exist. The Self—the inner wholeness—is petrified. Without the true masculine spirit and the true feminine love within, no inner life exists. If we try to make perfection outside, try to concretize our unconscious inner ideal, we kill our imagination. We are left holding life in our rigid molds. To be free is to break the stone images and allow life and love to flow.

The woman possessed by the Medusa/demon lover is an Andromeda still chained to the rock. She has not been born into time, and therefore does not experience being alive. Her authority consists of what she "ought" or "should not" do in the future, or the "if only's" of the past. Her authority for life takes on the form of rigid stone, rather than the living stone of personal relationship in the present. For her the stone of Christianity becomes the stone of the sepulcher, the dead stone of the law rather than the living stone of spirit. Life is ahead or behind, but never here. What she fails to understand is the paradox: to be in time is to be in the eternal. If she can contact her heroic animus, she will find him questing, not for the perfection of the world hereafter, nor for the nostalgic Paradise of times past, but for eternity in the present. He lives in the eternal Now. He loves the eternal virgin.

The image of the double-faced Janus head amplifies this paradox of eternity within time. Our month of January is named after the god Janus. One face looks backward to the past; the other looks forward to the future. To be identified with either face is to be captive in stone, victim of fixed laws and fixed authorities. A woman imprisoned in the stone attitudes of one or both of the Janus faces will say with Shelley, "We look before and after,/And pine for what is not";[12] the "not" she pines for is what Carlos Castaneda calls "the path with heart."[13] Only when the stone images are smashed will she be born into her capacity to love, into the eternal Now. The path that lies in the center of the Janus head is the ever-changing present. This is the eternity to which the Buddha refers when he says, "It may exist or it may not. But better the search than to dully agree with necessity." Necessity, obligation, duty—the standards of the past or the supposed future—are death to the human spirit. To be virgin we have to be ravished into Eternity, stripped of both faces of Janus.

So long as the woman is in the rock, she is not in touch with her own Being. She is the victim of the gods—the gods of rage, hunger and jealousy on the one hand, the gods of perfection on the other. She lives expecting the expected, trying to create the world her way. If she receives what she wants, she is happy; if not she is unhappy. She is a plaything of the gods, deluding herself into believing she is creating her own world. And if she is unfortunate enough to achieve the false godhead of her precious expectations, she may find herself alone with her gods, bereft of what she most longed for in life— loving and being loved.

On the other hand, if she abdicates her throne, then her creative spirit, rather than soaring with the gods from one judgmental affect to another, will wield his golden sword, split open her armor of fear and free her into Life. Freed from her gods, she joins the race of "mere humanity." With arms wide open she welcomes Life and Love and whispers from her heart:

> *Take me to you, imprison me, for I*
> *Except you enthrall me, never shall be free,*
> *Nor ever chaste, except you ravish me.*[14]

She is a human being, and being human she is able to give and to receive the greatest of all human gifts—"I love you as you are."

Sleeping nude.—Auguste Renoir. (Private Collection, Switzerland)

# Notes

CW – *The Collected Works of C.G. Jung*

**Preface**

1. Robert Graves, *The Greek Myths*, vol. 1, p. 46.
2. John Keats, "Ode on a Grecian Urn," lines 27-30.
3. Thomas Merton, *Zen and the Birds of Appetite*, p. 1.

**1. Introduction**

1. Ernest Becker, *The Denial of Life*, p. 24.
2. Jonathan Swift, "A Beautiful Young Nymph Going to Bed." ("Caelia" is a pun on the word "caecum," meaning "the blind gut; the first part of the large intestine, which is prolonged into a cul-de-sac." –O.E.D.)
3. Shakespeare, *Hamlet*, act 3, scene 1, lines 62-63.
4. Joseph Chilton Pearce, *Magical Child*, p. 22.
5. Ibid.
6. Ibid., p. 46.
7. Ibid., pp. 24-25.
8. Shakespeare, *Macbeth*, act 5, scene 5, lines 26-28.

**2. Ritual: Sacred and Demonic**

1. Paul B. Beeson and Walsh McDermott, *Textbook of Medicine*, p. 1375.
2. *Toronto Star*, Aug. 10, 1981 (quoting study at Clarke Institute of Psychiatry, Toronto).
3. David M. Garner and Paul E. Garfinkel, "Socio-cultural Factors in the Development of Anorexia Nervosa," *Psychological Medicine*, vol. 10, 1980, p. 652.
4. Jung, *Letters*, vol. 2 (1951-1961), pp. 623-625.
5. *Alcoholics Anonymous*, p. 59.
6. See, for instance, Jung, *The Structure and Dynamics of the Psyche*, CW 8, par. 242, and *Civilization in Transition*, CW 10, par. 659.
7. For an in-depth discussion of religious ritual, see Mircea Eliade, *The Sacred and the Profane: The Nature of Religion*.
8. For a fuller discussion of the Eye of the feminine, see Penelope Shuttle and Peter Redgrove, *The Wise Wound: Menstruation and Everywoman*, pp. 189-190, and Sylvia Brinton Perera, *Descent to the Goddess: A Way of Initiation for Women*, pp. 30-34.
9. Marie-Louise von Franz, *Shadow and Evil in Fairytales*, pp. 215-216.
10. Pearce, p. 209.

### 3 Addiction to Perfection

1. John Keats, "Ode to a Nightingale," lines 66-67.
2. John 3:3.
3. Jung, *Aion,* CW 9ii, par. 123.
4. James Joyce, *Portrait of the Artist as a Young Man,* p. 215.
5. See Mircea Eliade, *Rites and Symbols of Initiation,* pp. 92-96.
6. Maurice Buxton Foreman, ed., *The Letters of John Keats,* p. 112.
7. John Donne, "The Ecstasy," lines 69-76.

### 4 Through Thick and Thin

1. Shakespeare, *Macbeth,* act. 1, scene 5, lines 38, 42, 13-14.
2. Ibid., scene 7, line 31.
3. Jung, *Symbols of Transformation,* CW 5, par. 457.
4. Sandra Gilbert and Susan Gubar, *The Madwoman in the Attic,* p. 86.
5. Viktor Frankl, *Man's Search for Meaning,* p. 125.
6. Marie-Louise von Franz, *Alchemy: An Introduction to the Symbolism and the Psychology,* p. 215.
7. Matthew 10:39.
8. Louis Aragon, *Henri Matisse: A Novel,* p. 21.
9. Von Franz, *Alchemy,* p. 212.
10. Ibid., p. 219.
11. Ibid.
12. William Blake, "Milton," 29:3, *Poetry and Prose,* ed. David Erdman.
13. Von Franz, *Alchemy,* p. 142.
14. William Butler Yeats, "Among School Children," lines 63-64.

### 5 Assent to the Goddess

1. See Jung, "The Visions of Zosimos," *Alchemical Studies,* CW 13, par. 138.
2. Marina Warner, *Alone of All Her Sex,* pp. 338-339.
3. Ibid., pp. 274, 276, 314.
4. M. Esther Harding, *Woman's Mysteries,* pp. 146-147.
5. Proverbs 8:23, 30.
6. Von Franz, *Alchemy,* p. 252.
7. Matthew 9:17.
8. Joan Chodorow, "Dance Movement and Body Experience in Analysis."
9. Jung, "Commentary on 'The Secret of the Golden Flower,'" *Alchemical Studies,* CW 13, par. 30.
10. Perera, pp. 44-45.
11. Jung, *The Development of Personality,* CW 17, pars. 84, 87.

12. Barbara Hannah, *Jung, His Life and Work: A Biographical Memoir,* p. 188.

13. Russell Lockhart, in a lecture at *Insights 1980,* Toronto.

## 6 The Myth of Ms

1. Mircea Eliade, *Sacred and Profane,* pp. 33-34.

2. A classic example is Mary Daly, the feminist author of *Beyond God the Father,* whose reputation has thrived on the basis of vitriolic diatribes against men.

3. Bruce Lincoln, *Emerging from the Chrysalis,* p. 78 (quoting *The Homeric Hymn*).

4. Jung, "The Problem of the Attitude-Type," *Two Essays on Analytical Psychology,* CW 7, par. 78.

5. Donald Lee Williams, *Border Crossings: A Psychological Perspective on Carlos Castaneda's Path of Knowledge,* p. 48.

6. See, for instance, Jung, "Psychological Aspects of the Mother Archetype," *The Archetypes and the Collective Unconscious,* CW 9i, pars. 196-197.

7. For a discussion of the "two children" motif, see Nathan Schwartz-Salant, *Narcissism and Character Transformation,* pp. 159-164.

## 7 Rape and the Demon Lover

1. Jung, *Memories, Dreams, Reflections,* pp. 199-200.

2. Jung, "Psychological Aspects of the Mother Archetype," *The Archetypes and the Collective Unconscious,* CW 9i, par. 185.

3. Hannah Arendt, "Understanding and Politics," *Partisan Review,* vol. 20, no. 4, (July-Aug. 1953), p. 392.

4. Hannah Arendt, *Men in Dark Times,* p. 97 (the quote is from "The Blank Page," a short story by Isaac Dinesen).

5. Jung, *Psychology and Alchemy,* CW 12, par. 559.

6. Emily Dickinson, *The Complete Poems,* p. 148.

7. Ibid., p. 323.

8. Jung, "The Psychology of the Transference," *The Practice of Psychotherapy,* CW 16, par. 419.

9. Dickinson, p. 42: *Our lives are Swiss—*
   *So still—so Cool*
   *Till some odd afternoon*
   *The Alps neglect their Curtains*
   *And we look farther on!*

   *Italy stands the other side!*
   *While like a guard between—*
   *The solemn Alps—*
   *The siren Alps*
   *Forever intervene!*

10.  Erich Neumann, *Depth Psychology and the New Ethic*, pp. 65-66.

11.  Eva Metman, "Woman and the Anima," p. 12.

12.  Jung, *Symbols of Transformation*, CW 5, par. 273.

13.  R.D. Laing, *The Voices of Experience*, p. 82.

14.  Ibid., p. 83.

15.  Von Franz, *The Feminine in Fairytales*, p. 78.

16.  Ibid., p. 85.

17.  Jung, "The Psychological Aspects of the Kore," *The Archetypes and the Collective Unconscious*, CW 9i, par. 316.

18.  Pearce, pp. 145-146.

19.  Von Franz in *The Way of the Dream* (film in preparation).

## 8 The Ravished Bride

1.  Erich Neumann, *The Origins and History of Consciousness*, p. 54.

2.  Robert Rosenblum, *Cubism and Twentieth-Century Art*, pp. 10-11.

3.  Esther Harding, *Woman's Mysteries*, p. 157.

4.  Jung, *Psychology and Alchemy*, CW 12, par. 192n.

5.  Jung, "The Psychology of the Transference," *The Practice of Psychotherapy*, CW 16, par. 454.

6.  Harold Bayley, *The Lost Language of Symbolism*, part 2, pp. 74-75.

7.  James Joyce, *Ulysses*, p. 774.

8.  "Transverberation of the Heart of Saint Teresa," in *Three Mystics*, ed. Father Bruno de J.M., p. 78.

9.  Matthew 5:17.

10.  John 8:7.

11.  W.H. Auden, "Birthday Poem," from the last stanza:
> *O stand, stand at the window*
> *As the tears scald and start;*
> *You shall love your crooked neighbour*
> *With your crooked heart.*

12.  Percy Byshe Shelley, "To a Skylark," lines 85-86.

13.  Williams, p. 37.

14.  John Donne, "Holy Sonnets," No. 14, lines 9-14.

# Glossary of Jungian Terms

**Anima** (Latin, "soul"). The unconscious, feminine side of a man's personality. She is personified in dreams by images of women ranging from prostitute and seductress to spiritual guide (Wisdom). She is the eros principle, hence a man's anima development is reflected in how he relates to women. Identification with the anima can appear as moodiness, effeminacy, and oversensitivity. Jung calls the anima *the archetype of life itself.*

**Animus** (Latin, "spirit"). The unconscious, masculine side of a woman's personality. He personifies the logos principle. Identification with the animus can cause a woman to become rigid, opinionated, and argumentative. More positively, he is the inner man who acts as a bridge between the woman's ego and her own creative resources in the unconscious.

**Archetypes.** Irrepresentable in themselves, but their effects appear in consciousness as the archetypal images and ideas. These are universal patterns or motifs which come from the collective unconscious and are the basic content of religions, mythologies, legends, and fairytales. They emerge in individuals through dreams and visions.

**Association.** A spontaneous flow of interconnected thoughts and images around a specific idea, determined by unconscious connections.

**Complex.** An emotionally charged group of ideas or images. At the "center" of a complex is an archetype or archetypal image.

**Constellate.** Whenever there is a strong emotional reaction to a person or a situation, a complex has been constellated (activated).

**Ego.** The central complex in the field of consciousness. A strong ego can relate objectively to activated contents of the unconscious (i.e., other complexes), rather than identifying with them, which appears as a state of possession.

**Feeling.** One of the four psychic functions. It is a rational function which evaluates the worth of relationships and situations. Feeling must be distinguished from emotion, which is due to an activated complex.

**Individuation.** The conscious realization of one's unique psychological reality, including both strengths and limitations. It leads to the experience of the Self as the regulating center of the psyche.

**Inflation.** A state in which one has an unrealistically high or low (negative inflation) sense of identity. It indicates a regression of consciousness into unconsciousness, which typically happens when the ego takes too many unconscious contents upon itself and loses the faculty of discrimination.

**Intuition.** One of the four psychic functions. It is the irrational function which tells us the possibilities inherent in the present. In contrast to sensation (the function which perceives immediate reality through the physical senses) intuition perceives via the unconscious, e.g., flashes of insight of unknown origin.

195

**Participation mystique.** A term derived from the anthropologist Lévy-Bruhl, denoting a primitive, psychological connection with objects, or between persons, resulting in a strong unconscious bond.

**Persona** (Latin, "actor's mask"). One's social role, derived from the expectations of society and early training. A strong ego relates to the outside world through a flexible persona; identification with a specific persona (doctor, scholar, artist, etc.) inhibits psychological development.

**Projection.** The process whereby an unconscious quality or characteristic of one's own is perceived and reacted to in an outer object or person. Projection of the anima or animus onto a real women or man is experienced as falling in love. Frustrated expectations indicate the need to withdraw projections, in order to relate to the reality of other people.

**Puer aeternus** (Latin, "eternal youth"). Indicates a certain type of man who remains too long in adolescent psychology, generally associated with a strong unconscious attachment to the mother (actual or symbolic). Positive traits are spontaneity and openness to change. His female counterpart is the **puella,** an "eternal girl" with a corresponding attachment to the father-world.

**Self.** The archetype of wholeness and the regulating center of the personality. It is experienced as a transpersonal power which transcends the ego, e.g., God.

**Senex** (Latin, "old man"). Associated with attitudes that come with advancing age. Negatively, this can mean cynicism, rigidity and extreme conservatism; positive traits are responsibility, orderliness and self-discipline. A well-balanced personality functions appropriately within the puer-senex polarity.

**Shadow.** An unconscious part of the personality characterized by traits and attitudes, whether negative or positive, which the conscious ego tends to reject or ignore. It is personified in dreams by persons of the same sex as the dreamer. Consciously assimilating one's shadow usually results in an increase of energy.

**Symbol.** The best possible expression for something essentially unknown. Symbolic thinking is non-linear, right-brain oriented; it is complementary to logical, linear, left-brain thinking.

**Transcendent function.** The reconciling "third" which emerges from the unconscious (in the form of a symbol or a new attitude) after the conflicting opposites have been consciously differentiated, and the tension between them held.

**Transference and countertransference.** Particular cases of projection, commonly used to describe the unconscious, emotional bonds that arise between two persons in an analytic or therapeutic relationship.

**Uroboros.** The mythical snake or dragon that eats its own tail. It is a symbol both for individuation as a self-contained, circular process, and for narcissistic self-absorption.

# Bibliography

*Alcoholics Anonymous.* Cornwall Press, Cornwall, N.Y., 1939.

Aragon, Louis. *Henri Matisse: A Novel.* 2 vols. Trans. Jean Stewart. Harcourt Brace Jovanovich, New York, 1972.

Arendt, Hannah. *Men in Dark Times.* Harcourt Brace Jovanovich, New York, 1968.

Atwood, Margaret. *You Are Happy.* Oxford University Press, Toronto, 1974.

Bauer, Jan. *Alcoholism and Women: The Background and the Psychology.* Inner City Books, Toronto, 1982.

Bayley, Harold. *The Lost Language of Symbolism.* Rowman and Littlefield, Totowa, N.J., 1974.

Becker, Ernest. *The Denial of Death.* The Free Press (Macmillan), New York, 1973.

Beeson, Paul B., and Walsh McDermott, eds. *Textbook of Medicine* (14th Edition). Saunders Publications, Philadelphia, 1975.

Blake, William. *Poetry and Prose.* Ed. David Erdman. Doubleday, Garden City, 1965.

Bruno de J.M., Father, ed. *Three Mystics: El Greco, St. John of the Cross, St. Teresa of Avila.* Sheed & Ward, New York, 1949.

Chodorow, Joan. "Dance Movement and Body Experience in Analysis," in *Jungian Analysis.* Ed. Murray Stein. Open Court, La Salle, 1982.

Dickinson, Emily. *The Complete Poems.* Ed. Thomas H. Johnson. Little, Brown and Company, Boston, 1960.

Donne, John. *Selected Poems.* Ed. Matthias A. Shaaber. Appleton-Century-Crofts, New York, 1958.

Eliade, Mircea. *Rites and Symbols of Initiation: The Mysteries of Birth and Rebirth.* Trans. Willard R. Trask. Harper Torchbook, New York, 1958.

————. *The Sacred and the Profane: The Nature of Religion.* Trans. Willard R. Trask. Harcourt Brace and World, New York, 1959.

Eliot, T.S. *Selected Poems.* Faber and Faber, London, 1954.

Foreman, Maurice Buxton. *The Letters of John Keats.* Oxford University Press, London, 1947.

Frankl, Viktor E. *Man's Search for Meaning.* Simon & Schuster Pocketbook, New York, 1963.

Gilbert, Sandra, and Susan Gubar. *The Madwoman in the Attic: The Woman Writer and the Nineteenth-Century Literary Imagination.* Yale University Press, New Haven, 1979.

Graves, Robert. *The Greek Myths.* 2 vols. Penguin Books, Harmondsworth, 1955.

Hannah, Barbara. *Jung, His Life and Work: A Biographical Memoir.* G.P. Putnam's Sons, New York, 1976.

Harding, M. Esther. *The I and the Not-I* (Bollingen Series LXXIX). Princeton University Press, Princeton, 1965.

———. *The Way of All Women.* Harper Colophon, New York, 1975.

———. *Woman's Mysteries, Ancient and Modern.* Longman's Green & Co., London, 1935.

Joyce, James. *Portrait of the Artist as a Young Man.* Penguin Books, Harmondsworth, 1960.

———. *Ulysses.* The Franklin Library, Franklin Center, P.A., 1976.

Jung, C.G. *The Collected Works* (Bollingen Series XX). 20 vols. Trans. R.F.C. Hull. Ed. H. Read, M. Fordham, G. Adler, Wm. McGuire. Princeton University Press, Princeton, 1953-1979.

———. *Letters* (Bollingen Series XCV). Trans. R.F.C. Hull. Ed. Gerhard Adler and Aniela Jaffé. Princeton University Press, Princeton, 1974.

———. *Memories, Dreams, Reflections.* Trans. Richard and Clara Winston. Ed. Aniela Jaffé. Fontana Library (Random House), London, 1971.

Laing. R.D. *The Voices of Experience.* Pantheon Books, New York, 1982.

Lincoln, Bruce. *Emerging from the Chrysalis: Studies in Rituals of Women's Initiation.* Harvard University Press, New York, 1981.

Mechthilde of Magdeburg. *The Revelations (The Flowing Light of God).* Trans. Lucy Menzies. Longman's Green, London, 1953.

Merton, Thomas. *Zen and the Birds of Appetite.* New Directions, New York, 1968.

Metman, Eva. "Woman and the Anima." Guild of Pastoral Psychology, Lecture No. 71, London, 1962.

Neumann, Erich. *The Child.* Trans. Ralph Manheim. Harper Colophon, New York, 1976.

———. *Depth Psychology and the New Ethic.* Trans. Eugene Rolfe. Harper and Row, New York, 1973.

———. *The Great Mother* (Bollingen Series XLVII). Trans. Ralph Manheim. Princeton University Press, Princeton, 1972.

———. *The Origins and History of Consciousness* (Bollingen Series XLII). Trans. R.F.C. Hull. Princeton University Press, Princeton, 1970.

*Norton Anthology of English Literature, The.* Ed. Meyer Howard Abrams. W.W.Norton and Company, New York, 1975.

Pearce, Joseph Chilton. *Magical Child.* Bantam New Age Books, New York, 1977.

Perera, Sylvia Brinton. *Descent to the Goddess: A Way of Initiation for Women.* Inner City Books, Toronto, 1981.

Rilke, Rainer Maria. *Selected Poems.* Trans. Robert Bly. Harper and Row, New York, 1981.

Rosenblum, Robert. *Cubism and Twentieth-Century Art.* Harry N. Abrams, Inc., New York, 1966.

Schwartz-Salant, Nathan. *Narcissism and Character Transformation.* Inner City Books, Toronto, 1982.

Shuttle, Penelope, and Peter Redgrove. *The Wise Wound: Menstruation and Everywoman*. Penguin Books, Harmondsworth, 1980.

Te Paske, Bradley A. *Rape and Ritual: A Psychological Study*. Inner City Books, Toronto, 1982.

Von Franz, Marie-Louise. *Alchemy: An Introduction to the Symbolism and the Psychology*. Inner City Books, Toronto, 1980.

——— . *The Feminine in Fairytales*. Spring Publications, Zurich, 1972.

——— . *Shadow and Evil in Fairytales*. Spring Publications, Zurich, 1974.

——— . *The Psychological Meaning of Redemption Motifs in Fairytales*. Inner City Books, Toronto, 1980.

——— . *The Way of the Dream*. Windrose Films, Toronto (in preparation).

Warner, Marina. *Alone of All Her Sex: The Myth and the Cult of the Virgin Mary*. Quartet Books Limited, London, 1978.

Williams, Donald Lee. *Border Crossings: A Psychological Perspective on Carlos Castaneda's Path of Knowledge*. Inner City Books, Toronto, 1981.

Woodman, Marion. *The Owl Was a Baker's Daughter: Obesity, Anorexia Nervosa, and the Repressed Feminine*. Inner City Books, Toronto, 1980.

Yeats, W.B. *The Collected Poems*. Macmillan Company, New York, 1938.

# Index

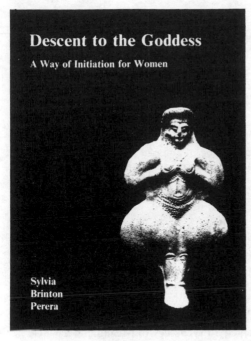

**6. Descent to the Goddess: A Way of Initiation for Women.** $10
Sylvia Brinton Perera (New York). ISBN 0-919123-05-8. 112 pages.

This is a highly original and provocative book about women's freedom and the need for an inner, female authority in a masculine-oriented society.

Combining ancient texts and modern dreams, the author, a practising therapist, presents a way of feminine initiation. Inanna-Ishtar, Sumerian Goddess of Heaven and Earth, journeys into the underworld to Ereshkigal, her dark "sister," and returns. So modern women must descend from their old role-determined behavior into the depths of their instinct and image patterns, to find anew the Great Goddess and restore her values to modern culture.

Men too will be interested in this book, both for its revelations of women's essential nature and for its implications in terms of their own inner journey.

"The most significant contribution to an understanding of feminine psychology since Esther Harding's *Way of All Women.*"—**Marion Woodman,** psychoanalyst and author of *The Owl Was a Baker's Daughter.*

# Studies in Jungian Psychology
# by Jungian Analysts

**LIMITED EDITION PAPERBACKS**

*Prices quoted are in U.S. dollars (except for Canadian orders)*

### 1. The Secret Raven: Conflict and Transformation.
Daryl Sharp (Toronto). ISBN 0-919123-00-7. 128 pages. $10

A concise introduction to the application of Jungian psychology. Focuses on the creative personality—and the life and dreams of the writer Franz Kafka—but the psychology is relevant to anyone who has experienced a conflict between the spiritual life and sex, or between inner and outer reality. (Knowledge of Kafka is not necessary.) Illustrated. Bibliography.

### 2. The Psychological Meaning of Redemption Motifs in Fairytales.
Marie-Louise von Franz (Zurich). ISBN 0-919123-01-5. 128 pages. $10

A unique account of the significance of fairytales for an understanding of the process of individuation, especially in terms of integrating animal nature and human nature. Particularly helpful for its symbolic, nonlinear approach to the meaning of typical dream motifs (bathing, beating, clothes, animals, etc.), and its clear description of complexes and projection.

### 3. On Divination and Synchronicity: Psychology of Meaningful Chance.
Marie-Louise von Franz (Zurich). ISBN 0-919123-02-3. 128 pages. $10

A penetrating study of the meaning of the irrational. Examines time, number, and methods of divining fate such as the I Ching, astrology, Tarot, palmistry, random patterns, etc. Explains Jung's ideas on archetypes, projection, psychic energy and synchronicity, contrasting Western scientific attitudes with those of the Chinese and so-called primitives. Illustrated.

### 4. The Owl Was a Baker's Daughter: Obesity, Anorexia Nervosa, and the Repressed Feminine.
Marion Woodman (Toronto). ISBN 0-919123-03-1. 144 pages. $10

A pioneer work in feminine psychology, with particular attention to the body as mirror of the psyche in eating disorders and weight disturbances. Explores the personal and cultural loss—and potential rediscovery—of the feminine principle, through Jung's Association Experiment, case studies, dreams, Christianity and mythology. Illustrated. Glossary. Bibliography.

### 5. Alchemy: An Introduction to the Symbolism and the Psychology.
Marie-Louise von Franz (Zurich). ISBN 0-919123-04-X. 288 pages. $16

A lucid and practical guide to what the alchemists were really looking for—emotional balance and wholeness. Completely demystifies the subject. An important work, invaluable for an understanding of images and motifs in modern dreams and drawings, and indispensable for anyone interested in relationships and communication between the sexes. 84 Illustrations.

### 6. Descent to the Goddess: A Way of Initiation for Women.
Sylvia Brinton Perera (New York). ISBN 0-919123-05-8. 112 pages. $10

A timely and provocative study of women's freedom and the need for an inner, female authority in a masculine-oriented society. Based on the Sumerian goddess Inanna-Ishtar's journey to the underworld, her transformation through contact with her dark "sister" Ereshkigal, and her return. Rich in insights from dreams, mythology and analysis. Glossary. Bibliography.

7. **The Psyche as Sacrament: C.G. Jung and Paul Tillich.**
   John P. Dourley (Ottawa). ISBN 0-919123-06-6. 128 pages. $10

An illuminating, comparative study showing with great clarity that in the depths of the soul the psychological task and the religious task are one. With a dual perspective, the author—Jungian analyst and Catholic priest— examines the deeper meaning, for Christian and non-Christian alike, of God, Christ, the Spirit, the Trinity, morality and the religious life. Glossary.

8. **Border Crossings: Carlos Castaneda's Path of Knowledge.**
   Donald Lee Williams (Boulder). ISBN 0-919123-07-4. 160 pages. $12

The first thorough psychological examination of the popular don Juan novels. Using dreams, fairytales, and mythic and cultural parallels, the author brings Castaneda's spiritual journey down to earth, in terms of everyone's search for self-realization. Special attention to the psychology of women. (Familiarity with the novels is not necessary.) Glossary.

9. **Narcissism and Character Transformation: The Psychology of Narcissistic Character Disorders.**
   Nathan Schwartz-Salant (New York). ISBN 0-919123-08-2. 192 pp. $13

An incisive and comprehensive analysis of narcissism: what it looks like, what it means and how to deal with it. Shows how an understanding of the archetypal patterns that underlie the individual, clinical symptoms of narcissism can point the way to a healthy restructuring of the personality. Draws upon a variety of psychoanalytic points of view (Jungian, Freudian, Kohutian, Kleinian, etc.). Illustrated. Glossary. Bibliography.

10. **Rape and Ritual: A Psychological Study.**
   Bradley A. Te Paske (Minneapolis). ISBN 0-919123-09-0. 160 pp. $12

An absorbing combination of theory, clinical material, dreams and mythology, penetrating far beyond the actual deed to the impersonal, archetypal background of sexual assault. Special attention to male ambivalence toward women and the psychological significance of rape dreams and fantasies. Illustrated. Glossary. Bibliography.

11. **Alcoholism and Women: The Background and the Psychology.**
   Jan Bauer (Zurich). ISBN 0-919123-10-4. 144 pages. $12

A major contribution to an understanding of alcoholism, particularly in women. Compares and contrasts medical and psychological models, illustrates the relative merits of Alcoholics Anonymous and individual therapy, and presents new ways of looking at the problem based on case material, dreams and archetypal patterns. Glossary. Bibliography.

12. **Addiction to Perfection: The Still Unravished Bride.**
   Marion Woodman (Toronto). ISBN 0-919123-11-2. 208 pages. $12

A powerful and authoritative look at the psychology and attitudes of modern woman, expanding on the themes introduced in *The Owl Was a Baker's Daughter*. Explores the nature of the feminine through case material, dreams and mythology, in food rituals, rape symbolism, perfectionism, imagery in the body, sexuality and creativity. Illustrated.

13. **Jungian Dream Interpretation: A Handbook of Theory and Practice.**
   James A. Hall, M.D. (Dallas). ISBN 0-919123-12-0. 128 pages. $12

A comprehensive and practical guide to an understanding of dreams in light of the basic concepts of Jungian psychology. Jung's model of the psyche is described and discussed, with many clinical examples. Particular attention to common dream motifs, and how dreams are related to the stage of life and individuation process of the dreamer. Glossary.

14. **The Creation of Consciousness: Jung's Myth for Modern Man.**
Edward F. Edinger, M.D. (Los Angeles). ISBN 0-919123-13-9. 128 pages. $12

An important new book by the author of *Ego and Archetype,* proposing a new world-view based on a creative collaboration between the scientific pursuit of knowledge and the religious search for meaning. Explores the significance for mankind of Jung's life and work; discusses the purpose of human life and what it means to be conscious; examines the theological and psychological implications of Jung's master-work, *Answer to Job;* presents a radical, psychological understanding of God's "continuing incarnation"; and illustrates the pressing need for man to become more conscious of his dark, destructive side as well as his creative potential. Illustrated.

15. **The Analytic Encounter: Transference and Human Relationship.**
Mario Jacoby (Zurich). ISBN 0-919123-14-7. 128 pages. $12

A sensitive and revealing study that differentiates relationships based on projection from those characterized by psychological distance and mutual respect. Examines the psychodynamics activated in any intimate relationship, and particularly in therapy and analysis; summarizes the views of Jung and Freud on identification, projection and transference-countertransference, as well as those of Martin Buber (I-It and I-Thou relationships); and shows how unconscious complexes may appear in dreams and emotional reactions. Special attention to the so-called narcissistic transferences (mirror, idealizing, etc.), the archetypal roots of projection and the significance of erotic love in the analytic situation. Glossary. Bibliography.

16. **Change of Life: A Psychological Study of the Menopause.**
Ann Mankowitz (Santa Fe). ISBN 0-919123-15-5. 128 pages. $12

A detailed and profoundly moving account of a menopausal woman's Jungian analysis, openly facing the fears and apprehensions behind the collective "conspiracy of silence" that surrounds this crucial period of every woman's life. Dramatically interweaves the experience of one woman with more generally applicable social, biological, emotional and psychological factors; frankly discusses the realities of aging, within which the menopause is seen as a potentially creative rite of passage; and illustrates how the menopause may manifest, both in outer life and in dreams, as a time of rebirth, an opportunity for psychological integration and growth, increased strength and wisdom. Glossary. Bibliography.

*All books contain detailed Index*

**TERMS OF SALE**

**PREPAID ORDERS ONLY**
(except Booksellers and Libraries)

Orders from outside Canada pay in $U.S.

*Full credit on return of books damaged in post*

**POSTAGE AND HANDLING**

Add 80¢/book (Book Rate) *or* $3/book (Airmail)

*No charge if ordering 4 books or more*

**DISCOUNTS**
*(all postfree, book rate)*

Prepaid Orders, any 4-6 books: 10%
Any 7 books or more: 20%

Retail Booksellers: 40% (60 days)
*Booksellers Prepaid Orders: 50%*
Libraries (direct orders): 10% (30 days)

**INNER CITY BOOKS**
**Box 1271, Station Q, Toronto, Canada M4T 2P4**
**(416) 927-0355**